MR AMBASSADOR

Portrait of Sir Carl Berendsen by Red Moore, reproduced with kind permission of the Laking Family.

MR AMBASSADOR

Memoirs of Sir Carl Berendsen

EDITED BY HUGH TEMPLETON

VICTORIA UNIVERSITY PRESS

TE WHARE WĀNANGA O TE ŪPOKO O TE IKA A MĀUI
VICTORIA
UNIVERSITY OF WELLINGTON

VICTORIA UNIVERSITY PRESS
Victoria University of Wellington
PO Box 600 Wellington
vuw.ac.nz/vup

First published 2009

National Library of New Zealand Cataloguing-in-Publication Data

Mr. Ambassador : memoirs of Sir Carl Berendsen / edited by Hugh Templeton.
Includes index.
ISBN 978-0-86473-584-3
1. Berendsen, Carl. 2. Ambassadors—New Zealand—Biography. 3. New Zealand—Foreign relations.
I. Templeton, Hugh, 1929-
327.930092—dc 22

Printed by Astra Print

CONTENTS

EDITOR'S NOTE

Everyone who was associated with Berendsen carried away memories and stories that became part of an anecdotal treasure chest from which in due course others drew liberally. A small selection from that common store is presented throughout this book.

PREFACE

Sir Carl Berendsen KCMG (1890–1973) was the founder of New Zealand Foreign Policy. This Australian New Zealander, who claimed Australians and New Zealanders were the same people, was a dynamic thinker, an outstanding administrator, a gifted writer, and a considerable orator. Few civil servants before or since have addressed both Cabinet and Parliament; few have made or been involved in making so much and such important policy; and few have had such a significant influence on New Zealand and its international relationships.

The Berendsen career is a remarkable story of the growth of a youngster in the transformatory decade of the 1890s, of his emergence to manhood in the golden age before the Great War, and of a unique career in the New Zealand public service, administering great affairs as New Zealand evolved as an independent State.

By a combination of luck and good judgement Berendsen's talents and intellectual gifts, written and oral skills, personal links, energy and life experience led him at each stage of his career, and even in the Great War, to positions where, by skill and judgement, he could assist decisively in the making of a new nation. His career took flight in 1926, with the establishment of the Imperial Affairs Section of the Prime Minister's Department under Gordon Coates, whose Prime Ministership saw New Zealand, after Massey's signing of the Treaty of Versailles, take its first hesitant steps towards nationhood.

As New Zealand High Commissioner in Canberra, Berendsen was involved in the drafting of the ANZAC Pact of 1944, confirming New Zealand's most important relationship. By the time he retired in 1952 from his flamboyant Ambassadorship in Washington, Berendsen had been involved with Fraser in significantly shaping the United Nations Charter. As Ambassador in Washington Berendsen was engaged in the initial talks that led to the ANZUS Pact of 1951. When the New Zealand Government asked him to sign both the ANZUS Pact and the Japanese Peace Treaty, he crowned his career, with his stellar speech to the San Francisco Peace Conference, 'the most widely publicised and approved of all the hundreds' he had made.

So important is Berendsen in the evolution of New Zealand as an independent nation that I finally acceded to the request of Professor Vincent O'Sullivan, then Director of the Stout Research Centre at Victoria University of Wellington, to edit for publication Berendsen's somewhat difficult Reminiscences.

With Vincent O'Sullivan, Professor Margaret Clark, and others in the Stout Centre, I had, in a minor capacity as a representative of the Association of Former MPs, helped in organising the Stout series on New Zealand Prime Ministers. We saw them as lively contributions to our history while the colleagues of principal players were still alive and could use their personal experience to illumine the careers and policies of each Prime Minister and the Cabinet Ministers with whom they had served. In 1997, we had held a specially illuminating seminar on Peter Fraser, our great wartime Scots New Zealand Prime Minister. Berendsen, of course, had worked closely and travelled extensively with Fraser. I had just finished a book on my own family, trying to put the Templetons of Southland into context for my clan and the province they had helped, over some 140 years, to develop. Was it not time to put Berendsen's Reminiscences into the public arena?

For thirty-odd years Berendsen's Reminiscences, as he had called them, had lain in the Beaglehole Room at Victoria University, to be mined by historians. Ian McGibbon had edited the Berendsen–McIntosh correspondence between the two founding figures of the New Zealand Department of External Affairs, and shapers, under their Ministers, of New Zealand foreign policy. *Undiplomatic Dialogue* appeared in 1993. This fascinating volume contained the letters exchanged between 1943 and 1952 by Berendsen, after he went as High Commissioner to Canberra, and Alister McIntosh, who succeeded him as Head of Department in Wellington.

The problem with Berendsen's Reminiscences was clear enough. Sir Carl had written somewhat expansively of his times and activities. More difficult, he had divided his Reminiscences into two parts: a lengthy narrative, and a series of essays on major public figures he had known. He had also tired and left the story hanging; a meal as it were, without the brandy and cigars.

Initially I recoiled from Vincent O'Sullivan's suggestion. Then one night I woke with a possible answer. I recalled the advice of one of my friends and advisers for my own writing. 'Don't put it all in. Think of telling the story for an intelligent twenty-year-old niece who never knew a Muldoon.' Or, in this case, a Berendsen niece, for whom Carl's life and times were as remote as the moon. So, in however limited a fashion, I have tried, under the demands of a potential publisher, to put myself in Berendsen's place. I have been able to edit, shorten and collate his Reminiscences into a Memoir while, to an absolute degree, retaining his distinctive language.

This story of a remarkable life and significant career lies at the heart of the New Zealand nation, small as he always emphasised, but distinctive, that evolved in Berendsen's lifetime. The strands of that story are so strong and colourful that Vincent O'Sullivan, with his writer's eye, was right in wanting them teased out into the open while those who, like Tom Larkin, knew and worked with Berendsen, were available to analyse, describe and comment.

Given the difficulties for him, I am immensely grateful for Tom Larkin's decision in effect, to double the value of the Memoirs. His beautifully insightful essay is the ideal complement to Berendsen's own story. Written in repose, in a distant time, after long reflection, and with loving care, Tom brings to life, with telescopic exactitude, Berendsen's idiosyncratic genius. My brother Malcolm was right in insisting that Tom present the portrait. It lives and glows and laughs even at a third time of asking.

The Larkin portrait blends with the important article that Professor Ann Trotter published earlier. With her kind agreement we can offer the reader in the one volume an historian's view of the great Berendsen in action as a nation maker as we entered our Elizabethan age.

I need to thank Margaret Heywood too, for providing from her own political experience as adviser to Norman Kirk and as his Diarist, an invaluable eyrie counterpoint to our essayists. My debt to her is for assisting our publisher Fergus Barrowman and me to finalise the text. Her insistence too on extensive footnotes added value in illustrating the kind of people with whom Berendsen worked and moved. 'If I don't know about Ward and Coates and Frank Thomson, General Richardson and O.F. Nelson, let alone the Salisburys and Clarendons, what will future readers think?'

In preparing the footnotes, I am specially grateful for the skill and friendly patience of the librarians of the General Assembly Library's Upper Room, particularly Felicity Rashbrooke and Katherine Close. Long may they flourish. The equally generous help of Nicola Frean of the Victoria University Beaglehole Room was a vital first step. With my fixed computer, I could not have married Berendsen's twin volumes without her providing me with a copy of the full text. In my time I have owed much to the generosity of librarians like those of my Alma Mater, John Harris, Basil Dowling and David Esplin at Otago, as well as to Vincent Quinn of Balliol College, and now Mary Laking at Foreign Affairs. It's heart warming, given the pressures in writing and publishing, to find the tradition flourishing fifty years on.

My warm thanks are due to the Foreign Affairs establishment and recorders, Sir George Laking, who urged me on, my brother Malcolm, Simon Murdoch, Karen Bolger and Neil Robertson for their support, and in Simon's case for underwriting Victoria University Press's publication, and Sir George Laking, Mary Laking, and the Laking family for the use of his Berendsen caricature.

A good cartoonist catches at the soul and the mind of players like Berendsen, as well as at the politics and diplomacy of an age. For the latter, might I recommend for later generations John Lewis Gaddis's *The Cold War: A New History* (Penguin, 2005). Succinctly Gaddis provides the focus for a Berendsen – whose flesh had crawled in Nazi Germany and Peronist Argentina – in combat on the international stage with Soviet 'thugs and gangsters'. To catch at the intensity of the Cold War, I have used *Punch* cartoons I grew up with to illustrate its fraught diplomacy. Not once but thrice – in Korea, in Berlin (where at the height of the crisis, ready to advance, Soviet Colonels slept under their tanks), and in Cuba – the thunder of a third world war rumbled ominously. Some are still grateful for the nuclear stalemate, that 'frightful fiend', that saved us from Armageddon.

Hon. Hugh Templeton

I was sitting with Berendsen at the Assembly and listening while he spoke about his love of baseball. Then, foolishly, I repeated something I'd read that 'in baseball, so little happens on the field that the grandstand is an appropriate place for meditation and prayer.'

He exploded. 'Oh! What bloody nonsense! That's not baseball! That's cricket! And you'd better take Keith and get out to the Polo Grounds and learn what you're trying to talk about!'

So next day, with his son Keith, I went to the Polo Grounds to see the Giants play the Dodgers. There were a lot of famous players on show. Johnny Mize hit a ball further and higher than I'd ever seen – and still was caught. Leo Durocher, the Giants manager, hit a spectator and was suspended. It was a great great day and I reported enthusiastically, next morning.

'Told you so!' he said.

Tom Larkin

CARL BERENDSEN: A RECOLLECTION

BY TOM LARKIN[1]

Late in 1951, after nearly nine years representing New Zealand at the highest diplomatic level in Canberra, Washington and the United Nations, Carl Berendsen wrote to the Minister of Foreign Affairs, Frederick Doidge, saying that, in the years ahead, he would not wish 'Just to rust away, amusing myself' and suggesting a number of things within the Government's competence that he might like to do.

He expected a considered reply to his proposals but received none. Nor were his abilities ever used again by any Government.

One of his suggestions, however, was that 'I might write a little, if anybody were interested.'

And that is what he did, the result being his massive and hitherto unpublished 'Memoirs of an Ambassador'.

He talks there of reading Dickens with his mother and, in recalling those days, he must have been all too conscious of the Dickensian features of his own early life.

There was a gifted father, who drifted in and out of his family's orbit in constant pursuit of some new promise-laden enterprise that always in the end yielded failure. Berendsen once likened his father to Micawber,

1 Tom Larkin is one of a small band of university graduates who had served in World War II and who were recruited by Alister McIntosh, Secretary of External Affairs, immediately after the war to form the nucleus of New Zealand's career diplomatic service. They were a multi-talented group. Tom himself is a man whose keenness for sporting activity – he was a cricketer and rugby player of no mean ability – was matched by a love of English and American literature, and exceptional writing skills of his own. For family reasons he spent most of his career at a senior level in the home office, playing a key role in the development of New Zealand's foreign policy and in the maintenance of standards among the more junior recruits who followed him into the service. His integrity and devotion to principle were, and are absolute. Only towards the end of his career in 1971 did he accept an Ambassadorship, where his and his wife Sarah's contribution to the strengthening of New Zealand's relations with Japan has recently been recognized by his appointment as an Officer of the New Zealand Order of Merit. It was entirely appropriate that after his retirement from the Ministry of Foreign Affairs he should be appointed to represent the public interest on the Press Council, in which capacity he served for twelve years. At ninety his memory remains as clear, his judgements as perceptive and his writing skill as keenly honed as ever.

and there was more than a touch of Micawberian grandeur in such moments as that in which he saw his father ostentatiously tipping a steward, with possibly the last money he had, before travelling steerage from Wellington to Sydney.

There was the contrast between the excitement and beauty of Sydney, and the cold and cheerless surroundings of Waimumu, Mataura and Gore.

There was the sequence of homes, some in Australia, full of middle-class comfort provided by generous relations, others, in New Zealand, crafted by his father, and permitting only an isolated, scrabbling and hard-won existence, in which it was sometimes his mother, at her Singer sewing machine, who was the main breadwinner.

And throughout all this, there was his own unending determination in the face of poverty ('None could have been poorer than we') his mastery of a variety of practical skills, his physical stamina, and his development of scholastic abilities that in the end enabled his escape to Wellington, and to new opportunities and hope.

Berendsen arrived in Wellington aged fifteen and a half, as a cadet in the Department of Education. When he left in 1943 to be New Zealand High Commissioner in Canberra he had established a background of experience and achievement that had no counterpart in the New Zealand public service and equipped him supremely well for what was to come.

In the Department of Education and particularly in his work on the School Journal he had developed a respect for clarity and the right word in the right place.

He had been in the army in the early days of World War I and was present at the bizarre moment in 1915 when a German battlecruiser entered and circled the harbor at Apia and then left while New Zealand soldiers looked on. This was as close to combat as he got. But that early experience and later a training appointment in London gave him a view of service life and organisation and, although at a lower level, a taste of leadership.

As a Master of Laws in the Department of Labour he contested many cases before the Employment Court without, he claimed, losing any. 'It was there,' he wrote, 'that I made good friends, learned to despise my enemies, and to believe in the fundamental goodness of human beings.'

Among his friends were several (Paul Verschaffelt, H.H. Cornish and the Freybergs) destined to occupy places of influence in the public service and in the country at large. It was on the advice of Verschaffelt, the head of the Public Service, that he applied for the post of Imperial Affairs Officer in the Prime Minister's Department. He described himself as having 'intelligence, industry, integrity and interest in the proposed position'.

On his acceptance, he was shown a pile of documents relating to his new work and told 'There you are Berry. They're all yours!'

His first obligation was to prepare briefing papers and speech notes to assist his Prime Minister Gordon Coates at the Imperial Conference of that year. In the process it was probably Berendsen who learnt most.

At that time New Zealand had no diplomatic service, was represented only in London, received its information on international affairs solely from Britain, and, when it had comments to make, made them solely to Britain.

As Imperial Affairs Officer Berendsen was responsible for handling correspondence and giving advice on imperial and international affairs It was up to him, if he were so inclined, to suggest new approaches.

In the years that followed, he shouldered an increasing range of responsibilities, ranging from the Samoan Mandate and Island Affairs (in the late twenties) to control of the Prime Minister's Department (in the mid thirties) to the Organisation of National Security and the War Cabinet (in the years before and during the War).

He worked fast and virtually unaided, his usual response to new problems being simply to call for his typist and start dictating.

He was often abroad at Imperial Conferences and the League of Nations where he met (and was frequently unimpressed by) many of the leading statesmen and officials of the day.

In the thirties he deplored what he saw as the dominant developments of the time – the rise of the dictators, the retreat of the democracies, and the passivity of the world community as represented in the League of Nations.

He formed strong opinions about the response needed in the face of the dangers that threatened ('They're selecting their partners' he wrote in 1934), and he described events abroad for successive New Zealand governments in language that was candid and sometimes bleak.

With the election of a Labour Government in 1935, his ideas took hold. He was a conservative with a deep distaste for the social and economic theories of the new administration, which he judged later as 'appallingly mischievous in matters of internal politics'.

But it was they who were willing, from conviction, to proclaim and defend the measures he identified as necessary if the dangers confronting the world were to be arrested. In 1936, he drafted, and the Government endorsed, proposals for the reform of the League of Nations. These ideas appear, in League circles, to have had all the impact of a bubble on a harbour. But they provided the basis for New Zealand's response, in the League and elsewhere, to the sequence of crises that followed – Italy's invasion of Ethiopia, the civil war in Spain, Japan's attack on China, and the partition of Czechoslovakia.

They also marked out a clear difference of approach on New Zealand's part from that taken by Britain and other Commonwealth countries. (Typically, New Zealand alone of Commonwealth countries did not send a congratulatory telegram to Chamberlain after the Munich Conference opened the way to the sacrifice of Czechoslovakia.)

In 1938 Berendsen wrote a most significant memorandum to the Prime Minister, Michael Savage.[2] He recalled that over the past three years, the New Zealand Government had declined to support any policy designed to weaken collective security under the League, to diminish still further the sanctity of international agreements, and to reward any state of affairs brought about by aggression. But the time had come, he contended, at which, in view of the imminence of war, the government should subordinate that approach to the over-riding necessity of ensuring the survival of Britain and the Commonwealth.

It is a splendid memorandum, drafted in language that is lean and powerful and all of a piece with a statement which Berendsen delivered to the Pacific Defence Conference, held in April in the following year, in which he emphasised the frailty of defence planning reliant on the Singapore base and on expectation of the timely arrival of a British fleet.[3]

2 C.A. Berendsen to M.J. Savage, 14 October 1938 PM 85/1/1. See *Blue-Water Rationale: The Naval Defence of New Zealand 1914–1942*, by I.C. McGibbon (Wellington: Historical Publications Branch, Department of Internal Affairs, 1981)

3 Speech by C.A. Berendsen to the Pacific Defence Conference, 14 April 1939, C4-E5 PM 86/27/10.

His memorandum to Savage ended with a significant assertion. 'I have held these views for a considerable time and have expressed them as forcibly as possible from time to time as occasion arose and, while I may be entirely wrong, I am perhaps the only official who has had the opportunity of forming an opinion based on the knowledge both of the Foreign Affairs side and the Defence side of the Dominion's activities.' It was a fair claim.

So it was that, in 1943, when Berendsen was appointed to represent New Zealand in Canberra, the only uncertainties about the move were why it was made (he was not well and his relations with Peter Fraser were strained) and whether his abilities and experience would have appropriate scope in the new setting.

In Canberra it was not roses all the way. 'I have never allowed myself as an Ambassador,' he wrote once, 'to be ignored or indirectly insulted or imposed upon when insisting upon the dignity of the country I had the honour to represent.'

From that standpoint he twice threatened to return home (and to publicise the reasons) if the Australian authorities did not accord New Zealand its proper place at an Anzac Day ceremony, or assist him to overcome difficulties over appropriate housing.

He also had to cope with Australian displeasure over New Zealand's decision to retain its division in the Middle East rather than transfer them to the Pacific as Australia had done. He had a low opinion of the Australian Prime Minister, John Curtin, and the Defence Minister, Fred Shedden, and dealings between them were limited and sour.

Otherwise Australians made it easy for him in his efforts to keep his government as fully informed on Australian affairs 'as if they themselves were in Sydney, Canberra or Melbourne'. He was in great demand for speaking and other engagements and he responded readily to many aspects of Australian life. He had, after all, been born in Australia and claimed to be 'the possessor of a pure Australian accent'. He was a co-signatory of the Canberra Pact of 1944 and although in private correspondence critical of what he saw as Australian pretension and pushiness, supported the assertion of Anzac interests in the post-war Pacific.

All in all, in his first performance as a New Zealand diplomat, he was versatile and confident and well prepared for the appointment which followed, as New Zealand Minister in Washington DC.

In Washington and, before long, in New York following the foundation of the United Nations, he was close to the centre of great events.

At the United Nations, in its early stages, Peter Fraser and Berendsen pressed again for a system of collective security based on the principles they had advocated in the thirties. Berendsen took particular aim at what he saw as 'mortal weakness' in the United Nations Charter and as derelictions on the part of other members of the General Assembly. In speeches that abounded in power, derision and wit, he displayed a theatrical side that helped win attention to his views (even if in some quarters, his histrionics were dismissed as 'demagoguery' and 'clowning').

He was constantly enraged by the so called 'Veto', the Charter provision subjecting Security Council action to unanimity among the five Great Powers. He described its marriage to the Charter as a 'shot gun wedding' that reduced the Security Council to the level of a police department or fire brigade that could only operate when least needed. He vowed to speak against it wherever he had an audience, even if only at a wedding, and he once did exactly that.

He had other targets – the Soviet Union and its satellites which, he asserted, were bent solely on 'mischief'; those members of the General Assembly who preferred words to action and shrank from commitments that would give meaning to their declarations; attempts to retreat in mid-stream – as on Palestine, where his famous speech is thought to have swung the resolution to sustain Partition – from decisions painfully achieved; and, ultimately, Communist China, which he condemned as an aggressor following its intervention in the Korean War.

Berendsen balanced his jeremiads against the deficiencies of the Charter with declarations of support for the UN's fundamental purposes. 'I'd give my right hand to see this organisation succeed,' he once proclaimed, and the moment was captured in a photograph in Time magazine, showing him, arm extended, over the caption 'Offered, a right hand'.

His performance did not escape criticism. He was often fractious over instructions he did not like. 'I am the only delegate in the world,' he declared once, 'who in the space of twenty-four hours has been told to vote against, abstain, and vote for.' That was a situation in which his objections prevailed, but where they did not he obeyed his instructions scrupulously.

J.V. Wilson, with long experience of international organisations, felt that his criticism of the Veto was overdone. Some commentators disliked his hectoring tone and anti-Soviet stance. And there were times when he missed the opportunity to be silent.

But overall it would be hard to question the skill and tenacity with which he presented New Zealand's views on the problems of the world.

Because of the demands made upon him in New York by the United Nations General Assembly, the Trusteeship Council and his nominal responsibility for the operation of the New York office, much of his time in any year was diverted from Washington, where he was elevated from Minister to Ambassador in 1948.

But he was no longer a one-man band, as he had been for so long. He was supported now by people appointed from the Department of External Affairs and open to their suggestions and advice. Their contribution did not divert him from continued prodigious effort on his own part but it enabled him to handle more effectively the work in Washington for which he had been initially appointed to the United States.

Berendsen's original assignment to Washington was extended several times so that when he finally left, early in 1952, he had served longer in the top post than anyone else has done. His labours and his often emotional reactions to the stresses involved took a toll of his health – he developed a stomach ulcer, and treatment of a throat ailment added a rasp to an already rough-edged voice.

His work in Washington involved several fields of endeavour – to interpret the United States to New Zealand and New Zealand to the United States; to perform a killing social round; to represent New Zealand at international conferences in the capital and elsewhere; to make New Zealand known; to make friends; and to leave a pleasing impression on the country at large.

In all these settings he made a mark and fittingly he ended on a high note. His last major appearance was at two conferences which he felt marked the pinnacle of his work – the signing of the ANZUS Treaty, which brought New Zealand under the American security blanket, and the Japanese Peace Treaty, the soft terms of which were the price paid by New Zealand and Australia for the security guarantee.

Berendsen left Washington soon after, well known as the result of his constant appearances on radio and television, and his crafty timing of them. He had given over 500 speeches, had been to hundreds of cities and towns and had visited every state but Arkansas. And year after year, he had reported to Wellington on the great issues of the times, urging always that for New Zealand 'to do the right thing was the right thing to do' and defining 'the right thing' in terms that did not always win ready acceptance in Wellington.

Berendsen had a distaste for dictatorships that was formed in the early years of his responsibility for New Zealand's international affairs. He was contemptuous of Mussolini's aspirations for empire in Africa and, in 1938, was glad to escape what he described as the 'fetid, fermenting hotbed of hatred and aggression of Hitler's Germany'. So it was that years later when he visited the Argentina of the Peron dictatorship, he was vividly reminded of those early distasteful impressions of totalitarian Germany. Ultimately it was against the Soviet Union under Stalin that, year after year, he directed his distrust. He saw the USSR (and later Communist China) as characterised by 'rule by jackboot', as engaged in a conspiracy against world peace, as aimed at chaos abroad and as presenting the world at large with a choice between the secret ballot and the secret police. Against all this, he saw no alternative but support for American policy which he defined as 'infinite patience but complete firmness.'

The most powerful (and intemperate) expression of his views on measures needed to resist Soviet aggression was contained in a memorandum of 14 March 1950.[4] In this he described the Soviet Union as led by 'thugs and gangsters' assisted by the 'pestilential disease of international communism' and he appeared prepared to accept a number of unlikely treaty partners for New Zealand provided a security relationship with the United States could be obtained. For any student of the language of persuasion, there is a striking contrast between the heated assertions of this memorandum and the control and power of his comparable statement in 1939 about the strategic choices before New Zealand.

4 See Robin Kay (ed.) *The ANZUS Pact and the Treaty of Peace with Japan* (Wellington: Government Printer, 1985), Document 198, p. 522.

By 1950 constant speechmaking at the United Nations and elsewhere had had conspicuous effects on his writing style.

His drafting methods in the thirties were described by an associate (W.G. Stevens) in these terms: '"Take a letter Madame," he would say, tap the edge of the desk with a pencil, look into the distance, and dictate a statement with balanced phrases that well nigh sang themselves onto the paper.'

Berendsen claimed that his best speeches were extempore and unrecorded and he certainly spoke effectively off the cuff. But in most contexts where he was speaking on behalf of New Zealand or attempting to change its policy, printed texts were essential. And it was there that, over the years, he displayed certain rhetorical flourishes and stylistic tricks which, while originally designed to catch and hold an audience's attention, became regular and recognisable features of his memoranda and letters.

Berendsen was celebrated for the statement: 'If you look at a thing and it's 51% black and 49% white, then, for Christ's sake, its black!' That was essentially the standpoint of an advocate making the most powerful possible case and it provided the footing from which he assailed the Veto and the Russians and the Communist world.

But for someone who had a reputation for directness and candour, it is surprising that much of what he wrote and said was subject to reservations and restraints.

In the long sequence of letters that he exchanged for many years with Alister McIntosh, a frequent feature of his style was a long sentence full of dashes and brackets, in which some central and profound assertion would be hedged around with qualifications and asides before leading on to an admission of the possibility of error, followed by a denial of the admission.

He loved to confront his audience with questions as though he expected them to rise and give him a reply, and sometimes he answered himself.

Once after describing (in stark terms) the living conditions confronting the Japanese he asked: 'What are they going to do?' And answering himself he went on: 'I'll tell you what they are not going to do – that's starve with a smile!'

A variation was for him to pose a question, admit that he didn't know the answer and then, pointing aggressively at his audience, proclaim 'And you don't know either!'

In support of his arguments, he would claim the agreement of 'all sensible people' – 'everyone here' – 'all right thinking people' – 'any sensible person' – 'anyone who faces the facts and is not deaf or blind'. And of those who did not agree with him, he would suggest a lack of sanity, or a simplicity 'the order of which does them no credit' or placed them 'beyond the realm of logic or argument'.

Though conscious of their abilities he was suspicious of drafting suggestions from his advisers, whom he divided into those (the pushers) who would have him say things he didn't want to, and those (the shushers) who, he said, hardly wanted him to say anything at all. 'There you go,' he would say, 'cutting out all the best bits.'

Certainly there were occasions when restraint would have served him well. One such time was in 1947 during a General Assembly debate on the Palestine problem when he urged that, while the report of a special committee was being awaited, every effort should be made to establish an atmosphere of peace and quiet.

'This is a plea,' he said as he embarked on a prolonged passage of the purest purple, 'that should be unanimously supported by the Assembly, supported by every Government, broadcast through the world, emblazoned on every Journal's headline, endorsed in every pulpit, repeated in every school and adopted by every public speaker on this great and solemn problem: that all right-thinking people through out the world should so comport themselves during the next few pregnant months as to ensure that the enquiry would be conducted in that atmosphere of calm and peace which alone can enable the task to be performed and a solution to be attained which would bring justice to all and relief to suffering humanity. All hands should be held, all voices stilled, except in considered and responsible argument before the Committee which is to be established. I most solemnly urge magnanimity, patience, and moderation on the part of all, so that a true truce of God can be established during the months to come, that all will refrain from any provocation or exacerbation, by word or deed, in their consideration of this great and agonised human problem . . .' And so on.

There are other speeches or writings or passages within them, where his language was similarly overblown.

But all in all, when the United Nations was in its formative stages, when the post-war world was being reshaped, and stubborn issues were first under scrutiny, some of his statements were among the finest of his time and fully reflective of his determination that New Zealand should hold a good name and be heard on the international stage.

When diplomats are appointed to represent their countries abroad, they are expected to learn and appreciate, as much as they can, the things and activities that are valued and significant in the country to which they are assigned. In most countries, sports are among such activities but not all diplomats find it easy to develop, or even to feign, interest in them, especially when they differ from those played at home.

No such problem confronted Berendsen. As a boy he had played cricket in Sydney, with his cousin Oswald Asher, who later became prominent as a spin bowler at the top level, though the records do not support Berendsen's assertion that Oswald played for Australia.

In Wellington Berendsen represented the University clubs at rugby and cricket, and he was wicket keeper in the Wellington representative side. In the United States, he became passionate about baseball, was friendly with sports writers like Bob Considine, biographer of Babe Ruth, and read the *New York Times* sports pages as avidly as he did the political columns.

He had vivid memories about his days as a sportsman and a vast array of anecdotes (the day he scored eight runs from a single stroke; the football that burst; Al Gionfrido's catch off Joe DiMaggio) from which he liked to draw lessons that applied more widely:

'A man who does not warm to a sporting contest is half dead.'

'A skilled workman at any sport or work is joy to behold'.

'Football is like life. Things can happen of which one is completely unaware, until one is devastated by their impact.'

In the early days of his career, Berendsen was not a naturally gregarious man but later, and particularly in response to the general demands of diplomacy, he developed a somewhat rowdy conviviality that left no hosts in doubt that he was there and had honoured their invitation.

He also liked to 'act out' his store of personal, political and sporting anecdotes with a variety of gestures and facial expressions that inevitably caught the attention of all around and gave him an air of comicality quite at variance with his solemn or angry moods.

On one occasion, at lunch, when he could be heard and seen not only at his own table but by people close by, a small boy appeared at his elbow:

'Please sir' he said 'Can I ask you a question?'

'Of course. Of course. What's the question?'

'Please sir, I wondered are you a famous film star?'

'A pardonable error. Who do you think I am?'

'Well sir, I think you might be Groucho Marx!'

'Mmm. Well run along now.'

From time to time, in his reflective moments, Berendsen liked to tell of his earliest days, of his father and mother and of 'that little boy' who had made the trajectory from the dredge at Waimumu and 'the house of packing cases' to where he now was. No one hearing those stories could be other than quiet and thoughtful.

Berendsen was angered that, after his retirement, Foreign Affairs did not seek his opinion or include him in activities other than the Christmas party. On that occasion it was always possible to know that he had arrived, for there would be something like a small explosion as he and Lady Berendsen entered in a physical flurry and with loud expressions of enthusiasm at the sight of old friends.

Some of the most charming pages of the Memoirs are those describing Berendsen's courtship, marriage and adventures through life with Nellie Brown, who entered his vision at the age of sixteen and never left thereafter.

For Berendsen it was love at first sight. For Nellie it took longer. But from the time she accepted his offhand proposal 'What about getting married sometime?' until the end, she was his close companion and the love of his life.

He wrote of her that 'she cringes and screams from any bird, even a sparrow, even a bug, even a moth or a lady-bird, any animal, even a fawning and playful puppy or a tired old horse, including everything that lives except a man, and she fears no man and no woman.' She had tastes and interests that he did not share and some that he professed to scorn. She liked classical music which he claimed to 'detest' and rejected in favor of 'waltzes and marches'. 'Tchaikovsky?' he asked when she invited him to listen. 'Who's that? Someone in the New York office?' She liked to visit churches. He said that he preferred a fish shop. He was no linguist and she learned Spanish and, in situations where he withdrew helplessly, was skilled in getting results, even if her knowledge of the local language was rudimentary or non-existent.

In areas of importance to him she was constant and sustaining and she remained calm when he declared, as he often did, 'Something's bound to go wrong!' She also rode calmly through storm periods of semi-comic abuse that he would direct her way. 'Nellie, I'll slit your bloody throat!' he threatened when she interrupted a billiard game.

On another occasion, in a show of legs and underwear she donned her shoes and stockings in a New York taxi. 'Good God, woman,' he yelled, 'do you want to scarify the whole city?'

Another time she witnessed a robbery at gunpoint in the Rockefeller Plaza. As Berendsen appeared racing across the concourse with arms and coat flying she said in a rather chatty way:

'Carl! Carl! What do you think? There's been a hold up!'

'I'll say there's been a bloody hold up!' he roared. 'I've been waiting for you for half an hour!'

To any spectator of such exchanges, it was possible to forget that she was Lady Berendsen. But in all the settings, human, domestic, social and official, that demanded that they stand together, she measured up unfailingly.

It was not in Berendsen's nature to stifle unhappy memories, overlook slights, or mollify grievances. Rebuffs and difficulties encountered at school stayed vividly with him forever.

He did not keep diaries but his memoirs in their extended form are full of precise recollections of the service, or lack of it, accorded him in hotels, ships, airlines, railways, taxis and elsewhere. When attention fell below his standards, he was likely to see this as an aspersion not only towards him but in some ways towards New Zealand, and he would make his displeasure known.

In his time in the United States he built up a store of complaints over staffing decisions, contradictory or non-existent instructions, and particularly financial issues such as superannuation. In 1948 he wrote that his grievances totalled more than fifty, old and new, 'dead and alive'.

He did not conceal his anger over them from his staff, who became accustomed to his laments about the incompetence and hostility of what he termed 'that amorphous thing Wellington'. 'Wellington' became for him not merely the architect of his concerns but also the symbol of inadequacy.

When I first went to work for him in 1949, he staged a pantomime. 'So you're from Wellington?' he asked in a pretence of surprise. 'Well let me share a little confidence with you. In my view, and I've not always been wrong, nothing good and nobody good ever came out of Wellington!'

In another pantomime he would say 'Wellington think they've got all the cards! But . . .' and here he would tap the pocket of his jacket, demonstratively, 'I've got the bloody Joker! My resignation!' It was not a card that he ever played or was likely to.

But he retained his sense of injury to the end and in his last letter to McIntosh before leaving Washington he spoke of completing his service abroad 'with a sense of both resentment and indignation at obvious and demonstrable injustice'.

Alister McIntosh, who had for years been the main recipient of his complaints and had had the responsibility of coordinating and communicating the response from Wellington, said about him: 'His judgment goes to pot when personal interests are involved.'

Of his performance on New Zealand's behalf, the assessment was very different.

Everyone who worked for Berendsen was changed in at least some way by the experience. No one was able to escape his rage, for he could generate storm clouds in moments. And some have said that the tempests were easier to bear than his apologies, which could be long and sentimental.

He was complex and his faults were there for all to see. But he had vast abilities, his example was inspiring, and some of his less obvious qualities – loyalty, kindness, and a basic impulse towards fair dealing – were acknowledged and valued by those who knew him for long.

There has been no better evaluation of him than Alister McIntosh's simple conclusion that 'he was a very good thing' and that 'no one in the field of foreign affairs made such a dent on people and policies as he did.'

Early in 1956, President Nasser of Egypt nationalised the Suez Canal, which hitherto had been under the control of an International Authority designed to assure ships of all nations of unimpeded passage through the Canal. The move evoked outrage, particularly in Britain and France, and led them later in the year into the idiocy of colluding with Israel in attacking Egypt and occupying the area round the Canal, a situation from which they were rescued only through the replacement of their troops by a United Nations Force.

Sometime in August, I had gone to what was then the Post Office in Featherston Street in Wellington and was accosted by Berendsen, on the steps, on a wild and windy day.

'What are you people up there doing?' he said angrily. 'He's getting away with it – kit and caboodle!'

'Who do you mean?'

'Nasser of course!'

'Well,' I said, 'I've just been to the Suez Canal Conference. That may lead to something.'

'Who was there?' – and then as I gave him names, he gave his evaluation:

'Anthony Eden – Good man, once!'

'John Foster Dulles – Good man!'

'Selwyn Lloyd – Brain like a peanut!'

'Robert Menzies – Gasbag – clever though!'

And so on till I reached Krishna Menon of India.

'Menon!' he said. 'Well the most charitable thing I can say about Mr Menon is that he's only as evil as he looks!'

'Well then,' he said. 'That's not much of a crew!' He was quiet for a moment.

'Oh well,' he said then, 'the world's going to hell in a bucket anyway!' With that he plunged off, down the steps, into the wind.

I saw him several times after that. He was pleased that his son Keith was my mother's doctor. I was present when he and Nellie had their exchange over the 'hold up' in Rockefeller Plaza. When I got married they had us to lunch and gave a generous present. And early in the seventies, when they came to Japan, I asked him if there was anything we could help him to see – Kabuki or the Folk Art Museum?

'Oh God no!' he said. 'I don't go for that sort of stuff! Besides, Nellie and I have got tickets for the Takarakuza Girls!' (They were a Japanese imitation of the New York Rockettes.) So on that culturally unregenerate note, he left.

He died in 1973. Nellie stayed on in the house in Wai-te-ata Road and from time to time came knocking at our door as, somewhat dishevelled and full of spirit, she continued to climb the hills and pathways of Kelburn.

I have read, talked and thought about him many, many times. And of all the memories that I have of him, the image that returns most insistently is of the moment on the steps of the Post Office in Featherston Street, as he headed off into the wind, as always, battling against the elements.

BOOK I

THE MAKING OF AN ADMINISTRATOR

1890–1926

It was in the Basin Reserve that I hit an eight.

I mean an eight.

I got the ball away to fine leg for three, the return was outthrown, and we ran three, when it was again thrown wildly and we ran another two. Eight for one stroke seemed pretty good to me, but I was greatly deflated next day when the papers reported that 'Berendsen hit the only eight of the day.'

'Of the day' be it noted.

'Of the century' I felt.

Carl Berendsen

CHAPTER 1

SYDNEY

I was born in Sydney, Australia, in the suburb of Woollahra, on 16 August 1890. My first recollections are of an old galvanised-iron shed and of men busily heaving sacks of coal into the steam engine of a train. There was a barnyard rooster, coloured in a mix of red and yellow, and a black dog. Vaguely I have memories of a military review with soldiers in red uniforms.

In the half light of an early morning, my mother would put on an outer garment over her nightdress. Lying beside my father I could feel his face cold and fresh. There, a few doors on the Bondi side of Moncur Streets, the house of my birth, my first home, still stands. Even then I had the impression that all was not well. These were the days of financial panic when thousands like my father were ruined by the depression.

My next memories are of the Sydney suburb of Waverley. There my father had turned to the prospects of making a living from poultry farming. One cherished memory remains of the suburban lamplighter on his rounds in the late dusk. A sadder one is of the man arriving with the Singer sewing machine. My mother was never to be relieved from the burden of making a poor living from this Old Man of the Sea.

After the poultry-farming incident, I have a recollection of a grain dealing business, and then – my father had this habit of disappearing – of living alone with my mother in a lodging house in Paddington. We then went to live with my mother's brother, Philip, and his wife Florrie at Burwood, six miles out of Sydney. Despite our petty and limited life my uncle and aunt believed themselves to be among the more fortunate of the community, and we were happy there. In our own backyard, their son Oswald and I, restricted to each other's company, invented games which absorbed our leisure and enthralled our spirits. In particular we invented a kind of cricket with a tennis ball. We played this game day in, and day out and year in, year out. Perhaps it was this early training that took Oswald into the Australian cricket eleven, as a slow bowler, and me into the Wellington Plunket Shield team, as a wicketkeeper.

Tales and the early simple children's stories were a great delight. We were entranced, and as soon as we could make out the words, reading, with understanding parents encouraging us, and providing cheap books, became a constant joy. My uncle's shop was a tiny little affair, but with its window of large glass containers of coloured liquids, the traditional mark of the chemist's shop, quite entrancing. On the right was the customer's counter, while opposite stood the show case for the goods he sold, including his own brand of cough mixture, and at the back the dispensary for medical prescriptions.

It was at Burwood that my school career began. To a greater or lesser degree each of my ten schools was a terror and a misery. Until the very last I hated school, and I never heard the usual claptrap that school days were the happiest days of one's life without disgust and contempt. My infantile agony of ignorance and inferiority burned itself into me, and remains with me as at least equal in its distressing effects to any of the more substantial sorrows of later years. The pain still remains. I must have been a particularly timid child because I carried about a terrifying fear that I should have to leave the infant school. It made me so agitated that I deliberately gave wrong answers to tests. The teacher told me in sympathetic tones that I should have to spend a little more time in the infant school, and I had to dissemble my relief and gratification.

When I did graduate from the infants, the terrors and perils of the transition did not match the worst of my anticipations. I took a retiring and bashful part in the common games of the school, in so far as games could be played without instruments or equipment. I gradually learned to take an interest in my lessons, slowly gathering some degree of confidence. Our daily work was done on slates and the hideous screech of the slate pencil remains with me still. The slates were dealt out indiscriminately with each child left to spit on his slate and wipe it clean with his fingers. I never had the courage to protest or to use a sponge. School did teach me much about the futility of human anticipation.

My main recollections of this period relate to the shop and the home to which it was attached. In the interests of trade my uncle had to keep his shop open for urgent needs and to match the competitor down the street. It also meant putting up with the unreasonable demands of some in the medical profession. Fortunately my uncle was lifted out of this petty little rut with an offer to manage the chemist's branch of a substantial store in Sydney. At a salary of five pounds a week, this was luxury, on a modest scale. The household soon moved nearer to Sydney itself, to a new home that was not much better than the one we had left at Burwood, but it was roomier and of course nearer my uncle's new place of business.

Before we left Burwood I began to read and have memories of newspapers and illustrations of the Spanish American War. I dimly remember Queen Victoria's Jubilee and the early stages of the Boer War. We were intensely patriotic, and I recall the scene of popular hysteria in one of the Sydney theatres as the orchestra played 'Soldiers of the Queen' and 'Sons of the Sea' to a tableau of flags. It is strange how melodies and scents become fixed to scenes and events. 'Soldiers of the Queen' means to me the Boer War; 'The Honeysuckle and the Bee' takes me to the Fourth Street school in Woollahra; 'Tipperary' to the agonising years of World War I; the 'Missouri Waltz' to the troopship *Briton* returning from that war; 'Bye Bye Blackbird' to the *Aquitania* in 1926; and 'Valencia' to the *Makura* in 1927.

The new house we entered was by coincidence in Glenmore Road where my mother and I had once lodged. At Glenmore Road Public School, where the headmaster went off to the Boer War in charge of one of the contingents, I was not so miserable as at Burwood. Still I loathed school, as I did the congregational Sunday school to which my mother sent me. I do not think that I was sensibly handled, for there began a contempt for the scriptures that has plagued me ever since. In the course of time I went to many Sunday schools but I learned nothing from them. Rightly or wrongly I did not insist on a Sunday school regime for my own children, though they both took it and neither profited any more than I did.

At Glenmore Road we were not far distant from Warialda, the home and surgery of Uncle Will and Aunt Sara, and there with the children of our own age we spent many a happy hour. Here my cousins, Marjorie and Oswald, and I had childish tea parties, amply supplied with sweets through Marjorie's extraordinary purchasing ability. Out of one penny she could provide eight separate kinds of comestibles. Those were the days when a farthing was a real thing.

Warialda was for years a kind of second home to Mother and me.

I remember the constant drama of Uncle's patients coming and going, and even one of his colleagues lancing a carbuncle on his arm. I recall long evenings in the little backyard, which, with all its petty aspects, was a haven of refuge and peace, a good and steady background which must have been beneficial to us children.

It was at this time that my father came into my life again in a new capacity. Somehow he had prepared himself to take a kind of professional role in the mining industry. As an engineer, with an engine driver's certificate, he was now engaged on a large gold mine at Galley Swamp in the back of New South Wales. Life at Galley Swamp, when I went to visit him, was fascinating to a youngster. Father lived in a wattle-and-daub hut. It was just one room with a kind of hammock for beds and with cooking done on the open fireplace in a camp oven. Father, who had an infinity of gifts – short of the essential ability to make a living – even baked our bread, and I have eaten none better. The refrigerator was the nearby creek, while our icewater was provided by the efficient and simple container, the canvas water bag, which by some miracle of evaporation gave cold water at all times through its canvas spout. Water was caught in barrels from the iron roof, and if it ran short, then one just reduced the washing.

There was nothing of a town at Galley Swamp and little to complicate life. At the mine, one man who had some authority eventually gave Father the chance of renting one of the few regularly built houses. My mother made meticulous enquiries as to the prospects of the mine and then came up and we were all installed in this little home. It was equipped with electric light; the first time that I, or any of us, had ever seen this modern miracle.

Then without warning the mining company went into liquidation. Father went into the blue again while Mother and I returned to Uncle Philip and Aunt Florrie. For my part I could say I had lived in the Australian bush, a natural and healthful life, with a minimum of necessities; and I had experienced the distinctive aroma of the country homes of New South Wales. At Galley Swamp I learned something real of men and women, and something of the importance of water to a community.

I also hated the Galley Swamp school less than any other school I ever attended. Now that I was growing up and community games began to appeal, the games at this school began to mean more to me. I was asked to play in some Homeric cricket contest in which the accident of fate led me to partner the local champion. They could not get me out and I held on while scoring two runs. This little triumph has remained with me while thousands more important have passed to yesterday's seven thousand years. In Galley Swamp too I found with glee I could, besides kittens, keep birds as pets: budgerigars and a cockatoo, and a magpie named Charlie.

Back again with the family in Glenmore Road, my principal recollections are gustatory. Our Chinese fruit peddler would hand out his Christmas offering of goodwill, a jar of preserved ginger. I loved it then and I love it still. My second adventure into the realm of the gourmet was the discovery of ice cream. Perhaps it was only just invented. It was at this time that Oswald and I fell to the lure of the popular games: tops and marbles and hoops. We maintained links too with my mother's numerous brothers and sisters in Randwick and Camden, some thirty miles away, and in Lithgow, fifty miles from Sydney by rail. Some of the Lithgow ways were very grand, as the family maintained a much higher standard of living than we had been accustomed to.

Then my uncle moved to Moncur Street. The new house was large enough and my uncle's remuneration adequate enough to allow of a resident domestic servant. We were definitely rising in the world, with congenial neighbours, including a rollicking sea captain who commanded a large passenger ship plying between Sydney and North America. Our own street nevertheless shocked us by producing an actual case of bubonic plague during the epidemic that occurred at that time. With all Sydney we were inoculated against the plague.

At this time we began to join organised games in Centennial Park. My first place in a team of any kind was as a supernumerary in a locally organised cricket group. Despite this, we did not escape persecution. The enemy was in no way evil or especially cruel. Life is made that way; it is cruel to some in the world of man, and in the whole world of nature. Let those who can explain a world based on the survival of the cruel, on life maintained by the consumption of other animals; in a world of incredible and constant ferocity. It is remarkable that theology gives such an inadequate explanation of a world built on such principles.

At the time, my uncle's household had arrived at some degree of financial and social success, and to mark this, Oswald and I were sent to a private school. The games were excellent but the education itself was absurd and contemptible. Nor did I learn much more at the Fourth Street school in Woollahra. One tremendous advantage, however, was our proximity to the Sydney Cricket Ground, a mile away. We saw all the great players in a halycon period for cricket: Trumper, Duff, Noble, Kelly, Gregory, Hill, Iredale, Jones and Howell among the Australians, while McLaren, Jessup and Ranji are vivid memories among the visitors. And football was also a joy, though rugby was not strong then in Australia.

Cricket and football were my early loves but I have learned to enjoy many games in many countries. Any man who does not warm to a sporting contest is half dead. I certainly wish my uncle could have lived to see his son Oswald play cricket for Australia.

One thing that was not so pleasant in the 1890s was toothache. This was a perpetual agony. Nothing has altered the lives of ordinary men and women in my lifetime more than the improvement in dentistry, and the relief the dentist has given from the constant pain of earlier days.

Living in Moncur we went invariably to two beaches:, Bondi, where I learned to swim, or Rose Bay. At Bondi there was nothing then but a tram, an hotel, and a swimming baths. At Rose Bay there was nothing at all. The little beach that has now become one of the largest flying boat centres in Australia was wooded and secluded.

Sydney as I have known it has always been a huge metropolis, with a beauty and a personality entirely individual and striking. Some of Sydney's early architecture is of such beauty that one day some discerning person will purchase and protect these older dwellings. The old steam trams may have given way to electric trams, the old horse buses may have gone, and the horse cabs may have been replaced by motor taxis, but the people seem no different. I think that they actually were very much the same then as now. Of course they looked different, at least the ladies did at a time when there was no nonsense about lipstick and make-up, or painted fingers and toenails, or smoking or drinking. Women of all kinds still wore their own hair, and all of it, curled up on top of their heads and surmounted by a huge hat. Today of course the many high buildings in the central area give Sydney much of the appearance and skyline of San Francisco, but the inner self of this lovely and historic city remains unchanged and individual.

Sydney is still a part of me, and a very dear part indeed.

CHAPTER 2

SOUTHLAND

Father now came into my life again. He had installed himself in the New Zealand dredging industry, and in some extraordinary way made himself sufficiently skilled to be entrusted with the command of one of the largest dredges in Southland. So Mother and I sailed to join him in a new land romanticised by tales of the Maori and moa. We had first class berths on the Union Company's *Warrimoo*, which ran between Sydney and Dunedin, by way of Wellington and Lyttelton.[1]

At Wellington we saw horse-drawn trams for the first time and felt we had come to a very bucolic country. Friends in Wellington took us about for the day, while in Christchurch a visit to the Canterbury Museum began a hatred of museums which has lasted throughout my life.

At Dunedin Father met us. It is as if a line – a firm black line – were drawn separating our Australian existence from this new and bewildering experience in a new and incalculable land. Father took us to the vaudeville and here, at ten years old, I spent the night in a room by myself. It was a landmark. I connect sleeping alone with this new land, as if it were a special kind of New Zealand custom.

Next day we travelled south by train. At Gore, as bubonic plague was still a complication, we were met by the local health officer. We then left the train at Mataura, scarcely a metropolis now, then no more than a township built around a river crossing, a freezing works and a paper mill.

The dredge was six miles away from this centre of civilisation, in the then repulsive locality of Waimumu, in a narrow valley between two small and low hills, covered with that tussock which is so pervasive and so destructive of beauty and utility, with marsh, swamp and petty

1 The Union Steam Ship Company (1875–1971) was founded in Dunedin for the coastal trade and played an important role in New Zealand for a century in maintaining key ferry services from Wellington to Lyttelton and Wellington to Picton. In 1876 the company began shipping services to Australia; in 1881 to the Pacific Islands; in 1888 to Calcutta; from 1910 to 1936 to San Francisco and 1901–46 to Vancouver. See Duncan Haws, *Merchant Fleets No. 32: Union Steamship Company of New Zealand* (TCL Publications, 1997).

and dirty streams. Here four or five dingy galvanised-iron erections, the gold dredges, belched forth smoke while screaming with the efforts of hauling iron buckets of soil from the depths to be sieved.

It was winter time, and cold beyond anything we had known. Truly the surroundings were discouraging, but the house was the crowning blow. It was not even a shack, its two small rooms made, not of brick or stone or timber, or even wattle and daub, but of wheat sacks. Now I must not be misunderstood. The house was a wonderful achievement of Father's. He had no money. He longed for family life again. So he built a home with his own hands. Its appearance was appalling, but roofed with iron, whitewashed, clean, neat and tidy, the whole thing was completely watertight, windtight and effective. The furniture similarly was all of Father's construction, and again entirely sufficient and comfortable.

We lived here for more than a year. We had little money, but we lacked for nothing, the large roaring fires making the place warm and cosy. What are now regarded as elementary necessities we proved with our own hands to be nothing but surplusage. There was hardship, but nothing due to our accommodation, and nothing that was not bearable, as a test of character and endurance. I laugh in contempt when I hear of the hardship involved in modern day life, even for the poorest. None could have been poorer than we. How creditable it is to a democracy that a child such as I, a stranger with no money and no influence, could have risen to some of the highest positions in the land.

Mother soon became adept at the housekeeping the circumstances demanded. The household washing was done in kerosene tins outside, sometimes in the snow. Rugs and mats were made of skins and sacks. Even winter clothing was made from skins shot by Father and tailored by Mother. Much of the food too was homemade with game from the area: hare and rabbit, wild pig and deer, eels and trout. Mother made bread and scones and all the delicacies she learned from the wonderful Scottish housewives who abounded on the farms of that area.

The whole thing was hard on Mother. She worked with more intense effort than ever before, and both she and I suffered from the stinging, biting agonies of the Southland winter. I often wonder whether the climate has not changed, for there seem to be no such blizzards as we went through, but there need be no doubt as to the severity of the weather.

The dredge was a constant source of interest to me. It consisted of two pontoons, between which ran an endless chain of buckets. A dredge was able to operate with just enough water to fill a pond of sufficient size to float the pontoons. This pond was made along the track of some little stream. After that the dredge, like a snail, carried its own home wherever it went, so long as there was water to keep the pond full.

The dredge operated throughout twenty-four hours with three shifts. Each shift had a fireman in charge of the boiler, and a winch man who moved the dredge as required. He was responsible for scooping up soil to be deposited into a tubular revolving screen. This sieved out the finer matter while rolling the stones and debris out onto a moving line of smaller buckets to be deposited as 'tailings'. The sieved material then fell onto a sloping table floored with netting over which a stream of water played. This separated out the heavier material including the gold. Once a week this mesh was taken away to be 'retorted' with quicksilver until the quicksilver melted, leaving as residue only the gold.

Our Waimumu dredge was the largest and most successful of the four or five in the Waimumu valley. In good weeks we would get some forty or fifty ounces of gold, which Father and I took into the bank at Mataura each Monday morning. My problem then was getting to school each day in Mataura. For this purpose a pony was purchased. So every morning that bitter winter, and the summer that followed, I rode my pony to school, six miles in and six miles back.

I quickly found that one cannot keep warm on a horse, and I suffered severely from cold and rain and snow. Despite predominantly unhappy memories, it was a good school, and I was well taught, better than in any of the Australian schools. The headmaster was a worthy old Scot. He was a good disciplinarian and he ran a good school.

Indeed I found the teaching of English in that predominantly Scottish community to be most competent and inspiring. This was true at Mataura, and later at Gore, where I went to the District High School on one of the first free places, which did so much to improve the standard of education in New Zealand, and without which I could not have continued my schooling.

For a time I boarded, before going to and from Gore daily. Every morning I rose before five, hours before daylight in the Southland winter, a very severe one that year. I would go out in the dark, and often the rain and the sleet and the snow, find my pony, catch him (not always the easiest of tasks), currycomb him, feed him and water him, come in to my breakfast, saddle up and leave at six; ride six miles into Mataura in all weathers; stable my pony; go another eight miles in the train to Gore; walk a mile to the school; and repeat the whole process after school, arriving home about seven, hours after nightfall.

I think that little boy had something of character and something of determination, for despite this rigorous regime I did not, however inclement the weather, miss one day, though I never was, nor ever became, a lover of horses.

Soon something went wrong, as it always did where Father was concerned, and we left the dredge. I never learned the cause but my principal reaction was a happy receptivity to the attractions of the softer and easier life in the township.

According to his nature Father took a lease of the finest residence available in Mataura. Fowls were purchased, and we started a new trade. Father went about things with his usual initial enthusiasm, and his constant intense labour; and Mother according to her nature took her full share in the care of the poultry, as well as the cooking and the household chores, while I attended school and did what I could when at home.

Mother toiled also in collecting fruit, as it became ripe, and selling it to whoever would buy. The grapes were entrusted to me to sell in Gore, and how I hated this. But I did it. Here we lived, if precariously, at least with some comfort. The house itself was pleasant and modern; it had running water piped in from a spring, and an imposing view over the Mataura valley.

Mataura was almost entirely a Scotch community. I have the highest regard for the Scotch but no one could describe them as companionable to strangers, or easy to know. Although we never felt really at home in the community, slowly we made friends, some of whom remained for many years to come.

To find a more suitable place for a poultry farm, we soon moved to Glen Stuart, an old farmhouse and fifty acres of land at Ferndale, some three miles from Mataura. Here for a year or two Father made a serious attempt to create a paying business. Of course it failed because it was economically hopeless in Southland as it then was, and because of Father's qualities.

Father was a tall and heavy man, not fat, but large and straight, blond and handsome. Until we went to New Zealand I did not see much of him, and I never did know him well, or perhaps understand him at all. Father was an exotic product. He never fitted in with his surroundings. From his few comments Mother and I understood that he had been born in Sweden and that he came from a wealthy landed family. We knew that he had been married previously, and that I had a half sister. There was no connexion at all between the Swedish and Australian families, nor did we hear anything of the northern group until one of Hedwig's children wrote to me just before my sixty-fourth birthday.

I think Father's people were of aristocratic origin and that others of the same name emigrated from Sweden to seek a new mode of existence in the new lands at the ends of the earth. I had the impression that Father had a general cultural education and some military training. Father never did earn his bread, though he was the hardest-working man I ever knew, and within his limits, one of the most competent. He loved to have me as a kind of assistant to hold and hand his tools. He was thorough in everything.

Why then did he suffer so much humiliation? The first reason was his tantalising and dominating personality, the second his mental inefficiency. Yet he appreciated good literature and had a remarkable facility for adding up. It was his judgement that was unsound. He lacked the ability to organise himself in the affairs of men.

Regarding himself as a superior being, he just could not mix on terms of equality, and still less of subordination. He could not even see that he was less bright than many of his supposed inferiors, nor could he come to an accurate appraisal of the prospects he faced. He never took account of petty book-keeping, and revolting economic facts, while he pursued will-o'-the-wisps. I never met a man more competent with his hands, or less capable of arriving at a sensible appreciation of any problem.

Father was not a likeable character. His temper was short and his patience with his inferiors limited. He was apt to roar forth his disapprobation with no apparent reason. At all times he must have felt a sense of frustration that he should have been brought down from his family pedestal. Added to Mother's strong personality, Father's nature and weaknesses did not make for a happy married life.

Mother was a much finer character in every respect. Short, dark, highly intelligent and sensitive, she had a stronger personality than Father and could carry her determination through to the end. She was mentally alert, extremely capable, quick and accurate in her judgement, and of a courage of quite epic quality. I never knew a woman who so gallantly battled against the odds, and, though sadly battered, came out triumphant in the end.

Ours was not a happy family. It was hard for love to flourish year after year in dependence on the charity of others and in soul-destroying toil. Mother could not respect her husband and resented his domineering ways. Things would have been better managed if she had had control. But Father had to be master or nothing. He would not even deign to consult, and her inability to confer made her frantic with frustration. Not the best tempered of women, she became loud in her complaints. Unhappily my parents clung together under the blows of fate. They could see no way to break the chains they had themselves forged.

At Ferndale, we were financially embarrassed to the extent that arrangements were put in hand for me to take up an apprenticeship as a cabinetmaker. My school results had been respectable but not outstanding so I was prepared to face life as a cabinetmaker if it would bring my trifling wages into the family purse. But fate intervened.

When my secondary studies began at Gore District High School, I found great gaps in my education. I had not had the grounding in some subjects, particularly mathematics. I simply could not understand algebra, geometry and trigonometry. The headmaster at Gore was a good teacher of English but a poor teacher of other things. The second teacher in the secondary class was much out of his depth.

I did know, however, that I was not a dunce. Moreover I was greatly encouraged by the other teacher. This lady took me under her wing and coached me where I was weakest. With her help, in the first term examinations I came top of three of the eleven subjects, and in the final examination at the end of the year, top of all eleven.

Such was the astonishment at this dramatic effort by a newcomer that the gold medal as dux was only awarded after much debate. It was a fine performance, on which I can congratulate that little boy fifty years after. It gave me a self-confidence that carried me well in later years, though at the time it made me the most arrant and objectionable of adolescents, convinced that I alone knew everything that ought to be.

At the end of the year I sat the matriculation and civil service examinations. To my surprise I did handsomely in both. I even obtained astonishingly good results in algebra and calculus, subjects in which I knew nothing at all. Passing the civil service exam in twenty-sixth place meant that I would be offered a place in the civil service.

By the end of my schooling I had greatly improved my standing with my schoolfellows. This was because I was good at games. I played cricket, and given my Australian approach, better than the country boys at Gore. One could not exaggerate one's standing as a member of the eleven. I played too with success as a footballer, as a wing or fullback in the back line. Skill in games did much for my morale and it was sweet to see those who had derided me fawning on one of the school's athletes.

The organised excursions of the day to watering places like Colac Bay or the Bluff or Queenstown added salt to our humdrum lives and gave us all geography and civics lessons of lasting value. They also built up my rather timid ego while giving me a wider horizon. I saw how other people's lives were conducted.

At the same time I had to contend with life at Ferndale: the agonies of trying to clean boots, the exasperation of turning the wheel of the butter churn, and the utterly laborious task of hand milking, with the cold and the dirt, and the ill humour of the cows. Cleaning the fowl houses was one of my pet aversions. Feeding, collecting eggs, killing and plucking chickens, carting the coal and the feed in our little dray, and chaffering around the neighbourhood for the purchase of birds, all fell to my reluctant lot.

But there were compensations, including birdnesting and rabbiting. Birds' eggs brought me a regular income, but from rabbiting and the breeding of ferrets I made a great deal more. My ferrets became a happy and profitable hobby. During a day we could catch anything from twenty to a hundred rabbits, so the money was a great help to the household.

Money could also be had helping the neighbouring farmers with their sowing and harvesting. I ploughed, harrowed and operated most kinds of horse-drawn implements, thinned turnips, dug potatoes, stooked, threshed and made hay, a task commonly painted as idyllic, but hard and unpleasant work. I did not like haymaking – in fact I did not like farm work, though I enjoyed cutting wood for the fires, and found a special pleasure in pick and shovel work. We named our wheelbarrow Melancholy after the song 'Away with Melancholy' that teased David Copperfield during homework. Mother used to read us Dickens every night when there was no more work to do.

At Glen Stuart I had no horse, but Father purchased an old bicycle. Bicycles were the latest fashion and were a matter of great moment in the community in those days. It was the sporting thing to have one, and bicycle races were the cause of much excitement and some betting.

We actually made some friends at Glen Stuart and, amidst the apprehensions of recurrent failure, had much fun and contentment. In particular I remember with special affection the first two of many dogs I learned to love and cherish. My love for these two dogs entirely supplanted my earlier affection for birds. I never had another bird for a pet. We also had an amusing young pig, who attached herself to us as one of the household. The other unusual character was our aged horse. Aged he was, but he could, and did, do all our work, even carrying coal from Mataura. Father, who had a happy knack for appropriate nomenclature, called him Trampas after a character in *The Virginian*, then a very popular novel by Owen Wister.

The countryside itself I greatly enjoyed. I roamed the foothills and never lost the sense of freedom where to be found wherever man has not defiled the handiwork of nature.

Amid much therefore that was pleasant, more that was bearable, and some that was detestable, we lived at Glen Stuart, clouded with that apprehension of failure. For the poultry farm would not do, and had to be abandoned. It was at that point, when all seemed black and hopeless, that Mother came driving up the road waving a newspaper. It was the result of the civil service exam. A way out had now shown itself, and a certain, if very small, income, was now assured in the great world of the capital.

CHAPTER 3

WELLINGTON

In due course I received an official telegram from Wellington offering a cadetship in the Department of Education. The opening salary was forty pounds a year, with a lodging allowance of twenty-five pounds. This total of sixty-five pounds, with an annual increase of ten, was destined to keep me, and then Mother, and for a time Father, by dint of the strictest economy. When my parents set up home in Wellington and the lodging allowance disappeared, we were brought to painful straits. I wore the clothes in which I had come to Wellington until they wore out. I spurned advice to dress more like other people; I had not the money.

On departure my father actually came in the train as far as Gore. This was unlike him, as was, still more, his emotion. He was openly distressed, while, God forgive me, I was elated. At last I was to be free from control. I did resent his authority, which was not always wisely or gently applied. His love for me was revealed at infrequent times. It always had a most moving effect on me, and left me infinitely sad for what might have been.

The train moved out of Gore, leaving Father to make his way home, while I soared into life. I travelled first class, as became a budding civil servant, for in those days the civil service was a service of gentlemen, and gentlemen of superior intelligence. It was a distinguished section of the community. Today when it just another trade union, something has been lost.

I remember my exultation clearly, as I remember the demeanour of the only other occupant of the birdcage carriage. Not one word did he give, this man who, I learned later, was the well-known Head of a Government Department. I realised then that perhaps the great world would be less receptive to my genius than I had imagined. I was a forlorn and agonised waif adrift on an uncharted sea.

How was I to find an hotel? How was I to catch the train and find the ship in Lyttelton? I had never had the confidence or presumption to interrupt and ask for advice or instructions. At the Dunedin hotel the manager had no recollection of my father. As the place was full, I had to share a room with a member of the staff and then, in the morning, as I had insufficient funds, ask for the bill to be sent to my father.

At the Dunedin railway station I saw another cadet on the same kind of journey, and then, in Lyttelton, an old Gore schoolmate showed me the way to the Union Steamship Company's *Mararoa*. We came alongside the Wellington wharf on a bright, sunny, windy morning. It was 6 February 1906. I was fifteen and a half years old. From that moment I supported myself, and to a large extent, my mother and father. Happily for me I was met, and I am as grateful today as I was then to have all my fears removed when Mr McInerny, a relative of the Mataura policeman, and himself employed in the Department of Education, shouted my name from the wharf, and took me to the boarding establishment where he was staying.

Later Mr McInerny led me to the Presence. The Head of the Department received me with the reserve necessary to maintain dignity. I was allocated to the Superannuation Branch of the Department and set to work with some pages of figures. My immediate superior was a nice young woman who shortly after died of tuberculosis, which I learned was rife in that particular office.

I was then allotted the task of copying all the Department's outward letters, folding them into envelopes and posting them. In my spare time I was also the telephone operator but, as a new thing, this did not take me much from immediate postal duties.

These were the days before typewriters. I well remember the first machine being installed. Before shorthand was the regular thing, most official letters were written by the great hands of the great minds who drafted them. I was responsible for damping them, and pressing them on blank sheets of tissue, which made a good copy if one were skilled enough. I then passed them over to the Records Branch to classify and file.

It was a busy post and brought me into touch with most of the other officers of the Department. As gentlemen we had a comparatively easy time. We came to the office at ten in the morning and, with one hour for lunch, ceased work at four in the afternoon. Unlike the hoi polloi, we never worked on a Saturday afternoon, and we had paid holidays when no others enjoyed such a thing. We were led to believe that to be a civil servant was to be of the higher orders of the community, and I believe that to have been a good thing.

The city of Wellington in 1906 was smaller and had none of today's imposing buildings. Indeed it had some of the primitive remains of earlier days. A signal station on Mt Victoria informed the townsfolk of the arrival of ships. Courtenay Place was practically the waterline, and the present dock site, the Thorndon Esplanade. The city has spread upwards and outwards, the Hutt Valley out of all recognition, but essentially nothing seems to have altered. Money went further when a shilling an hour was considered good pay.

My personal life was chequered and at times embarrassingly unhappy. Despite my essential timidity, I had adopted an overbearing manner as a defence mechanism. My problems were bitter. First was the question of where I was to live. On this I had carried the strictest of instructions from my parents. I must not spend all my twenty-five shillings a week, for some would be needed for them. So I was to get board and lodging as cheaply as possible. How was a shy and inexperienced child to huckster around to meet their expectation of paying less than fifteen shillings a week? Instead I stayed with my kind friend McInerny in Hawkestone Street, with a rather superior clientele and an excellent table, at seventeen shillings and sixpence.

Later, when I was told I must pay a pound a week, I left for a much inferior place around the corner in Molesworth Street. Most of the guests were youngsters in some Government Department, with the doyen of the place, a Mr Buck, the chief letter carrier of the city, asserting that the sun revolved around the earth. The proprietors were among the hardest workers I have ever met.

The young and the elderly that I met at these two boarding houses were a wholesome group from whom I learned much that was good. We may have been unduly preoccupied with sport, but that is at least a healthy thing, and admirably calculated to form and develop character. Old McInerny, who fathered me at a time of great difficulty for such a tender, if noisy youngster, drank to excess, but he was a good and admirable person.

At the office it was not quite the same. The Head of my Department was a queer, introverted, self-centred man, who wore a beard and an air of superior reserve. I never could persuade myself that he was a great man, though I took good care to show him the same deference as the remainder of his serfs. The second in command was a baronet. Sir Edward Gibbs was at least a man. He was not very intelligent, but he was sound and true and sensible, and a good example for a youngster. I liked and admired Gibbs and I hope I learned from him.

The third man in the office was grotesque. He had a certain superficial ability, but a character so weak that he was terrified, not only of his senior officers, but of life itself. He bent and swayed to every breeze. There was no trusting him. He would lie and dissemble. His word was nothing. No one liked or trusted this unpleasant, frightened, rabbity little man who could have only risen so high under a system based on seniority.

When I had served my time in the stamp-licking Department, I was removed one step up into the Records Branch. This is a good system of preliminary training, but one of the least demanding of tasks. Usually one finds there a group of old hacks, or the more stupid of the newcomers. We had both classes in the enterprise to which I now lent some assistance.

The officer in charge came from a well-known family distinguished for its oddities. This man's peculiarity was a hatred of soap and water. He was a silly man, with all sorts of queer and senseless quirks of character. He did me no good, except that he taught me how not to behave. Still, from the very nature of the records work, I learned habits of order and system which have been most valuable to me.

Then I was moved to the Native Schools Branch. There I met two of the finest men imaginable. Frank Severne was a crusty old bachelor, but straight and honest. His was the responsibility for the administration of the Native Schools. Duty to him was more than a word. He did what seemed right, and what he did, he did well. 'Do it now; do it yourself; and do it as well as you possibly can' were his principles.

William Watson Bird, the then Senior Inspector of Native Schools, was another man of high and inspiring character. Bird was bright, breezy, straightforward and honourable, with a hatred of sham and a gift of rollicking humour. Bird looked on the world as a collection of jokes, some of them, such as our immediate superiors, in bad taste, but funny for all that. These two fine men personified for me what is manly and wise and true. Much of what is good in my life has come from them.

There too I had one contact, and one only, with one of the most famous of all New Zealanders. Richard John Seddon was the first of our 'do-gooders'. Now I am entirely in favour of doing good: I admire those who do good; and in my small way I have endeavoured to do good myself. I use the term 'do-gooder' to describe the busy bodies of our times, some visionaries, some highly self interested, who have put into practical application the depressing theory that the higher interests of mankind are served by using the tax powers of Government to take three pounds from Smith, who has usually earned them, to give two to Jones, who usually does not deserve them, and to fritter the other away in meeting the costs of this transaction.

On the whole I believe that the innovations of Seddon were right and proper, but the very success of these novel humanitarian steps tended to inspire the woolly minded all over the world. Seddon might indeed be described as the originator of the 'New Deal' or 'Fair Deal' 'Redistribution of Wealth' school which has done so much to change the face of the civilised world.

I can see Seddon now, as for the first and last time, I was ushered into his office one morning in 1906. A big man, burly and imposing in his bulk, with an ineffable and irresistible air of authority and confidence in his every word and gesture. Timidly I entered the regal presence. From the great man's violent reception of the document I innocently bore from the Department of Education I gathered that it was not pleasing to him.

The case was this. One of the small native schools in a remote part of the country needed a replacement. The inspectors had carefully scrutinised a lengthy list of candidates possibilities for this little post and picked out three outstanding candidates. The last on the list possessed no academic qualifications and had only just been released from prison for embezzlement. When the Premier appointed the gentleman from gaol, the Departmental officials had the temerity to return the papers to the Minister calling attention to Mr X's criminal record. I cowered in the corner while with a snarl Seddon grasped his pen and wrote once more in very large letters, 'Appoint Mr X'.

Nothing did as much as this incident to tarnish my early hopes of mankind. In one stroke my trailing clouds of glory were reft away, and I was forced gloomily to contemplate the possibility that the world was imperfect, and that in this wider life, which I had so lately joined, all might not be right and just and fair.

This was the beginning of a distaste and distrust with which I have learned to approach and judge the genus Politician. It may be that Seddon's action, wrong to the school and the scholars, was wholly atrocious. Certainly I cannot acquit him of politics in one of its most contemptible aspects. Nevertheless I can just conceive circumstances in which such a remarkable decision could in some measure be explained as an attempt by a Minister, knowing more of Mr X than did the Department, to help an innocent or repentant man.

My only other connection with Seddon was my attendance, in the dead of night, at the melancholy reception accorded to his remains on their arrival in Wellington after his sudden and unexpected demise at sea. A huge crowd had gathered at the wharf as the *Oswestry Grange* inched into its berth amid the wailing of a Maori tangi and the solemn strains of the 'Dead March'. The cortege, that followed the coffin, was lit by torches and kerosene lamps, and has lingered in my memory as a nation's farewell to one of its greatest sons.

Meantime at the office I continued with my training. Typing was one of the things that I took and at which I became quite good. I also learned Pitman's shorthand. My domestic life, however, was unhappy. My mother arrived and found a poor little room in Molesworth Street. My heart weeps now for her plight. When my father came up, we roomed first with a family in Brougham Street before moving to a cottage in Tasman Street, near the Basin Reserve.

I can remember taking holidays on the Wanganui River and on the farm of our Brougham Street family, but there were few other breaks in our daily routine. We were hard pressed for money, and our lives were straitened indeed, at a time when my father almost entirely gave up. His business enterprises did not last long, though he had resumed control of affairs, just as if they had not already overcome him many times.

Mother's solution to our financial difficulties at this time was to establish a boarding house for university students in Hawkestone Street. In an old, broken-down home, she earned a bare livelihood for the three of us. It was hard and unpleasant labour. So began a long period of years in which the presence of boarders or roomers meant we never really had a home to ourselves.

It was in these circumstances that I did most of my studying. My cadetship provided for continuing education, and my mother scraped the bottom of the barrel to enable me to go to university. I had of course passed the matriculation exam, but coming from an inefficient country high school, I was far from ready for university courses. Choosing to take arts, I found I could make no progress, because I could not understand mathematics. So I decided to take law. And for this I had to teach myself sufficient Latin to pass the elementary exam for a degree.

The struggle with Latin was good for me, I am sure, and my law course proceeded without setback to an LLB, and eventually an LLM, though I did not attain a First Class degree. It may have been that top honours could not be achieved working all day in the civil service. Life is made up of setbacks. So I put this little failure, a profound disappointment to me at the time, behind me and went on.

Although I was not one of the original students at Victoria University College, I was early enough to be with the first of them. It was then very much a night school, but in some degree, it was an inspiring experience. Certainly some of my success in the life of men was the result of something what I received, and put to use, from my university course.

The professors were not a clear or inspiring body of men. Brown, who taught Latin, was a dear old man, whom I loved. The Dean of Law, a fine man, I respected for his knowledge, but not for his teaching ability. The Professor of New Zealand Law was a brash man. The one real inspiration was the Professor of Philosophy.

Tommy Hunter was a fresh, stirring mind of liberal views, willing and unafraid to search for the truth. From him I learned more than from any other man before or since. His penetrating and enthusing personality did much to give life to my callow and fallow mentality. From him I took essential habits of orderly thought and systematic analysis. He taught me how to think; how to evaluate and classify my facts; how to weigh and balance contrary considerations; how to check and recheck; and how to avoid careless thinking: 'Get your facts; get them yourself; check them; check them yourself; check them again.'

Hunter knew the value of time and of focus. Never leave a problem: work through until you have a solution. Never accept a commonly accepted proposition and never be led astray by intellectual arrogance: we all make mistakes. Never assume anyone to be in error until you have proven the issue. Never assert a negative: it's difficult to prove. Never generalise from the particular: it's unscientific. Never particularise from the general: it's often misleading. Think everything right through; then when you have the truth you can take your position. Hunter was a great teacher and wonderfully rounded human being. Our country lost something of spiritual value when he died.

These were not easy times. To learn my Latin and keep up with my course, I had to rise at five and leave home after two hours of study, and walk up Glenmore Road – how names recur – to Victoria for the eight o'clock lecture. I then went to the office and then back to the university until eight, and then the walk home. During the university session I did this every day, for years. It called for one possessed of determination and industry.

All the time I had another demanding activity: sport. In effect I divided my life into two halves: on the one, hard work and my studies; on the other, organised games. By a happy dispensation I have always been reasonably good at games and have loved cricket and football. It was my good fortune to get into a rugby side that knew how to use its backs. A season in a good team did much for me. I knew what to do when the ball came to me. I set out with one thought: to get to the line. When a university club was founded I naturally joined, playing either as wing or, more frequently, at fullback.

It was my privilege then, the greatest of all times in New Zealand rugby, to meet some of the giants of rugby. This was the era of the 1905 All Black side, the best I ever saw. After their return, I played against some of the greatest of the Originals, including Wallace, Roberts, and Thomson. I played too, against many of those who were to replace the heroes of those days, as time has the habit of replacing the heroes of every age.

I could write a book on the great players. Of defensive players I would choose two, both fullbacks: Nepia of the Invincibles of 1924, and the 1950s New Zealand fullback, Bob Scott of the Kiwis. Both were nearly perfect in defence, and both were a joy to watch at all times. Of all-rounders I would choose Billy Wallace, one of the mainstays of the 1905 All Blacks. Of attacking players, the champagne of rugby, I would choose Bert Cooke. He was by all odds the quickest man into his stride and at his full pace the best I have ever seen. He was the quickest to see and seize an opening of any kind. Of forwards I also have one selection only, Arthur (Ranji) Wilson, who was everything, everywhere on the field, and a great toiler in the scrummage.

I was never even a good rugby player but I did have sufficient skill to play in the university's top team. I was a fast and determined aspirant for a touchdown, and a fairly solid and reliable fullback. But I was light, 140 pounds at the time, and so was the team as a whole. We were not very skilled, but we loved the game and took our lickings and occasional successes with resignation and composure. Football, I simply note, is like real life. It is full of unusual incidents. Things can happen of which one can be completely unaware until one is devastated by their impact.

My cricketing career was just as fascinating to me, and more successful than football. For that reason it was more enjoyable for me to play. I have long lost the patience to watch cricket as it is played today. We then went to the wickets to make runs. Nothing seems further from the thoughts of present day batsmen: if runs come incidentally, they seem to have no insuperable objection, but their main object is simply to stay in. Batsmen, once the pride and joy of their side, now pose and posture, and decline to play at anything that would not hit their wicket if left. Even the bowlers have found new methods of wasting time, with bowlers' runs being elongated out of all knowledge. Even the veriest minnow now takes his twenty or thirty paces, and stalks this distance at the pace of an undertaker. That the game has deteriorated as a spectacle is indubitable, but somehow or other I am sure cricket will live and once again be the delight it was in my young days.

Early in my stay in Wellington I recall vividly practising at the Basin Reserve. I first played for the Phoenix Cricket Club. It had some outstanding players from all of whom I learned something. Hickey and Gibbes were first class bowlers and Laws a good all rounder. I began as the third grade team wicketkeeper, but when the first grade wicketkeeper fell ill, I filled the vacancy. I have always had good fortune at critical times. I not only kept wickets well in that match but I made 48 runs in cheerful style. Thus I found myself a regular member of the first eleven and finished the season with quite good figures.

When the Victoria University College entered the competition, I transferred to that club. The Wellington coach, an Australian bowler called J.V. Saunders, was allocated to the weakest team in the competition, and it became my privilege to keep wickets to a much higher class of bowling than was otherwise to be found in the country. That season, when I had the advantage of Saunders bowling and coaching, I was selected for the Wellington provincial team. In the trial I did well behind the wickets, and also made some runs. I then had a fairly good season or two, and it is still a matter of pride that, for a quite lengthy period, I played in the best class of cricket that New Zealand can afford.

Saunders, in typical Australian fashion, played a game in which you asked no quarter, and certainly gave none. He was full of hints and stratagems to lure a wicket. If he appealed for leg before wicket it was for him a cardinal sin if I did not appeal also, with all my heart and voice, whether I thought it out or not. Blacklock, a most graceful batsman and excellent captain, had different standards. He drew a distinction between the laws of cricket and 'cricket'. Once an opposing batsman called for a quick run. Unfortunately his pads came undone. He stumbled and fell. The ball was returned to me. 'Don't break the wicket, Berry,' shouted Blacklock. 'Hold it.' And I did until the batsman got back in his crease. I always thought that was good sportsmanship. I learned something from it. I hope I always played as a sportsman would wish – in cricket and life.

In cricket, as in rugby, I had the good fortune to play against the best. New Zealand does not produce great cricketers, but one Wellington player was to rise to the height of fame in Australia. Clarrie Grimmett, born in Dunedin, was selected for a Wellington team just when he was developing his googly. I kept wickets for him, and neither he nor I had any real idea which way the ball was going to break; byes were plentiful. Grimmett was a quiet and modest boy, and we all took great pride in his subsequent astonishing success playing for Australia.

I had the usual young man's interests and struggles during the perplexing time of adolescence. I had formed boyish attachments, innocent and fleeting, for this girl, and that. I had read widely and largely rectified the astonishing shortcomings in education of the day in the facts of life. I have never been a handsome, or even an attractive person. Nevertheless I was gradually shedding my cruder qualities, though I was still unbearably self-satisfied, and always striving for public notice and approbation. I was constantly putting on an act. I was wrapped up in myself, and intolerant of of the world that was not me, brash, conceited and assertive. Had I met this young man, as he then was, I should have found him intolerable.

Yet it was not all bad. I was improving. Loud and assertive as I was, I retained a fundamental modesty. I could exult in my petty sporting successes, but I could not push myself forward, nor approach authority, except in fear and trepidation. I could not impose or interrupt. I could not shop, or ever count my change. Rank and official position daunted me. Only gradually did my reputation as a good player of many games allow me, as I recall with one of the Freybergs, to lower the spines of my bruised personality and slowly grow more human, more poised, more kindly, and better balanced.

I was now transferred from the Native Schools to a new branch of the Education Department. The School Journal had just been approved as a source of suitable reading for New Zealand's educational system. This was an excellent idea, and it has continued with conspicuous success until the present day. The first thing was to find a suitable Editor, an experienced teacher with some literary taste and ability. The senior officers of the Department all agreed on the best man, but the new Massey Government was quite shameless in devotion to the principle of the loaves and fishes. As a result the Minister of the day appointed the third choice.

Although he was a university graduate, the new Editor was an ignorant and somewhat childish man. He was weak and uncertain, and his effect on his staff was unhappy and disconcerting. His life was a perpetual flurry to keep in line with his surroundings, and particularly with his Minister and his heads of Department. But he did a good job. The Journal was an immediate success.

At that post I learned the fundamental difference between taking the final responsibility for anything, and merely doing something under supervision. In the Editor's absence I was once left in charge, and had to make a last-minute alteration in a text he had already approved. I made an error, and am still ashamed fifty years after the event. It was a small matter, but I got it quite wrong. It is all the more remarkable as no one ever mentioned the error.

I learned much from that incident. I learned to take the most careful precautions when personally responsible. I learned too, to be meticulously careful when asserting a negative. As it just cannot be proved, it requires the utmost care before its assertion.

The work on the Journal did not call for any special skill or knowledge, but it taught me habits of industry and application. Proof reading itself requires some degree of reliability. In front of thousands of readers and a discriminating and critical audience, we had to watch our grammar, our spelling, and our facts. I must give the Editor great credit for the admirable results he attained. Poor fellow, he was later to die by his own hand.

It was an unusual group of people in the Education Department. Tuberculosis, as I have stated, was rife, while two of my colleagues went insane. The great majority were simply uninspiring. Despite the shocking leadership, there was were enough people of superior intelligence to enable me to rub my wits with others to real advantage. From these young people in this poorly conducted Department were to come a distinguished band of senior officials, including Heads of the Treasury, the Air Department, National Broadcasting and the Public Service Commission.

There, in hackwork and dull routine, I spent ten of the most formative years of my life, while the world around me was reeling and tottering, to the ruin and destruction of so much that seemed eternal and unalterable. Though in my busy life I knew it not, love and war were to alter my whole existence, and both were upon me.

In 1911 the School Journal received its latest recruit, straight from school. She wore a wide sailor hat, a white shirtwaist, and a black skirt. Her face was round and chubby, her eyes almost black. She was sixteen years old. One hears of love at first sight, and many deride the existence of such a phenomenon. Those unbelievers are mistaken. I knew that very moment that here was fate, and I expected, poor simple soul, that she would know too.

Nothing of the kind. Miss Brown took a hearty dislike to me when I found, to my exasperation, that she was a careless officer and told her so. Long nights of happy social activities left her tired and listless, and less accurate and industrious than was desirable. She went blithely about her way, irrespective of my views, and ignorant of my affection and devotion. Apart from my inescapable official conversations, she would not speak to me at all.

At this time Mother's boarding house came to an end, and my father decided to go to Sydney. There he found a supervisory position on one of the Sydney wharves as a kind of watchman, guarding the premises and tallying the goods and vehicles. He held this post during the war, when such responsibilities were of considerable importance, and he held it well. It was a comfort that at long last he had found a post that he could hold with satisfaction.

To earn a living and maintain a home, my mother began a lodging house, a somewhat easier and pleasanter task than a boarding house. One had fewer critics, but enough worries, among a diversified and often distressed group. One family of genteel people stayed with us for years. We had another tragic little family from Liverpool who had come to the new world to escape the ravages of tuberculosis. How this family passed the medical exam I do not know.

Then we had a junior official from the Prime Minister's Department whose wife died in childbirth. The official, with his two little boys, then lived with us for years, eating at our table. While the father was at work, the boys were in our care. Like his political masters, this man had an extreme disregard for time. Mother found herself providing special meals when he deigned to enter. Still I became very much attached to his little boys, played with them, sang to them, told them stories and saw them through their infantile diseases.

For a time we even had with us the contractor who was building the new Parliament Buildings. As the Government had let the work on a cost plus ten per cent basis, the contract made him as rich as a gold mine, and soon wafted this family out of our home.

Before that I had finished my Bachelor of Laws. With the contractor's wife promising to manage our home, I induced my mother to take a holiday, which she desperately needed, with her family in Sydney.

While she was away, World War I broke out. When Mother came back I was gone, and the world was never to be the same again.

CHAPTER 4

SAMOA

From my earliest mental stirrings I have been fascinated by the interplay of nations, people, cultures and religions. History has always captured my imagination. As soon as I could think seriously I had followed from newspapers the growing threat to peace in the swelling power and ambition of the German people. I watched the Agadir incident of 1911 with the greatest anxiety, and I had come to the conclusion that a conflict must arise. I was not therefore surprised when the Germans seized on the Sarajevo incident to justify an attack on the democratic world. The ruthless rape of Belgium left me indignant and infuriated.

Here was something clear and indefensible. The world must meet this relapse into barbarism. It was for us to meet this evil thing, by force against force. Little recking the bitter agony and destruction that was to follow, I was impatient at Edward Grey's attempts in London at a last-minute solution. I thirsted to take my share in this modern crusade against evil, and in defence of freedom and truth.

I had just completed my law degree, and could now choose whether to follow that profession as my life's work. I badly wanted to take my chances in the law, but with Mother, and the life that was left to her, I could not. Holding this view, it is extraordinary that I rushed to enlist without consultation with Mother, on the very outbreak of war. At the last of several parties in our home during Mother's absence to celebrate my enlistment, Nellie Brown was there, and I took her home from this rather sombre little function.

At the barracks in Buckle Street I met many of my university and sporting friends. War is a terrible thing, but there was something in the highest degree satisfactory in answering the call of our country in a time of crisis. This feeling, almost of exaltation, is real and good and true.

My war services were entirely undistinguished and inadequate. The force I had so eagerly joined at the outbreak of war – my regimental number was 1/100 – was destined for nothing more dramatic than the seizure, without fighting, of the German colony of Western Samoa. That, as fate would have it, was the most useful thing I did during the war.

The Samoan interlude was interesting in a high degree. It was fortunate that there was no fighting involved, as we were largely untrained, and badly officered. We gathered in the barracks, were sworn in, matched up with clothing and equipment, farewelled at the Basin Reserve, and shipped aboard the *Moeraki* and *Monowai*.

On deck, after the evening meal, I was astounded to see two girls walking down the wharf, and one of them was Nellie Brown – my Nellie Brown. However she got there I never knew, but there she was, and my heart leaped up. She was there to farewell her brother, but she did see me, and waved goodbye. I can see her there now, sweet and dear to me, but as far as I could see quite unattainable.

We left Wellington, on an August afternoon in the fateful year of 1914, into a nasty sea. Seasickness is not a pleasant thing, especially in the rigours of a troopship. We did not know it, but the German cruisers *Scharnhorst* and *Gneisenau* from the Asiatic squadron were in the vicinity, and we had to sail to New Caledonia, to pick up the battle cruiser *Australia*, and an allied flotilla. Our armada then made its way, via Fiji, to Samoa, through some of the roughest seas I have ever experienced.

I shall not forget the lovely still dawn as we approached Apia that August morning. The little *Psyche* steamed into the harbour flying a white flag of truce. The German Governor Wilhelm Solf was inland at Vailima, Robert Louis Stevenson's old home.[1] We learned that no resistance was to be offered.

We went over the side and were towed to the beaches, where we made a wide sweep through the plantations and bush surrounding Apia. In the evening my company bedded down on a concrete floor in a public market on the front road of Apia. I was deputed to go off and managed, despite threats of a court martial, to buy some welcome coconuts. At the same time the Germans were pouring over Belgium

1 Berendsen must have been unaware that Solf returned to Germany in 1911. His Deputy, Erich Schultz-Ewerth, who took over in December 1911, Damon Salesa comments, was as able and as accomplished as Solf. Schultz-Ewerth was made Governor in June 1912. After the occupation he was deported and interned, but in some comfort, on Somes Island in Wellington Harbour.

using the steamroller tactics that were to astonish the world, both in that war, and in the later conflict that was still in the womb of time.

Boredom was the principal difficulty we had to contend with in that romantic isle. But there was much to enjoy. While Noumea was beautiful and Fiji attractive, Samoa surpassed them both. The high and bold mountain ranges are graceful and majestic, covered with lush and luxuriant verdure. The sparkling streams of clearest blue, the golden sands of the seashore, the dazzling white surf and the unceasing murmur of the coral reefs, the ineffable, lazy grace of the palm trees, the scent of the copra, the gentle song of the trade winds, the soft and variegated greens of the vegetation, the vivid colours of the flamboyant hibiscus and the ivory of the frangipani combine, in unforgettable charm, with the neat and picturesque native towns, the clean and handsome people, the thatched and attractive houses and the tidy village greens to render Samoa indescribably beautiful.

In the order of beautiful lands, the South Sea Islands are a thing apart. Honolulu has lost some of its charm by its sophistication. Tahiti and Samoa are more natural, while Rarotonga in the Cooks is the loveliest of them all. Truly these are lotus lands. One would ask nothing better than to spend a gentle and lazy life in surroundings of such extreme beauty. Even in the capacity of a soldier, my visit to Samoa left me with a love of the tropics, and of this soft and graceful land, that time has not withered.

At this point I have to observe that the more civilisation obtrudes itself in the South Seas, the less attractive the land and the peoples become. Europe has of course brought some degree of peace and order, and freedom from strife and murder, and even cannibalism. But apart from these basic gifts, Oceania and its peoples are best left to themselves. It is in this sense much to the credit of the present Administrations that their primary objective has been the defence of these peoples from Europeanisation. Later in my official capacity I was to learn how detrimental many of our European customs, and especially foodstuffs, can be to such peoples.

Every land has its drawbacks. Here it was mainly the mosquito. The buzz of the pest was everywhere, day and night. Sporadic efforts to eradicate or minimise the nuisance had failed everywhere but in the Panama Canal Zone. In a land such as Samoa, without money and with water everywhere, eradication seemed hopeless. As the Anopheles mosquito had never reached Samoa, the principal disease was not malaria, but filariasis, with its distressing symptoms of elephantiasis. Another terrible disease is yaws. Less serious ailments abounded. Truly all earthly paradises have their devil and their purgatory.

It was useful to me too, to see life in the army as one of the common herd. I learned early that men in the mass are good and sound and reliable, and even inspiring in their unselfishness and helpfulness. As the first volunteers, this may have been an especially fine body of men, but I learned to admire my fellows. One soon learns the real quality of a man in the crowded life of the army. Here I met some of the finest of mankind in the humblest of capacities.

Another valuable lesson was that every man, however modest, can teach us all something of value, as we learnt from a common wharf labourer. He taught us how to unload coal with the least effort on the *Monowai* in New Caledonia. I must have worked well that day for I found myself promoted to lance corporal. I did not appreciate the potentialities of the rank until I was in a group digging trenches in Apia Harbour. 'Come out of there, Corporal. Don't you know that NCOs are not supposed to work with the men?' That gave me a good tale for years to come.

Boredom was the principal enemy, as I have said, in our long stay on the island. At first the food was understandably bad, with our biscuit providing the daily entries for a weevil race. Once we had adjusted, these inexperienced men were well treated, given the incapacity of most of the staff. Gradually one became accustomed to being wet and even sleeping wet, living with scorpions and centipedes, and the thud of a falling – painful and possibly lethal – coconut.

To escape boredom I became the guard at Government House. Vailima was originally the home of Robert Louis Stevenson, so famous in literature and Samoan history. It is in a most delightful situation, some hundreds of feet up the mountain side for coolness, with an exhilarating view over the fronds and the bays, to the the distant horizon across the rolling sea. Cunning use has been made of a small stream to form a delightful little swimming pool, with a natural waterfall for a shower. Lawns and gardens and orchards provide choice tropical fruits and vegetables, shade and beauty.

A winding path leads up to Stevenson's grave on Mt Vaea. The grave itself had been allowed to drift into semi ruin, and the path was almost hidden in the undergrowth. Here on a small slab is engraved Stevenson's requiem:

> Under the wide and starry sky,
> Dig the grave and let me lie;
> Glad did I live and gladly die,
> And I laid me down with a will.
> This be the verse you 'grave for me:
> *Here he lies where he longs to be;*
> *Home is the sailor, home from the sea,*
> *And the hunter home from the hill.*

I am not an admirer of Stevenson's work, nor of the man, except for his courage. In Samoa Stevenson was an inflammatory element in the smouldering heat of Samoan politics. But he knew how, and where, to choose a home, and my sojourn there, although all too short, and spoilt by the arrival of senior officers, was highly enjoyable. At Vailima the first guard lived on the best of the land.

I next inherited from a sergeant, who thought he was doing me an injury, the leadership of a group providing sand from the Apia waterfront for our campsite. This was the softest and easiest activity with which I was ever entrusted. This pleasant task lasted for an astonishingly long time. I suppose we averaged less than a dozen cartloads a day, with all the real delights of what amounted to a permanent holiday, out of camp, in town, and at the seaside.

Then I found another tolerable occupation; membership of an outlying picquet. No one was clear about their purpose. We were several miles out in the country, where discipline became senseless and unnecessary. My function as second in command was to lead a patrol out to meet another. The walk was for two miles, through coconut plantations and bush, down to the seashore, where we waited comfortably for our opposite numbers. We did this three times a day: at dawn, quite delightful; at dusk, equally delightful; and at midnight, when I took special care to check the safety catches of the men.

That was a good job, while it lasted, but on return to ordinary duty the monotony became intense. So I became a member of the regimental signallers, which saw me through the rest of the campaign. I enjoyed this work, at which I became very proficient. It left me free to career about the island, so I became familiar with the lovely countryside around Apia.

We had one serious alarm when we were alerted, and moved off to the seashore, on word that German warships were approaching, as indeed they were. I happened to be corporal of the guard, and had to transport reserves of ammunition to the harbour trenches.

When we got to the seafront, there indeed were the German ships. Either the *Gneisenau* or the *Scharnhorst* had come right into Apia Harbour, and we had the uncomfortable experience of marching along the main road on the waterfront, out in the open, and under the muzzles of the cruiser's eight-inch guns, which swung round with us as we moved along. We were within easy machine-gun range, and no one has to this day explained why we were not molested. Perhaps the best explanation is that the ships were commanded by a man of high character, Admiral Graf von Spee. They had already communicated with some local Germans, at Mulifanua in the west of the island, and had learned that Samoa was now in British occupation. As the inhabitants were being well treated, any firing on us would have needlessly damaged the property of the German community around Apia.

Once arrived at our posts, we waited for several hours, with one ship in the harbour, and the others outside. The whole squadron then made off to the eastward, subsequently to destroy Admiral Craddock's British squadron, which gallantly attacked them, despite the absence of its most powerful ship, the *Canopus*, at Coronel, on the west coast of South America. The Germans were then annihilated by Admiral Sturdee's two battlecruisers, the *Inflexible* and the *Invincible*, at the Battle of the Falkland Islands.[2] I have never failed to thrill at the tragic drama of the German ships' recognition, in Stanley Harbour, of the tripod masts that indicated powerful and speedy battlecruisers. For the German squadron could neither escape nor defeat them.

---

2 The Battles of Coronel and the Falkland Islands (November and December 1914) were linked naval battles fought early in the Great War when Admiral Maximilian Graf von Spee's East Asiatic squadron was sailing home – via Samoa as Berendsen so vividly describes in the confines of Apia Bay – to Germany. Von Spee defeated Admiral Sir Frederick Craddock and his inferior squadron at Coronel, off the South American coast, but, scouting the Falkland Islands, was then chased and sunk by Admiral Sir Frederick Sturdee's superior squadron, led by the larger and faster ultra-modern battlecruisers, *Inflexible* and *Invincible*.

For our part, the visit of von Spee was not the only alarm we were to experience. Rumour seemed endemic in tropical places, especially small places, where nothing was certain. And we went through a tropical hurricane that was far from pleasant. At last the news came through that our little force was to be relieved by a specially enlisted body of older men. I guided one of their formations to their camps, and my exhilaration was high, until I learnt that I was not to be among the first shipload to return to New Zealand. Those who remained were, however, spared most of the daily tasks. I recall the beautiful calm mornings, as we ate our breakfasts in the open air. Then at last, we had the thrill of embarking, clearing the reefs and turning for the Apolima Passage, and for home, and to our reception and welcome by the Mayor, Sir John Luke, on the wharf in Wellington.

After an emotional reunion with my mother, I was recalled to Departmental duties. Most of my comrades went on directly to the Great War itself, in full recognition that what we had done was really nothing at all. I found it difficult to decide on my next course. Mother, I found, was deeply hurt by what she felt was my desertion of her, and she urged me most earnestly not to leave her again. I was also distressed.

Convinced of my selfishness in enlisting in her absence, I took the hard way of promising Mother that I would not again voluntarily join the forces without her consent. For her part I insisted that when, in the opinion of my country, my turn came for the army again, she was to make no objection. There we left it in the meantime – quite an unsatisfactory position, and an unhappy and unpleasant one for me, but in my special circumstances, I felt I was doing the right thing.

Looking back over the years I am not sure. It seems to me now to have been a close and dubious decision; whether one's personal and individual duty should outweigh one's national duty. Whatever the merits of the decisions I made, the line I took was not what I wished to take. I had indeed sacrificed my own wishes to my sense of filial duty.

CHAPTER 5

WARTIME INTERLUDE

So I went back to work, as did many of my colleagues, but I was not to remain long in the Education Department. During my Bachelor of Laws degree, soon to be extended to a Master's course, I had formed some close friendships. Among my friends at this malleable period of my life were Henry Havelock Cornish, an obscure teacher, and later to become a professor of law, Solicitor General and ultimately a judge; and Paul Verschaffelt, then a junior in the civil service, but destined to rise to be its highest officer as Public Service Commissioner.

We were all accustomed to study law and to spend our leisure together. On taking his law degree Verschaffelt moved to the Public Trust, and then into the Public Service Commission. Casting about to utilise my law degree, I was offered a legal post in the Department of Labour, no doubt through Verschaffelt. After failing to interest legal practitioners in my worth, I decided, with the comfort that soon I was due for the army again, to accept the risk of transfer to the Labour Department.

Before this I decided that I must do something about my increasingly irresistible affection for Nellie Brown. After my return from Samoa I was no longer her immediate superior. So I gradually improved the terms on which we met. Miss Brown was a very athletic girl who had represented Otago and Wellington at hockey, and even played internationally. She loved table tennis and I managed to get her as my partner and to win a final. This made a substantial step forward in her good opinion. I took every opportunity to meet and please her, joining in the constant balls and entertainments in which little Nellie Brown took an active part to raise patriotic funds.

The misery to me was that she did not go out only with me. The indefinite terms of my relations with this young lady preyed on my mind. One night I asked her to come to the movies, and then suggested a walk round Oriental Bay to view the lights of the city under the moon. We sat at the water's edge and I found myself, without any prior intention, asking her, when the war was over, to join her life with mine. 'What about getting married sometime?'

Nellie was amazed – I can hear her gasp of astonishment even now – but her amazement was no greater than mine. The most important decision of my life was made by some force stronger and wiser than I. A long silence followed. I think Nellie was puzzled how to handle the situation. Ultimately she gave me her answer. She would think it over. That seemed to me to be enormous progress. I had not dared for anything but a friendly rebuff. I took her home. We went out again the next night. Then she said she would become engaged to me, and see how it went. Very gently she kissed me. We were engaged.

After all these years my love, affection, respect and admiration for this young girl are unchanged. She made of me a better and a more understanding person. Even today I grieve to be separated from my partner and still find myself perplexed at the depth and tenderness of my affection. I thank whatever gods there be for giving me such a helpmate. My wife is not perfect, but she is as nearly perfect as any human being can be.

One of the most difficult tasks we had to face was to convince our friends that we were indeed betrothed. Miss Brown had been frank and outspoken in her contempt for me. People would not believe that Nellie Brown was entrusting her life to the brash, explosive, crude and noisy young man whom she had so disliked. It was many weeks before Nellie's parents could be brought to accept the fact of the engagement. Lovers of Jane Austen both, we smilingly compared our plight with that of Elizabeth and Darcy.

Almost immediately my fiancée went to Sydney to visit her favourite cousin and I was left bereaved. On her return I had the joy of taking her around my friends. They thought her lovely and confirmed my good opinion of them. With my mother I detected a shade of reserve at the news of my engagement. It had not occurred to me that she might be disturbed at this intrusion in her life. In the event the two women figuratively circled each other, before settling down into a kind of armed and friendly neutrality.

Nellie at once entered into every detail of my life, hearing me in my studies, and sharing in my induction into the Department of Labour. Here I began to meet men and women of the employing and working classes. This was a time when the wage earner was beginning to achieve that decisive position in our land that was to lift him from penury and dependence to predominance and comparative luxury.

By the time I joined the Department, much in the relations between capital and labour that called for redress, was being redressed, and for this real credit must be given to the professional labour leader. We were emerging from the period of sweatshops, the abuse of outworkers, and the elimination of the indefensible conditions of labour and remuneration, for the elimination of which the Department of Labour had been instituted.

No one could doubt the utility, or even the necessity, of much of the legislation we were called upon to administer. The state had to ensure that factories provided decent working conditions, employers paid adequate wages, and the community was protected from conflict between worker and employer, as set out in the Industrial Conciliation and Arbitration Act, one of New Zealand's greatest social experiments.

William Pember Reeves's far-reaching Act had provided that unions could by registration obtain the right to have wages and conditions of employment established by law. In return they abandoned their right to strike, with the agreement or award, as the law of the land, being enforced by the state. In theory this was an admirable system, but key unions, when dissatisfied with the award, or for any other reason, would strike regardless of legislation, which greatly increased the power of union officials as well as giving preference to unionists.

It was the duty of the Department to prosecute breaches of the industrial and labour laws, and strikers. As usual politics ensured that prosecutions for such fundamental offences were infrequent and ineffective. Irrespective of the irresponsibility of the typical politician, the hardship and damage to the community made strikes a highly potent industrial and political weapon. Almost always at the end of a stoppage one of the terms of settlement was that there should be no prosecution. In time the law against strikes became more of a farce than a deterrent, and thus one of the main reasons for the system went by the board.

In this situation one became accustomed to see workers claiming more than they expected, and employers disinclined to offer anything. On the whole the court tended to split the difference between the claims of the two parties, and the public interest was invariably ignored. The court's increases were simply passed on to the long-suffering consumer. The protection of the consumer might be the function of Parliament but I have so little confidence in politics and politicians, and so little respect for the work of Parliament, as I have contemplated it over so many years, that I despair of justice for the consumer.

CHAPTER 6

RECALL TO WAR

When I was recalled into camp, the Department, embarrassingly for me, appealed and delayed my return. No sooner did I find myself in uniform than, as a well-known athlete, I was posted to the instructional staff. It was astonishing to find how many gladiators were still out of uniform. In my case I was drafted into a physical training squad.

I found myself under the command of one of the most objectionable and yet most competent men I have ever met. Captain Brock was a British Sergeant Major turned officer, not the type for that, but certainly for teaching physical culture.

With a group of Sergeant Majors he put us through a most gruelling course. I do not ever remember being so exhausted as at the end of the second day of training. I literally could not lift my feet to climb the steps of the hut. No concession was made to pain and weariness. A week of it, I have to confess, left me in a state of physical fitness I had never before approached, and have never since exceeded.

On completion of the training we were ordered to work as instructors with the new reinforcements as they came in. Although I felt I should be doing something more directly concerned with the war, I found the work congenial. While the war took its slow and tragic course, I just had to carry on. As a member of a training squad I was even sent around the country raising money for patriotic purposes.

In order to see something of Nellie I took the law into my own hands to get the twenty miles between Trentham and, Wellington, and back again, before lights out. This meant pitting my wits against the military authorities. That was no contest at all. Anyone of a mentality adequate to keep them out of a lunatic asylum could defeat them, and I regularly did so, even making arrangements with the drivers of the leave trains.

While I was on the physical training staff, Nellie and I made up our minds to marry before I left New Zealand. That was against my wishes. I felt the uncertainties of war made it unfair to bind her to me until the future could be seen more clearly. But Nellie would have none of this.

We were going to marry now – and we did. She did not tell me then, but she also made up her mind that she would have a baby too – and we did.

We were married in St John's Presbyterian Church in Wellington, I in my uniform and she in a suit. Paul Verschaffelt was my best man and Vera Cunningham our bridesmaid. There were just a few friends and a lot of confetti, a tiny wedding breakfast, and a quiet departure by train for Plimmerton, where a friend had lent us a seaside cottage.

'Poor Nellie,' wept Nellie's mother. 'Lucky Nellie,' replied my indignant mother. How we laughed at the human absurdity of those two, for I never for a moment ceased to adore, or to obey Nellie, as this determined and capable young lady took control of our joint affairs and we embarked on the fairy tale of a wonderful life together, wonderful in the unbroken trust and confidence and love that has joined us.

The few fleeting days of our honeymoon were the happiest of my whole life. From Plimmerton we went onto Waitomo, and then to Rotorua, for a week or so of my final leave. Back in camp I was transferred into a reinforcement and sent to Featherston over the Rimutaka Range on the rack railway.

In that heartbreaking and godforsaken spot, our training was sound and good. I managed to get into town each weekend and then just before departure, Nellie came up to Featherston. When our train finally reached the wharf, I fell out of the ranks again and again to kiss her goodbye. If those responsible for war are held to account only for the miseries of countless partings, they have a heavy and unforgivable load to carry into the world to come.

We were excellently housed and fed on our 69-day voyage to London in the old *Matatua* on the voyage to London. The influenza epidemic was in its earliest stages as we left New Zealand, but I was fully recovered by the time we reached Fremantle and we faced the great rollers of the Southern Ocean. Because of the epidemic we were not allowed ashore in Durban or Cape Town, nor at Freetown. To all intents the war had ended when we arrived in South Africa, for at Freetown I was able to read the signals detailing the surrender of the German fleet.

Finally we had our first sight of the hallowed shores of England, so familiar to us in history and story. In the Portland Roads we saw American battleships coming in from the sea before we ran into the endless lights leading to the Thames. Here was the old world from which our ancestors for the most part had come. By troop train we then went to one of the most miserable places the lovely isle of England can show. Muddy, cold and isolated, Sling Camp in Wiltshire, some ten miles out of Salisbury, was dismal in the extreme.

What was worse, our reinforcement was superfluous, laggards in the field, inferior men moving among the warriors. These veterans of warfare were not willing to fall back into the ways of the camp, with its rigid routine and 'bullring', which, with a stupidity quite unbelievable, the camp authorities reinstituted. The long service men rioted quite seriously before the authorities learned their lesson. They then tried to institute an impracticable scheme of education. The attempt to force compulsory schooling down the throats of disgruntled soldiery was more than they could stomach, or the authorities impose.

Sling Camp was only seventy miles from London so I spent time there, staying in a flat belonging to a niece of my Uncle Will's, then a qualified physician employed at Bedlam. I wandered in a dream of delight about this lovely and historic city, and then managed to get down to Torquay in Devon.

Sling Camp on return seemed more insufferable than ever. I remember an emissary of authority formally inviting volunteers for the campaign in Russia. There was not one in the whole camp. Little was done except for a daily roll call. Most of us loafed about or spent our time at interminable games of 'two up'. My release from the distressing atmosphere of Sling Camp came when my Sergeant Major, who had come over in the same ship as me, ran up the slope to the Headquarters of the camp. 'Want to live in London?'

Tom Jordan was an unusual character, a leading legal practitioner, an admired rugby player, and later a most effective and autocratic Mayor of Masterton. Jordan was as distressed as I at our uncertainty and idleness. Looking for a means of escape from camp life, he had replied to a notice in General Orders calling for experts in electoral procedure to apply for seconding to the New Zealand High Commissioner's Office in London.

Tom had once acted as a scrutineer at some obscure booth in the Wairarapa, but I knew nothing about election procedures. To our astonishment, we were selected to go to London. There we told

Cecil Day, the officer in charge, that we knew nothing about election procedures but that as university graduates, with law degrees, we could handle the thing.

In London we were granted the rank of warrant officer, took board and lodging in Golders Green, and travelled by tube to Trafalgar Square. The work a few yards away at the High Commission Office was infantile. We had to arrange for the printing of papers and the provision of containers, and make simple arrangements for taking the soldiers' votes in the camps and on the departing troopships. We took it in turn to travel to the various ports, London, Plymouth, Avonmouth, Swansea, Cardiff, Liverpool, Glasgow, and others like Southampton.

In this way I learned much of officers, so called. Some who had kept themselves in some clerical post had become like emperors in their unapproachability, seemingly godlike in their own estimation. But I did get to many parts of the country, including the lovely Welsh countryside, that I would never have seen. As we really had little to do, we were able to roam around London, visiting all the renowned sights, and soaking ourselves in the history and majesty of this great and famous city. I even had my first experience of royalty when the Princess Royal served us at the YMCA and invited Tom Jordan and me to visit her at Windsor Castle, my first contact with the exalted of this world.

As a judge of oratory, and one of its martyrs, I was thrilled in 1919 to join a huge and enthusiastic audience at the Albert Hall to hear Herbert Asquith, one of the greatest orators of his time. Asquith's delivery was so slow and hesitant as to destroy much of the charm of his undoubted gift for the apt word and the striking phrase. In print, his speeches read like erudite and eloquent essays from a fine and fully instructed mind, and a most delicate understanding.

Of that impressive address, I carry the indelible recollection of one sentence only. Asquith was directing attention to the threat in the magnitude of armaments, and the temptation presented to would-be aggressors to seize power and destroy liberty – and perhaps even at that time to obliterate civilisation and even humanity itself. 'Mankind,' he said in that extraordinary slow and thoughtful delivery of his, pausing after each word as if to ensure that the next be exactly, perfectly what it should be. 'Mankind – is – *lisping* – the alphabet – of – *a long pause and shout* – annihilation.'

I place Asquith among the very few first rate speakers I have been privileged to hear – and I have been bedevilled by the shouts and platitudes of more speakers than I can or would remember. I would list as outstanding, two American Socialists, Walter Thomas Mills, who visited New Zealand when I was a young man, and later Norman Thomas, one of the most convincing speakers I have ever heard. General MacArthur, and General Romulo of the Philippines were also first class speakers. Few in New Zealand rank very highly on my list, such is the paucity of good speakers in our little land, though I have noted among our politicians men like Thomas Wilford and particularly John A. Lee.

Of a totally different and very special type, Lord Birkenhead was clearly ahead of others as an after dinner speaker. Franklin D. Roosevelt and the greatest of them all, Winston Churchill, the finest exponent of the English language I have ever heard, perhaps the greatest of all times, were of a higher and wider order. But it did me good to hear, so early in my life, one speaker of taste and perception, who could rouse the admiration and exercise the intelligence. London in 1919 gave me that privilege, and I have not forgotten it, nor lost my admiration for Asquith.

Through family connexions who moved among the influential circles of the British Labour movement – then growing but still without power or influence – I found it useful in my apparent career as a labour administrator to meet a number of the leading Socialists: G.D.H. Cole and his wife chilled me, and Marion Phillips repelled me. At the Fabian Society I met the two Webbs, whom I disliked: both of the very first intellect, but both, it seemed to me, machines, bloodless and without human emotion, planning for mankind as automata, and not as men and women.

I also met, and instantly disliked, George Bernard Shaw. I thought him a poseur. I have heard him speak more often than I would have wished. His wit no one can doubt; his sense one may, and should. Some of his judgements are utterly absurd and only one who has attained the position of a demigod, as Shaw has, could have uttered them and escaped ridicule or contumely. I have tried to read his plays – I cannot, though I can read their prefaces and enjoy and admire them.

We met other interesting people and I made some contacts with the officials in the Labour Department. Despite the humble uniform I wore,

I saw all that they had to show. I do not remember learning anything except their sensible habit of using different colours to distinguish the records of the various divisions, an idea that I tried without much success to introduce when I returned to my own Department in New Zealand.

Before that, I took part in the Victory Parade in London before the King and Queen and all the great Allied leaders. The fact that I personally had done nothing to bring about that victory did not lessen in my heart the sense of pride and gratitude that was so widespread that day, and so bitterly to be belied in the years to come.

The day of the election came at last. We were not particularly interested in the results for electorates but we were intensely concerned with the licensing poll. The vexed question of prohibition was a lively one, and the supporters, of whom I was one, had almost achieved their objective. Although I have enjoyed my share, I am convinced that alcohol is, on balance, an evil thing, responsible for much misery and degradation. Prohibition in a little island country, and with such a law-abiding people, would have been a more manageable and successful thing than in the huge United States with its traditions of law breaking still extant today.

The soldiers' vote, expected to be strongly in favour of continuance, would be decisive. The troops were understood to resent the poll being taken while they away serving their country. So after the New Zealand results showed a majority for prohibition of over the required sixty per cent, great care was taken to ensure that the camps voted right. In one of the few corrupt polls in New Zealand's history, the soldiers handsomely reversed the vote at home.

Irrespective of the manipulation, the troops were wholeheartedly in favour of the liquor traffic. Looking at our present disgusting drinking habits, I cannot help but wish that the cause had been successful. New Zealand and Australia are the only two countries in the world where the brutish swilling of beer and whisky show people who have no idea how to utilise the undoubted gifts of alcohol. What a distance we still have to go to learn to enjoy alcohol as the English or the Europeans do.

After the election we returned to Sling, hoping for an early passage to New Zealand. While we were waiting, no work of any kind was done. We would march out to plant potatoes and spend the day reading, walking, sleeping, eating and playing. There was no way the embattled veterans could have been moved to action. Of course it all became wearying beyond words and the authorities wisely gave everybody leave of absence and free transport throughout the United Kingdom. This got these idle men out of mischief and allowed this British group of men to familiarise themselves with their original point of origin, and their relatives, in a land they still regarded as Home.

We all took tickets as far as one could go, either to Inverness in Scotland, or Dingle in Ireland. I had this memorable jaunt to Dublin – where I saw something of Sinn Féin enthusiasm over the graves of the martyrs of the 1916 rebellion, and the dream of the fallen Irish destined to become a reality a few years later – to Belfast and Londonderry, and then to Killarney, to prove that the Emerald Isle is indeed one of the beauty spots of the world.

On my return I found that the authorities were urgently demanding my presence. At Headquarters no less a person than a General pompously claimed that he had instructions to send me home. It was of course my Department that had requested my immediate return and, unjust though it was to many who had arrived before me, my anxiety to rejoin my wife, and an infant immediately expected, overrode any tenderness of conscience. Here were orders that I could obey with alacrity.

I have never seen a countryside so lovely as southern England the morning we set off for Tilbury. The fields were painted a brilliant scarlet with poppies, set off by the vivid green of the fields and warm red of the loam. The world was opening up again, and we could see a future as free men, free to think as we liked, speak as we liked, and act as we liked, instead of being confined in the tight and often stupid control of untaught, thoughtless and ignorant men inflated with a little brief authority.

That experience in the army did, however, greatly inform my mind and character. The injustice and incompetence of my leaders made me, when I came to manage men, try to be reasonable, particularly to juniors and to the humble. I may not always have succeeded, but I became a more understanding person, because of that lack of understanding of the typical army leader.

So to Tilbury, and down the Channel, with little done to inform the troops of what was happening; and the troops in turn prompt to defeat attempts to parade or drill on the way to the Panama Canal and through the Pacific, calm, warm and pleasant. We arrived off Cape Palliser and hove to for the night. Early, very early the next morning, we approached Wellington Heads just as the Lyttelton Ferry had made the harbour, and we came home to one of the loveliest cities in natural beauty in the whole world – and I would not exempt Rio de Janeiro from that comparison.

My old friend Cornish had brought Mother to the wharf to meet me, as my wife, after the birth of our elder son, was not strong enough to come herself. I took it for granted that my mother would continue to live with us, and it was years before I realised that my wife longed for a home of her own.

So in the delight of my dear wife and little son, my undistinguished military service ended. I do not defend my record. Nearly everyone did better, but I find it difficult to see where I went wrong in this fundamental matter of conscience. I had volunteered very early and then, owing so much to my mother, waited my country's call. That decision I made in the best of faith and on balance was right. But there it is; I did not do nearly enough in that great crisis of human history. More than three years of military service left me with a deep sense of dissatisfaction, three medals and a sense of not making the sacrifice worthy of joining the Returned Soldiers' Association.

CHAPTER 7

THE DEPARTMENT OF LABOUR

The inconsiderate Head of my Department did not welcome me back but asked me to return to work the day after my return home. Like a fool I gave way to this unreasonable request when there was no real cause or reason. Those who make appointments to responsible positions should be careful to find suitable people.

That weekend my wife and I set out house hunting and found a little place, furnished, in Island Bay. It was a modest little home, cheap but pleasant, with room for Mother and the baby. We took it for a year, wondering if our exiguous income would run to it, but willing to take a chance. All of life in fact consists in taking chances. One must simply ascertain the degree of risk and take some kind of chance wherever one goes.

Island Bay is not one of the better suburbs in Wellington, but it does possess a nice sea beach, which our children grew to love, and which did them good. It is perhaps one of the windiest populated areas in the world but that is no doubt bracing and healthy. We grew so attached to the locality that we decided to build a home of our own there, greatly daring but encouraged by a small loan from my wife's parents. It was tiny, but roomy enough for us, with Mother, and our two children, when our second son was born. The whole thing cost us fifteen hundred pounds. It seemed a huge sum at the time.

How we worked over that little place. An old friend and I took turns working on each other's property. We dug, we raked, we planted, and we landscaped, and shifted earth by the ton until each of us had made civilised gardens of flowers and vegetables, on what had been gorse. I became quite a handyman about the house, fixing the washers, repairing the fuses, and plugging the leaks, for we had chosen slates instead of corrugated iron, and the diabolic wind blew water under them. There we lived for ten years, walking and tramping over the hills, until we felt the need to get nearer to my work, which had become more testing as the years went by.

At the office I had the partial confidence of our odd and difficult chief. Without consistent support from above, no one can confidently do supervisory work, but he stood by me adequately. There were many problems to solve in the Department. My contempt for some of its antiquated methods led me to institute a whole host of innovations, nearly all of which proved to be right and wise, however much they frightened and surprised my chief.

At first I made mistakes, for example in discarding checks essential to the prevention of theft. Over time we uncovered three breaches of honesty. I was never sure, and agonise now whether all three men were in fact guilty. I cannot exaggerate the distress these disgraces caused me. I felt they reflected on me because I was responsible for the discipline and routine, in fact, for the whole conduct of the office.

I also made mistakes in handling personal problems. At one point I found that official mail was disappearing. So I detailed one of the more promising youngsters the Department had recruited (at my instigation, to lift the general level of intelligence over the earlier political appointments), to check the matter. He found that our records officer was intercepting and hiding the correspondence. This man had simply got behind with his work. He became so horrified by what I would say and do that, in his panic, he had taken to destroying and hiding papers.

These unhappy incidents I hope made a better man of me. I certainly learned from my errors. I felt myself growing in stature, and becoming better prepared, every day, for the more serious problems of life in a Department with something like a dozen offices scattered throughout the country.

My function was to keep in personal contact with all these offices and their staff, to ensure efficiency in their application of the law and their inspection of commercial and industrial establishments, as well as in their office work. Many of these officers were political appointees, normally less qualified and less competent than staff selected by appropriate methods. A few indeed were misfits, and while some did their best, others did nothing.

The staff clearly needed steadying and strengthening. It became part of my duty to visit the Departmental offices. As Administrative Officer I was in effect troubleshooting when something went wrong, and in any case for two months of the year I had to travel round first the North, and then the South Island. I loathed this separation from my wife and family.

I hated too that the visits were inspections not only of the office, but also of the accounts. Unannounced I must walk into the office and, though I was not an accountant, demand the cash box and the chequebooks. I disliked acting the policeman when I lacked the instinct. Happily I never found evidence of financial failure, and simply dressed down any delinquents, made them make up any shortfall, or contributed a shilling or two of my own.

I was always on the look out for discourtesy. I would walk in anxious to stamp upon that callous indifference to the convenience of the public that is the mark of the uncivil servant. I have always felt this bitterly. But I never did find a case of it in my Department; I was almost disappointed, for I was ready to deal with it most vigorously.

I had to pass judgement too on their inspections and prosecutions. Whenever I saw an undue proportion of Chinese among those prosecuted, I became critical. This was a sign of inefficiency, as they were simply the easiest to catch. The various branches of the Department also varied considerably in their administration of the labour laws.

Many of the senior people in this relatively new Department had come from the labour unions, where an Oxford degree was not as valuable as commonsense and a sympathetic feeling for the worker. We felt that our principal objective was the protection of the worker, and not the employer. To this end the Department extended its tentacles in all directions, until it had gathered, under a wide umbrella, a diversified collection of responsibilities. Each year we extended their range, spawning new legislation as a fish spawns roe. Too many Government Departments share this tendency. It is salutary to ask ourselves how much of this waste matter is of any effect.

One function successfully grasped was the erection of workers' dwellings. I cannot imagine a man less fitted by nature and experience to guide such activity than my chief, nor why the experience of a Deputy Chief Inspector of Factories qualified him to build the houses. But build them we did, in hundreds, and charged the lucky tenants at cost.

I was dismayed to find myself the third member of the Board – for my drive, my chief explained. I did my best, but the work could have been done so much better. The architect was a poor ineffectual creature; the management was untrained and inexperienced, and therefore timid and uncertain; and our town planner spent his time dreaming and drawing. I did not enjoy my period as one charged with the responsibility of a huge building programme.

I also found myself as the official responsible for the initiation and administration of the first rent restriction legislation. I did not support these iniquitous measures. They were the brainchild of one of my betters. I was merely called upon to administer them, and administer them I did, despite my indignation and distress that we should have fallen so low in public morality. For the cost of assisting the underprivileged was not spread over the whole community, but unfairly placed on the landlord. Even worse were completely indefensible provisions depriving owners of the right to obtain possession of their property.

Another activity of the Department was of a different order of things. This was the registration of barmaids under one of the Blue Laws, for which New Zealand has been noteworthy. One such law prohibited the employment of women in hotel bars except for those already so employed. The law was already twenty-five years old, but there were still a number of elderly ladies for whom the Register of Barmaids was a valuable property to be jealously guarded. There was a good deal of quiet amusement in receiving these old, but still sidling charmers, some protecting their rights, others bogusly trying to get on the Register.

It did not take me long to establish a good working system in the office. As the years went by I was fortunate to work with some exceedingly competent colleagues and assistants in the Labour Department. Some of the young boys were outstanding. I hope I helped them by an example of industry and responsibility. My aim was to do each job as well as I could, by taking first things first, by never leaving till tomorrow anything that could be done today, and never leaving anything at all on my table at the end of the day. These quite pedestrian qualities are essential to becoming a competent officer, especially in controlling the work of others. In a large undertaking there must be an active management with constant supervision and direction. True efficiency required the pointing out of every single dereliction balanced by the appreciation of good work. I made it my practice never to pass over failure and never to omit congratulation for outstanding work.

I owed a special gratitude to the stenographers working with me in the Labour Department. They had to be able to type and write shorthand, be knowledgeable enough and courageous enough to prevent their chief falling into error, and act as his conscience and his reminder of all engagements and duties. By nature I drafted my communications and speeches at great speed. Many of these secretaries went on to become the trusted assistants of Ministers of the Crown.

It was at this time I had further contact with another Prime Minister and his Deputy, less satisfactory I might say than with my staff, and indeed reminiscent of that with Seddon not quite twenty years before. I was called into the august presence over something to do with the Holidays legislation, which the Department of Labour administered. The Prime Minister wished to mitigate the effect of the holiday by providing for special holiday pay at double or treble time. Mr Massey's wish was at variance with the terms of the legislation.

Being young in the ways of politicians I made the cardinal mistake of telling Massey that his understanding was erroneous, that the day was not a prescribed holiday, and that the action he contemplated was unnecessary. A Crown Law official corroborated my remarks. 'Not a holiday,' snorted the great man, 'of course it's a holiday.' We tried to show him the legislation, but this proved to be unnecessary. Politicians, and particularly Prime Ministers, are never wrong. The mighty did not need to consult documents. 'Not a holiday. Not a holiday; of course it's a holiday; what nonsense.' We left the Prime Minister's office much deflated by this absurd decision but with a new appreciation that we would have to spend more time and energy to handle erroneous decisions that sprang from the omniscience that comes of election by the people.

Meantime my chief decided to use me as a qualified lawyer to take the Department's principal cases in the courts. Our Inspectors of Factories were frequently lost when any question of law arose. They were liable, too, to be submerged by the more forceful legal defence counsel. Without consulting me, he had me admitted to the bar. The Crown Law Office, though not disposed to lose any of their prerogatives, agreed that my detailed knowledge of the labour laws was superior to theirs, and on their motion, I was admitted to the bar by Chief Justice Sir Robert Stout.

There I proceeded to take all the Department's difficult cases, appearing in all courts, except the Court of Appeal. I can perhaps claim to be the only man who ever practiced law in the courts who, despite having some tricky ones, never lost a case. The most frequent were against strikers, all in some degree important, some difficult and a few doubtful. Up to a point I enjoyed this work and I learned much from it. I did, however, get heartily tired of continually prosecuting. All my life I have hated retribution. Still my experience gave me a taste for the dialectics of the courts, which at times led me to hanker for a legal career, but I never dared take the financial risk.

We remained living at Island Bay for some ten years. There our elder son Ian survived a severe illness. But worse was to follow. Our second son Keith fell victim in 1925, at the age of eighteen months, to infantile paralysis. Our family doctor and then the consultant did not recognise the disease for a long time. Our little boy was then isolated in Wellington Hospital and we were quarantined. When we were released from control we had to set out out on a long road to save our infant son. In this we owed much to the skill and optimism of Dr Walter Robertson, the specialist orthopaedic surgeon at the hospital. It meant my wife taking him (by tram and on foot, for she would never drive) for massage every day for more than ten years. Today our son may be a better doctor for his own experience of pain and disability.

We had actually invested at this time in a motorcar from a small legacy my mother had received. The car, which I serviced and drove, was a famous Ford T. The old Tin Lizzie was a temperamental kind of thing with only two forward gears but it took us everywhere, though only at weekends. My mother adored the car, which gave her the feeling that she had at last arrived.

All this time my father had been maintaining himself in Sydney. When he fell ill, after some difficulties with my stupid chief, I crossed the Tasman on the Union Company's *Maheno*, through a fearful cyclone, and saw him and all my Sydney relatives. I found Father recovering, and as he did not suggest returning to New Zealand, after careful thought I left him there. He went back to work for a year or two and then, suddenly, he was dead and at rest. Poor Father; every single thing of any kind that belonged to him has disappeared from the face of the earth, and he lives only in memory, and in pity and sorrow.

At the office we had our own trials. During depressions, Government Departments were required to retrench severely. This was an agonising thing for me, as the officer responsible for administration, to do. I of course suffered no hardship myself. All I could do was contribute a fixed percentage of my income towards relief funds. This I must confess was heartbreaking work. It was a bitter period.

On the whole, however, I look back with some sense of satisfaction on my ten years of service with the Department of Labour. I did good work there, I learned much of benefit, I made good friends, I learned to despise my enemies, and I came to believe in the fundamental goodness of human beings. I have met few evil men on my own account before coming into contact with 'enemies of mankind' responsible for persecution, torture and murder. On the day of judgement I am sure petty sinners against our little man-made laws will be forgiven when the violators of the laws of God, who have desecrated the hearths of men and flouted the essential canons of kindness and decency, will be condemned. We are fallible folk in this world. We try to make our own codes of conduct, and to a large extent succeed. But there is a higher authority, and time will show the essential triviality of many of our rules, and the eternal verity of the more lofty and rarer qualities of true Christianity, of true brotherliness between man and man.

The years between 1890 and 1926 essentially made me what I am. As I look back, I suffered much, but little compared with the suffering of others. I toiled long and hard. I learned that whatever I was to have from life, I must earn myself; and that however hard I might try, there was nevertheless a destiny that shaped our ends, despite my own rough hewing. I was not anything much, but I had developed into something firm and solid, tempered by some pain and some toil. I was still selfish and conceited, but not as much as I had been, for I clearly realised my limitations. Confident, though still essentially modest and retiring, I was ready to bear a man's task in a man's world.

BOOK II

IMPERIAL AFFAIRS

1926–1943

Nellie Berendsen once said 'Carl admired Peter Fraser enormously – and never voted for him once!'

Berendsen did indeed have mixed views on Peter Fraser. He said that Fraser had great abilities and in many ways was a great man. He remembered too that in the early years of the war they had been involved together in dangerous situations. But Peter had habits, idiosyncrasies and working methods that he could not abide.

He himself always aimed to complete his working day in regulation hours, leaving a clear desk and the prospect of an evening's cosy domesticity with Nellie. For Peter Fraser the day would still by then be strenuously under way. He was ill organised and inconsiderate, and thought nothing of having someone reading telegrams to him after midnight. That was not a role that Berendsen cast for himself.

So it is generally believed that the conflict of temperament and methods was largely responsible for Berendsen's appointment to Canberra in 1943. From then on he and Peter Fraser appear to have worked well together in the formative years of the United Nations, when they were ardent spokesmen for New Zealand 'as a small power rampant'.

In April 1949, when Peter Fraser flew into New York he was immediately involved with a problem on which the New Zealand delegation needed guidance. The United Nations General Assembly was considering the future of what had been the Italian colonies in Africa, and its members were looking at a resolution based on a disastrous agreement between Ernest Bevin of Britain and Count Sforza of Italy that would have overridden quite bitter opposition to the return of Italian authority to any of its possessions. Under its provisions the constituent parts of Libya (Cyrenaica, Tripolitania and the Fezzan) would go to Britain, Italy and France, and Italy would have Trusteeship over Somaliland. Berendsen said that the plan was so bad that it made his ulcer squirt blue ink. But the British argued that control of Cyrenaica was vital to their interests in the Middle East. Within the General Assembly the voting balance was precarious.

The delegation met at once with Peter Fraser in his hotel room and discussed the issue for several hours. Peter was both benign and abrasive and no one escaped quizzing or derision. One way or another everything that could be said was said. Then at last he got up, saying 'I'm going to rest. You boys (this category included Berendsen, nearing 60, and the rest, about 30) . . . you boys wait a while!.'

So he withdrew and Berendsen said 'Now don't take any notice of that. I know my old man! He's not going to have a rest! He's going to go all over it again, by himself. And I think he'll come up with the right decision.'

About an hour later Peter came back proclaiming as he often did with an accentuation all his own 'Now I think we'll all have a ni-i-i-ice cup of tea.' And then he turned to Berendsen and said 'I don't think we should support the British on this.'

Berendsen was delighted but less so by the aftermath. Peter returned to New Zealand and then somehow something happened and Berendsen was instructed to support the resolution. He did so, every clause of it, and to his ill disguised glee, it failed.

Tom Larkin

CHAPTER 1

IMPERIAL CONFERENCE

Some ten years after entering the Department of Labour I had become its Deputy Secretary. Apart from my brief calls on Seddon and then on Massey, until 1926, I had had little to do with Ministers. This changed with the election of the Reform Government late in 1925. Early in 1926 I was astonished to receive a call from Frank Thomson, since Seddon the Principal Private Secretary to successive Prime Ministers. The new Prime Minister, Gordon Coates, had just appointed a man for whom I came to have boundless admiration as the Head of his Department. Soon I was to begin a life of diplomacy on the staff of the Prime Minister.

Despite my seniority, I still found it a trial to essay the sacred precincts of Parliament Buildings. There I was kept waiting for over an hour. When Thomson arrived we discussed the weather, sports, and the Labour Department. Only then did I discover that a new branch of the Prime Minister's Department was needed to take charge of foreign affairs and of relations with Great Britain.

In the 1920s, in the early days of Dominion status, New Zealand did not regard itself as an independent entity. To the disturbance of more self-conscious Dominions, New Zealand was a mere echo of London. Our limited contacts with foreign nations and the League were conducted through the High Commissioner in London, New Zealand's only official stationed abroad. The existing Department of External Affairs was to remain responsible for New Zealand's Island Territories, including the Mandate of Western Samoa. In the Prime Minister's Department we would establish a new section to handle the growing workload in foreign affairs.

Thomson made clear that the Public Service Commissioner had recommended me for this new post. By the merest chance of my studying law with Paul Verschaffelt, I received this invitation to develop New Zealand's first organisation to deal with foreign affairs. Thomson was a taciturn man. He gave me no indication of his thoughts and left me to go home to discuss the possibilities with my wife and mother. At the time I might expect shortly to be the next Secretary of Labour. Against this the work with the Prime Minister would be more interesting. Thomson had also indicated that I might expect a substantial increase in remuneration. This was very important to me.

Months went by, and nothing happened. I calculated that I was not the man, or that the plan was not to be adopted. But in the world I was about to enter this was just the normal way of doing business. Unexpectedly and without explanation Thomson invited me to come down and see the Prime Minister. Again I was kept waiting for over an hour. Finally Thomson came in, full of business, an indication, I learnt later, that he had been at Bellamy's imbibing whisky and the political chatter.[1]

Gordon Coates was no more businesslike than my other Prime Ministers. He always took time to get round to his appointments. At long last we entered the presence. I liked Coates at first sight, but I was surprised how little interest he showed in me, or in our new organisation. I imagine we were in his office for perhaps five minutes, admittedly a friendly five minutes. Nothing at all to the point was said and I left his office more bewildered than when I entered.

Again nothing happened for months. Then at long last my appointment as Imperial Affairs Officer was announced. This was a title I always loathed. Still I appeared at my new office with a new feeling of importance. I was about to embark on a man's work of real interest. I would march forward in collaboration with Thomson, and of course a Prime Minister, who, however casually, had selected me for my diplomatic career.

Frank Thomson, the most amiable as well as the ablest of men, took me to my office. Pointing to a huge pile of papers on the desk, chairs, and floor he said: 'There you are Berry; that's all there is; and it's all yours.' A great delegator, he meant it. He gave me no guidance. What I did was avail myself very frequently of his invitation to drop in and talk.

Thomson was a man who refused to be trammelled by any consideration of time or fettered by any anxiety. He never did anything

1 In Wellington, New Zealand's Parliament – the only one to do so – has perpetuated the name of the caterer at Westminster, Bellamy's, for its restaurants and bars.

in a hurry. Indeed he never took action if he could avoid it. His value was as a detached and sage adviser. His great gift was his capacity to put a brake on new and inadequately considered acts and policies. His long experience and faultless memory were linked to a delicate judgement and political sense. Frank Thomson was the *éminence grise* of New Zealand politics for thirty years. He was one of the greatest of New Zealanders, possibly the greatest I have known.

In my difficult formative years Coates had to suffer much from my inexperience but his trust helped me greatly. I formed a warm affection for this young and active Prime Minister, to whose initial assistance and encouragement and, when I needed it, defence, my career owed much.

My appointment also brought me into frequent contact with Sir Francis Bell, the long serving Deputy Prime Minister to Massey. By reason of his seniority, Bell exercised much influence and authority as the principal adviser of my new and vigorous Prime Minister. Much past his prime, Bell was now a spent political force, heavy and irascible, an overbearing old man, utterly intolerant of the views of others, and infuriated by any opposition, however logical. Bell had become a bully: the sarcastic, sneering, cutting type of bully, to be distinguished from the bellowing ferocious type of which the Labour movement would later provide some choice examples.

Bell never showed me any degree of courtesy. He was a particular terror to his Private Secretaries and Cabinet colleagues. In general they were afraid of his retaliation against any opposition to his views. As a result he was not a source of strength to Coates. The Prime Minister himself was not at all overawed by the old gentleman. He was fond of him and showed him much deference, but when Coates had made up his mind, he followed it, notwithstanding the echoing remonstrances of Sir Francis. The real problem lay in the bad advice Bell often gave Coates. This was conspicuously disastrous in respect to New Zealand's Mandate in Western Samoa.[2] For a variety of reasons, including some

2 The Treaty of Versailles 1919 placed former German colonies – and parts of the Turkish Empire – under the tutelage of Mandatory Powers. Western Samoa had been one of Imperial Germany's Pacific colonies 1900–1914. New Zealand claimed it in 1919 as a C-class mandate, i.e. to be administered as part of New Zealand. In 1945 this 'sacred trust' was transferred, as Berendsen discusses, to the trusteeship system of the United Nations. Samoa moved to independence in 1962, while the editor of this book was Deputy High Commissioner for New Zealand in Apia. See Mary Boyd, 'The Record in Western Samoa to 1945' in Angus Ross (ed.) *New Zealand's Record in the Pacific Islands in the Twentieth Century* (Wellington, 1969).

degree of stupidity among New Zealand officials, a serious revolt had broken out there.

Bell never understood the unhappy Mau affair; indeed he never troubled himself to investigate it closely.[3] This did not prevent him from being most insistent in the advice he offered to the Prime Minister. Its wrongs and rights were never understood in New Zealand. Bell's efforts succeeded in seriously embarrassing a Government which failed to solve these distressing difficulties before leaving office in 1928.

When I joined him in the latter half of 1926, Coates was a tall and handsome figure, in the full flush of manhood. In Massey's Administration he had made an excellent impression as a successful Minister of Public Works. New Zealand, somewhat in the doldrums, expected much of this young and vigorous Prime Minister with an admirable war record, and the rank and martial assurance of a Major.

Coates was a man of little formal education. There were large, and even astonishing gaps in his narrow field of knowledge. He had little book training, and was apt to belittle the man of learning compared with the man of experience. Demonstratively, even boastfully he preferred the University of the World to the University of New Zealand. My own modest academic record, together with the distinguished letters of Dr R.M. Campbell who joined his staff with me, must have given Coates some anxious moments. It says much for Coates's broadmindedness that despite our dubious academic past, he encouraged and trusted both of us to the full.

Coates was a competent Chairman and handled his Cabinet with sense and discretion, qualities sadly lacking in other leaders with whom I have been connected. He was very much the master in his house. With the exception of Bell and Downie Stewart, whose advice he sought and followed, his Ministers played minor parts.

Every Cabinet with which I have been associated tended to consist of two or three strong men. The remainder were camp followers, of

3 The Mau, or the Samoan League, rose out of the intrinsically political nature of Samoan society. Its campaigns of popular non-violent civil disobedience against the German administration in 1908 provided the basis for the Mau of 1925–30. Directed against the New Zealand administration, it involved boycotts, non-payment of taxes, and the setting up of alternative police and village committees of governance. It culminated in the Black Sunday demonstrations of 28 December 1929, in which Tupua Tamasese III was shot and died. See Michael J. Field's *Mau: Samoa's Struggle Against New Zealand Oppression* (Wellington: A.H. & A.W. Reed, 1984).

little weight or influence. Sometimes the junior members scarcely dared open their mouths. If they did, they risked an angry snub. All serious decisions were in fact usually made by the Prime Minister himself. Cabinet sadly was subject to a dilatoriness that detracted from the orderly and efficient transaction of the country's business.

Coates's most valuable quality was a certain flair – shared only in my experience by Peter Fraser – of leaping to the heart of any issue by intuition, and without apparent cerebral activity. Once he had made it, he would then stay with a decision, at least until he was convinced it was wrong and must be changed. These admirable qualities carried him over many awkward places, when a more rational approach might have taken him into serious difficulties.

On the whole Coates was a good judge of men, though he did make some bad errors in the choice of colleagues and subordinates. He had the sort of personal loyalty I was to see later in President Truman. Once he had given his confidence it was unlimited in scope and time. To an official that is a priceless advantage: to know that your leader will not, as so frequently I have experienced, change overnight. Assured of support from above, one is safe to proceed.

Coates knew how to assume responsibility for the actions of his staff, and, more important, how to delegate responsibilities. Only Savage among my Prime Ministers shared that essential magnanimity of mind that makes for a successful Administration, rather than the dilatory and fumbling ones that are characteristic of most of the New Zealand Governments I have served.

After Thomson left me, I started on the papers, aided by my staff of two: a clerk, Tom Sherrard, and Jean McKenzie, a stenographer. We had no guidelines. We were uncertain of what was required, or how to work. So we began by sorting the papers, and the spate of telegrams and despatches calling for action that we were astonished to find arriving daily.

Our principal cause of consternation was the approaching Imperial Conference.[4] The agenda seemed enormous, so I decided, as I was to

4 The Imperial Conference system (1911–1944) flowed out of the Colonial Conference system (1887–1911) developed to deal with issues of colonial defence, communications and preferences. The first Imperial Conference was held in 1911 and thereafter at regular intervals, viz 1921, 1923, 1926, 1930, 1932 (Economic Conference in Ottawa) and 1937, until subsumed by more regular meetings of Commonwealth Prime Ministers during World War II.

accompany the Prime Minister, to confine myself to the preparation of papers for the Delegation. This meant working day and night to understand what it was all about. I drafted short statements of the main considerations with recommendations on the line we might take. I recorded my ideas of our most natural policy and drafted speeches, which, I was astonished, were later used without alteration.

My first official journey abroad left a vivid impression on me. The Prime Minister and Mrs Coates, Frank Thomson and I, together with a stenographer, Miss Piper, and Mr Lewis, as baggageman, set out in August 1926 on the Union Company's RMS *Makura* on our month-long voyage across the Pacific and the United States to the United Kingdom. Coates was quite the worst sufferer from seasickness I have ever met. Once he was recovered we began what became practice for Imperial Conferences, our morning study of the agenda and the papers. I have often wondered about the value of these sessions. My experience was that our Prime Ministers, with the exception of Peter Fraser, knew little or nothing of the subjects they were crossing the world to discuss, and indeed cared nothing.

Let me stress that these meetings are essentially superficial so that a detailed knowledge of the subjects was unnecessary for harried and distracted people like our Prime Ministers. Even if most of them were ignorant, and contemptuous of their ignorance, competent officials were always available with the facts to see that the Chief did not make a fool of himself. Indeed at this time I cannot overstress the ignorance of their adviser having to do the best he could in the time available to deal with complex problems.

In the event we did not do so badly. We had to come to terms with the ill-drafted Treaty of Locarno, so full of ambiguities that it would not stand the test of time and aggression.[5] We learnt then, a point Coates took clearly, not to put our faith in pieces of paper in trying to keep the peace in a wicked world. We noted too that conferences came to agreements so wide and general as to be, in practice, meaningless and useless. I had to reach behind the words to the realities of our meetings.

5 The Locarno Pact (1926–1936) was a non-aggression pact with mutual guarantees of the Versailles settlement that took Germany into the League of Nations. It was a symbol of hope for an era of international peace and goodwill which ended in 1936 with Hitler's denunciation of the Pact, remilitarisation of the Rhineland, and countdown to World War II.

They taught me that peace and liberty depend on the spirit, not the letter; on the heart and the sword, not on the mind and the pen. That lesson is soon forgotten. Fortunately it was one which Coates, as a soldier, did not have to learn.

After crossing the United States, we took the *Majestic* to Southampton and eventually installed ourselves in the Hotel Cecil, one of the millionaires' hotels on the Strand, close to the New Zealand High Commission,[6] as the guests of the British Government. New Zealand's representatives were Coates and Sir Francis Bell, who joined us in London, supported by Thomson and myself as officials.

Prime Minister Baldwin led the British Delegation, with Austen Chamberlain as Foreign Secretary, Balfour as Lord President of the Council and Leo Amery as Colonial Secretary. Mackenzie King represented Canada, Bruce Australia, and Hertzog South Africa. The Irish group comprised O'Higgins, Desmond Fitzgerald, McGilligan and O'Neill.

The British Foreign Secretary led off with a lengthy *tour d'horizon* on foreign affairs. I still do not understand why it was necessary to painfully read this prepared statement aloud when we had copies in front of us. I did not greatly admire Austen Chamberlain, though I thought him a prince compared with his dismal brother Neville.

The question of real importance at this conference concerned the constitutional development of the Empire. What was to be the status of the Dominions? New Zealand, the most loyal and biddable of all these adolescent national entities, wanted no independence, theoretical or practical. We did not question the motives or intentions of those who did, but we were inclined to deprecate the campaign for a written formula establishing independence. Even with a high degree of interdependence, we feared this would disrupt the Empire or Commonwealth, the term coming into fashion for the wider association of British countries.

From 1926 there never was to be one single instance when the New Zealand Government was unable to do all, and exactly what it wished. On no occasion was any attempt made to deny its rights or to interfere with its exercise of those rights. All members of the British

6 During Berendsen's era, the New Zealand High Commission was housed at 415 The Strand, close not only to Downing Street and Whitehall, but also to other High Commissions, as well as to Simpson's Restaurant, and later the favoured hostelry of The Savoy.

Commonwealth were in fact, if not in theory, entirely independent, sharing only a common and valued Crown. In 1919 their separate signatures of the Versailles Peace Treaties had adequately recorded that fact.[7]

At this time there was no question of independence for other countries of the Empire. India was represented by the India Office and Ceylon by the Colonial Office, while Newfoundland and Rhodesia held a kind of quasi Dominion status alongside a number of observers, and a host of officials and constitutional experts.

The 1926 Conference was content to adopt the Balfour Declaration as a general statement of the relations between Britain and the self-governing Dominions. These entities were to be seen as fully autonomous in every respect of their internal and external affairs, and united solely by a common allegiance to the British Crown. The Declaration itself was then embodied in the Statute of Westminster. This left each country to legislate for its own situation. New Zealand did not do so for over twenty years, long after I myself thought we should have done so. In fact, of course, as distinct from theory, no material alteration was made from the position which already existed.

In so far as the Balfour Declaration was made to placate the Irish, this constitutional conference signally failed, but it was still an important conference. It had the additional advantage of providing invaluable contacts. I got to know people with whom I would in future be dealing or corresponding. It taught me, also, how clumsily the affairs of the world were managed. As the old Roman adage had it: 'If the world but knew with what little wit its affairs are conducted.'

Despite their reputations, I could not help but notice, for instance, that few of the great British political figures were men of particular knowledge or ability. To my shocked astonishment many giants had not only feet, but also heads of clay. Too often our talks seemed directed to

7 Thirty states, dominated by the Big Four – Woodrow Wilson of the United States, Lloyd George of Britain, Georges Clemencau ('the Tiger') of France, and Vittorio Orlando of Italy – produced the Versailles Peace Treaties in 1919, covering inter alia German reparations, the League of Nations, and the mandate system for the German colonies and Turkish provinces. Prime Minister Massey's signature of the peace treaties stands as the first formal step towards an independent New Zealand. See Austen Chamberlain, *Peace in Our Time: Addresses on Europe and the Empire* (London: Allen, 1928); Maynard Keynes, *The Economic Consequences of the Peace* (New York: Harcourt Brace, 1920); and Paul Mantoux (ed.), *Les Deliberations du Conseil des Quatre (24 mars–28 juin 1919)* 2 vols. (Paris, 1955).

a search not for truth or for reality, but for a formula. Usually we ended up with a resolution so broad, and so anodyne, as to be meaningless. Conferences may be essential but I do not admire them.

Coates carried himself surprisingly well in these discussions. He was a very poor speaker, as have been all my Prime Ministers. 'Very Farmer George, your Prime Minister, what?' said one of the officials, but Farmer George said what he had to say effectively enough. He made a good impression not only in the conference room, but also in the country, where his personal qualities made him very popular. Coates was a natural gentleman, with excellent manners and plenty of self-confidence, who got along well with people of all classes.

One mistake I made as a new broom had been to canvass other Departments on matters they wished raised in England. To my dismay I drew a large and mixed bag. Some I cleared up, some I carried a little further, and others I left just as they were. Many of these problems had been outstanding for years and were insoluble.

Prime Ministerial visits of this kind meant a constant round of entertainment. While I handled these problems in London the Coateses visited the great homes of England, Scotland, Wales and Ireland, the latter much loved of our Prime Ministers. The Delegations were of course received by royalty, and attended a range of Government and London Company dinners. Here I heard Lord Birkenhead, in parts genius, egomaniac, playboy, and larrikin, give quite the finest after dinner speech I have ever heard. Coates on this first visit was somewhat vulnerable to people who sought to attach themselves to the Delegation, and the functions to which we were invited, a mistake he did not make subsequently.

Of the great families I particularly admired the Cecils, and the Clarendons, for their tradition of cultured service to their country. There is nothing of the aristocrat about me, and I have no reverence for blood as such, but these people possessed ability and character to a high degree, and that I do admire. A class with wealth, confidence and standing in the community is well placed to study and ponder the complicated and vital questions on which our existence and our future depends.

I came to admire too the officials responsible for the hospitality the British Government extended to its distinguished visitors. Among the functions of these unusual and powerful men, generally distinguished military officers, was that of arbiter of protocol. On this, my first visit, the principal officer, Colonel de Satge, looking the pukka sahib if ever a man did, knew all there was to know on a subject of which I knew nothing. But I learned, and learned quickly and well, of de Satge, and of his successor, Rear-Admiral Bromley.

So we left for home on the *Aquitania*, in palatial suites provided by the Cunard line, spoilt by remarkable first class service that required all our sense of proportion to manage. In boisterous weather, the Prime Minister was seasick and could not enjoy much of this remarkable service, or the concerts at which musicians as distinguished as Fritz Kreisler and as well known as Nick Lucas, the original exponent of 'Bye Bye Blackbird', contributed.

After our arrival in New York, with its special beauty, we travelled to Montreal and made calls in Ottawa, before journeying across Canada by special train as guests of the Canadian National Railways. We came to appreciate both the size of Canada and the extremes of its winter climate. Our special car was then transferred to an American train for the journey south through the lovely green lands, like our own, of Washington and Oregon, the latter famous for its roses.

In San Francisco, where he was operating a political machine with effrontery and success, the assertive and gregarious Mayor Rolph, later to become Governor of California, took over the care of the Coateses. No one could help liking the strong, self-reliant Rolph, with his rough ability, and the drive and the thick skin, that had taken him to such high office. He had an absolutely infectious good humour and he loved people like Coates, who was in all ways very much of a man's man. The two got along famously. When he came to the wharf to say goodbye to the RMS *Makura*, he called out 'Captain Mawson, Captain Mawson, take great care of your ship this voyage: look carefully to the safety and comfort of your great Prime Minister.'

So via Papeete and Rarotonga we reached Wellington. I know nothing more affecting than the sight of one's own hometown and the happiness of seeing one's dear ones at the wharf. Coates was the kind of man who understood human beings. 'No work, no work at all today. This is a holiday. Come to the office tomorrow.' So I went home to the family to tell them of where I had been and what I had seen, look over the garden, settle in, and resume our natural and accustomed life.

Let me emphasise how much I had learned in attending this important Imperial Conference at the beginning of my diplomatic career. My first official journey took me out of the confines of a little country, where we are all inclined to become insular and fixed in our view. I had learned the manners and speech, and the customs and conventions of the wider world, and especially of that portion that professes to lead the thoughts and acts of men in organised communities. I had had the opportunity to gauge the magnitude, and the proportional importance of the questions of the day, and to learn how they were being faced or avoided.

To a considerable degree this experience gave me poise and balance. I had become knowledgeable in the ways of the diplomatic and political world. I had learned to mix with the great and powerful, and to talk with the learned. I had gained experience of highly formal functions and how to host great dinners and receptions, and eat and drink with the connoisseur. Thus began, for this boy from the house of sacking on the Southland dredge, my long and testing career in diplomacy.

CHAPTER 2

'SAMOA MO SAMOA'

On resuming work in Wellington I found myself assuming responsibility for a wider and wider range of activities. Perhaps I had made a good impression on Coates and Thomson. Perhaps it was that Thomson had resolved to retire. In any case I found myself shouldering practically every problem coming into the office and, for a long time as the deputy to the Prime Minister, taking an inordinate share in the Government of the country.

All sorts of matters came to me and I handled them as best I could, without worrying the Prime Minister or Thomson for unnecessary instructions. I got along well enough and soon the press, who know everything, made it a practice to come to me every noon and evening to learn what had been going on, and what they could say about it.

So began my long and intimate relationship with the press, at home and abroad, that has left me full of admiration for the ability and responsibility of the profession. Cynical they are, as men of intelligence must be with the limitations of truth, and the fragility of the philosophies of the politicians. But there are no fools and no cheats. Never once in my long experience was I misrepresented by the press or had a confidence betrayed. I have the greatest admiration for journalists everywhere, working as they do at high pressure, with the temptation of handling much confidential material.

Among the problems I found myself taking on my shoulders was Western Samoa. Serious trouble had broken out with the indigenous inhabitants campaigning against the New Zealand Administration. Polynesians of the most admirable type, the Samoans had been so long isolated in their tiny islands that Samoa had grown in their eyes to be the centre of the world. Conquered from time to time by neighbouring peoples, the Samoans under their three princely families, each contending for primacy, had always regained their independence, and lived according to Samoan custom, as fixed and rigid as the laws of the Medes and Persians.

In the late nineteenth century these little islands had become the plaything of the great powers, who nearly came to war over their respective claims. As a result of a compromise, Samoa was divided up between Germany and the United States. The Samoans never acquiesced in the division of the spoils. From time to time they gave trouble in both areas. The Germans banished a number from the West, while difficulties in Eastern Samoa led to the suicide of one the American Governors. After our occupation in 1914 New Zealand's military administration conducted the Government until the peace treaties allotted New Zealand the League Mandate. New Zealand's military was then replaced by a civil administration.

There can be no doubt as to the excellence of New Zealand's intentions, nor indeed the success of the Administration in its early stages. Much was done for the Territory and its inhabitants under the benevolent administration of the New Zealand Administrator, Major General George Richardson, a soldier with a distinguished career during which he had risen from the ranks.

Richardson was a man of high moral character. Initially he strove with the greatest success for the welfare of the fifty thousand Samoans entrusted to New Zealand. Unfortunately he was to fail not because of any fault of character or intention, but because of the nature of the Samoans, coupled with his own want of local knowledge. His intelligence and his knowledge lagged behind his rectitude. He failed to see he had trouble on his hands, trouble of a most serious order, until it had got beyond his control.

Many have attempted, and some with the utmost confidence, to expound the basic cause of the uprising, but none in my opinion adequately. Much of the trouble was due to the nature and history of the Samoans themselves. Their system of native Government incorporated ancient and sanctified traditions and conventions embodied principally in the concepts of 'Tumua' (Orators) and 'Pule' (Chiefs or Elders) linked to a subsidiary system of authority contained in the Fono of Faipule (House of Chiefs). This was a kind of House of Representatives chosen according to Samoan custom by the villages. In developing their rule, the German Administration had exorcised the powers of the Tumua and the Pule and developed instead the authority of the Fono of Faipule. This system the New Zealanders largely continued.

Reduced to simple terms, the Samoans resented these changes. They were imposed by ignorant alien hands faced with the impossible task of incorporating Samoan custom into a German, and then a New Zealand Administration. Too often the Administrations chose the wrong men as officials; too often they acted without the concurrence, or even the knowledge of the Samoans themselves; sometimes they acted wrongly; and altogether they acted much too fast. In his zeal for prosperity and self-government, General Richardson had the fervour of the missionary. He made the mistake of trying to do in less than a decade what would have normally taken fifty years. Indeed it might not have been safely achieved in twice that time.

The difficulty was not that Richardson was evil; he was simply not very bright. Good and high minded, he was deluded by the plenitude of his good intentions, his early success and his ignorance of the extent of the problems he faced. An uncultured but masterful man, with no knowledge of Polynesia, his Proconsular status destroyed his sense of proportion and reality.

The New Zealand Government also proceeded in reliance on its good intentions, and its assumed success, by no means as complete as generally believed, in its largely British settlers adapting to the Maoris, and the Maoris to the Pakehas. This would not have been irremediable if we had discovered our error in time. That may, however, have been too much to expect of officials, with no special qualifications for the task, who made no attempt to seek the collaboration of those with experience in Maori Affairs.

The fact is our External Affairs officers were quite unqualified for the task. Its Head had graduated from the ranks of Private Secretaries. He might claim some knowledge of politicians, but none of Polynesians. His Deputy was an intelligent and unbalanced troublemaker. New Zealand simply had no expert knowledge available anywhere. All this might have have proved of negligible importance but for one critical factor, the antagonism of the powerful trading community in the Territory. On analysis, this ill will was greatly to the credit of the Administrator. He was trying to protect the ordinary Samoan from the depredations of two large firms which purchased copra from Samoans at low prices, and then sold abroad at world prices.

Of these firms, one was entirely Samoan. O.F. Nelson, the owner of the Samoan firm, was a remarkable character, half Swede and half Samoan. I see him as half patriot and half mischief-maker. His enmity for the Administration was unquestionably the deciding factor in the Samoan revolt, the Mau.

The plot was simple. Richardson felt the Samoans were not getting an adequate price for their copra. Why not bring the whole trade under the control of the Administration? The trading firms naturally objected. Nelson then used his wide authority with the Samoans to intrigue against Richardson. It became a personal conflict between Richardson, a simple, good old man, and O.F. Nelson, a wily and wealthy merchant of great ability and great bitterness.

The personal conflict ran against the backdrop of the Samoan constitutional delight in controversy and intrigue. Politics was the national pastime. Before Richardson knew he was in trouble the whole Territory was aflame. The Samoan association, the Mau, adopted a motto 'Samoa mo Samoa' ('Samoa for the Samoans') and a uniform with a light blue lavalava and headgear. As he became aware of what was afoot, Richardson began to send home excited and contradictory despatches proposing the deportation of malcontents to end this stupid and superficial affair.

At this stage Coates became disturbed. Despite Bell's confidence in Richardson, he told me to see what I could make of the whole affair. There was not much I could do. I read the despatches, studied Samoan history, and talked to the Wellington officials, naturally resentful of my interference. I was just forming some opinions when Richardson called hysterically for warships for the protection of life.

Cabinet met with some haste. As things were, no one except Bell had much confidence in Richardson. It was generally felt that a change in control was essential. In the meantime a call to protect life must be answered. The navy was summoned. Our two cruisers, the *Dunedin* and the *Diomede*, were little but fast.[1] Orders were despatched to Commodore Swabey, and I was told – the first of two occasions on which I was sent with a cruiser on a mission for my Government – to

---

1 HMS *Dunedin* (1924–37) and HMS *Diomede* (1926–35) were two 4700-ton fast D-class cruisers of eight ordered in 1916–18 with a crew of 450 and six-inch guns. Launched after World War I, the *Dunedin* and the *Diomede* served in the New Zealand Division of the Royal Navy, and gave notable service at Napier after the earthquake on 3 February 1931.

accompany the ships to Samoa. The Prime Minister asked to be advised daily of what I thought of things and assured me he would stand by me – as I knew he would.

The Government hoped to keep the matter secret until the ships had arrived in Samoa, so I travelled in the guard's van to Auckland. To avoid the press I then transferred, out the back of the station, to the *Philomel* to await the arrival of the *Dunedin*. Commodore Swabey picked me up in the stream and, without refuelling, set off as instructed to Samoa, arranging for a tanker to bring fuel to Apia later. After we rendezvoused with the *Diomede* we made full speed – nearly thirty knots – to Samoa.

On the way the Commodore received long telegrams from Richardson urging haste and containing a long series of detailed plans. As they called for more men than were available, Swabey, who had been instructed to use his discretion, made up his mind that he would do nothing until his arrival in Apia. There the Commodore and I went ashore with Richardson's Aide de Camp, Captain Ross. We were met by large numbers of Mau supporters in their blue uniforms, who accompanied us in a friendly body to the Central Office.

There we met with Richardson. I handed him the intimation of his recall, and told him that the Government looked to Swabey to handle the situation. He took this surprisingly well, but at the subsequent meeting with his officials behaved as though he was still in command. After hearing him calling for this or that to be done, I had to tell him that the navy was in command. Reproachfully he turned on me: 'I didn't want that to be known.'

What was agreed was that the Administration could not allow the Mau to continue flouting the law by parading in their proscribed uniform. Next morning sailors and marines landed and began rounding up all those who were wearing the blue. Soon on a piece of open ground we had a milling throng of some hundreds. No one then knew what to do. The Samoans were not upset. They were perfectly free to come and go. Indeed more and more came to join the group under guard. As it was a hot tropical day the navy had to bring in a water cart, and the civil power realised that they had no prison available for these blue hordes.

That meant a night in the open air, no great hardship in Samoa. The prisoners were then installed at Mulinu'u, a peninsula just out of Apia, and something of a national shrine.[2] A fence was constructed, but the affair became quite ludicrous when those desiring to leave the camp merely walked to the water's edge and paddled out. At the weekend the Samoans found it inconceivable that the Administration could deprive them of the inalienable right to attend the Saturday night movies. Soon the yeoman of signals was reporting 'Mau liberty men going ashore, Sir'. On both Saturday and Sunday night the camp was empty. On Monday they were all back, with their families, large numbers of them. The thing was, from the Samoan point of view, almost too good to be true. Here were quarters provided by the Government at traditional Mulinu'u, and food – the ship's biscuit and bully beef that are the height of delicacy to the Samoan palate – and all free.

Ultimately court was held. All these people were found guilty and sentenced to imprisonment. General Richardson then pardoned the lot; and we were as we had been. Authority had been vindicated, or ridiculed, as the case might be.

The navy itself was not free from the bungling endemic in such an atmosphere. This happened when they went to arrest Tupua Tamasese, a prominent Samoan out of one of the three princely lines, whom the Mau stalwarts had persuaded to give up his job to become the titular Head of the Mau. Tamasese had resisted the Mau with tears, but argument and force prevailed upon him to abandon the grocer's life he loved, for the career of a national hero, and an early and tragic death.

When the navy seized Tamasese, sympathisers rallied around and rescued the young man. This was bad, very bad, but no one knew what to do next. Any attempt to rearrest him might lead to serious bloodshed. Wellington was no help. In the uncertainty created by the approaching change of Administrators, and perhaps of policy, matters dragged on without decision or action.

Meantime the *Dunedin* used up sixty years of carbide to keep its searchlights playing on the main street of the little township at night. For our part General Richardson and I were separately sending long telegrams every day to Wellington. He still felt the situation was well under control. If he were left alone, all the difficulties would disappear.

---

2 Cape Mulinu'u, in Apia Harbour, is a national shrine, the burial place of great chiefs, the centre for national celebrations such as Independence Day, and the traditional seat of Samoan Fonos and now Parliament.

Sir Francis Bell, who admired the old man, strongly supported him. No one else did. While I deplored the uncertainty and stupidity that had allowed the situation to become as bad as it was, I was not prepared to start a war, for that is what it meant, until I and my seniors had a better idea of what it was all about, and what, if anything short of force, could be done to cure things.

The uncertainty of the situation led Commodore Swabey and me to decide against drastic action until after discussions with the Government. When Wellington agreed, we sailed from Apia for Wellington in the *Dunedin*, leaving the *Diomede* to handle any potential disturbances. We could not resolve a situation of such complete confusion by any quick stroke. This would need long and patient efforts at reconciliation, and the steady reintroduction of authority.

After a most violent storm off East Cape we reached Wellington on a typically windy day and went straight to Cabinet to report. My estimate and that of the Commodore was true enough, but things in Samoa went, as they have a habit of doing, from bad to worse before the Government appointed a new Administrator.

Colonel Stephen Allen, with a distinguished military career, was an old friend of Coates. He was taciturn and retiring, but he had a keen brain and devastating wit. His policy was to hold the situation quietly, and by patient firmness to restore respect for authority.

This policy might well have been effective but for the efforts of Nelson and his European and half European supporters. They kept the fires of rebellion alight. Despite being banished to New Zealand, Nelson, who was a wealthy man, spent freely to appeal against his banishment. In court I saw him baffle one of our quickest witted Crown counsels. Michael Myers may have taken Nelson, one of the wiliest of men of men, too lightly. Myers after all had none of his knowledge of Samoa or the situation there, and Nelson simply danced round his Crown examiner with the greatest of ease.

Nelson then went on to institute a newspaper, the *Samoa Guardian*, whose bitter invective, without any crippling regard for the truth, was remarkably effective in creating support for the Mau, particularly in the New Zealand Labour Party. Nelson's campaign led to renewed agitation in Samoa and began to attract international support.

When the Head of the Department of External Affairs retired,

Coates insisted on appointing me as the Secretary of the Department.[3] This created some administrative complications but led me to propose an enquiry into the somewhat Gilbert and Sullivanish administrative machine in Western Samoa. In 1928 the Coates Government appointed Paul Verschaffelt, Public Service Commissioner, A.D. Parkes, Head of the Treasury, and me as Commissioners to survey the Territory, and judge the technical competence and efficiency of the Administration and its officers.

We 'three wise men' sailed in the *Tofua*, visiting Tonga en route, and there hearing with incomprehension of the defeat of the Coates Administration. The Liberals under Sir Joseph Ward had won the famous 'seventy million pounds victory' which we had assumed would damn its sponsors. The facts showed that we had held too high an opinion of the electorate.

After some hesitation we decided we should carry on as if no political change had taken place. After arriving in Apia we paid our official calls. The smaller and less important the place, the more particular one had to be as to form and ceremony. Then we got down to work. Though at times humorous, our hearings proved on the whole most unpleasant.

Technically the Administration had run to seed in a most astonishing way. As a result the 'three wise men' found much to marvel at and much to condemn. We discovered a top-heavy, inefficient, happy-go-lucky administrative machine. Some of the oddest people were employed in the most unbelievable posts. All were receiving treatment of such generosity by New Zealand standards as to make a post in Samoa a prize. In spite

---

3 New Zealand has had two Departments of External Affairs. The first was set up to deal with New Zealand's responsibilities in the Pacific Islands, including the Cook Islands. In practice this Department dealt only with the mandated territory of Western Samoa. In 1943 it was renamed the Department of Island Territories responsible for both Western Samoa and the Cook Islands. The second was recommended by Berendsen and established by the External Affairs Act 1943 to provide the institutional framework for the conduct of New Zealand's expanding international relations. As its Secretary, and after 1945 as head of the Prime Minister's Department, McIntosh shaped our foreign service. See p. 1 of M.J.C. Templeton (ed.) *An Eye, an Ear, and a Voice: Fifty Years in New Zealand's External Affairs 1943–1993* (Wellington: Ministry of Foreign Affairs and Trade, 1993) and p. 3 of Ian MacGibbon (ed.) *Undiplomatic Dialogue: Letters between Carl Berendsen and Alister McIntosh 1943–1952* (Auckland: Auckland University Press, 1994). The Department of External Affairs became the Ministry of Foreign Affairs (1969–1988), then the Ministry of External Relations and Trade (1988–1993), then the Ministry of Foreign Affairs and Trade (1993–present). In 1975 the Department of Island Territories was absorbed back into the Ministry of Foreign Affairs.

of a few competent officers the whole thing had become 'Fa'a Samoa' – easy going, tomorrow will do, it doesn't matter very much.

What we found too was a 'pukka sahib' mentality that had flowered like the tropical jungle. Petty officials were sporting in an unwonted luxury compared with the way they would have lived in New Zealand. Even the junior white officials employed servants, while practically every single member of the local civil service was in debt to the Administration, sometimes for startlingly large sums. Loans were used in any direction that might add to comfort, but largely to purchase motorcars unaffordable in New Zealand. The European officials even had themselves exempted on medical grounds from the prohibition on alcoholic liquor.

The Commission spent a busy month examining and excoriating these comic opera conditions. There is something about small isolated tropical countries that leads to a lack of proportion, a magnification of problems, and a disposition to gossip and quarrel spitefully. With the support of Colonel Allen, we effected considerable changes. Despite the expense we moved to rotate seconded officials every two or three years. We did face attack from Bell in Parliament for 'not understanding tropical conditions' but any fuss soon blew over, as our investigation, based on the principles of good administration, was so demonstrably to the public benefit.

As Head of the Department of External Affairs, I found I had become responsible for the Samoan banana business. General Richardson had developed this to provide a settled form of income for the Territory. The Samoans had planted their bananas, but sadly I found that the Department had decided to build a special vessel rather than rely on private enterprise for transport. The officials who managed this exercise were babes in the wood. They had no knowledge of the shipping or refrigeration issues involved in building the *Maui Pomare*, nor in ensuring that the vessel paid its way. So when I took the ship over I made sure it was on a trial basis. I had to see if we could put the enterprise on a proper footing.

The Department of Scientific Research was asked to find out why the fruit was going bad. This they quickly tracked down to the gases emanating from the bananas, a problem that was quickly easily solved by allowing the utmost ventilation.

The ship was a different issue. I had no knowledge whatever of ships. So I forced the experts to form a committee and meet each month – and actually meet on the ship itself, when it came in – to study the problems on the spot. I warned the officers that their jobs were in jeopardy if the results did not get better. I then made some changes in staff and took steps to correct an obvious slackness by insisting on punctuality. At four o'clock each every fourth Tuesday I ruled that I expected four things to occur simultaneously: the town clock to strike four, the ship to strike eight bells, the engine room to telegraph half astern, and the Blue Peter to come down from the mast. This took their fancy. Almost at once they achieved and took pride in a perfect four-point departure.

In tightening up the discipline of the crew I had the invaluable help of an important labour leader, Fintan Patrick Walsh. He was then the chief official of the Seamen's Union. He got the message across that the crew had to be on time and then, when the crew tried to demand payment for unconsumed meals, turned up in person and dramatically put a halt to that form of indirect theft. Discipline tightened up and the ship ran according to schedule.

The ship even began to pay – and pay properly, with everything covered. We did this by insisting on full cargoes. This was in the interests of Samoa, which needed to sell the fruit for revenue; and of New Zealand, which needed the fruit.

The sale of the bananas – more than two million each voyage – also fell to me. I put them up annually by public tender, and thus assured the grower of his returns, and the New Zealand consumer of the lowest overhead costs.

To assist the ship to pay its way, we even fitted it up for passenger tours. We filled up the cabins with twenty-six passengers at twenty-one pounds for a twenty-one-day cruise, with two days ashore at Apia and one at Niue. This tipped the balance. With care and drive, the ship worked at a profit, a fact which I put to the Public Accounts Committee with some satisfaction.

Later the new Labour Government was to insist on an absurd scheme establishing a uniform price for bananas all over the country. Cheaper bananas for all were to be subsidised by Auckland. I was glad to sever all connection with what had once been a sensible and useful activity. Largely I believe because a close relative of one of the Ministers had his own interests to serve, our little venture became nothing more than a Government ramp.

At the time the 'three wise men' were in Samoa, Colonel Allen found that the adherents of the Mau were openly flouting the authority of the Administration. He took the course then of quietly arresting the Head of the movement, Tupua Tamasese. As he could not be kept in Samoa with its inadequate prison, he was sent with me to New Zealand.

This voyage was to make a good deal of grief for me. The Mau sympathisers and the *Samoa Guardian*, without a vestige of truth, claimed that I had treated Tamasese with great cruelty. We did handcuff him briefly on departure on the advice of the Chief of Police. This was to prevent him swimming ashore. Tamasese, a nice simple lad, enjoyed a voyage on which my wife and I fed him consistently with ice cream and soda pop, of which he was inordinately fond. Both at Suva and then at Auckland the police were tardy in taking him off my hands, so I had a good deal to do with him.

When in New Zealand, Tamasese, with Nelson, mounted appeals which made a considerable stir there and in Samoa, and indeed abroad. After his release, Tamasese returned home to a truculent Mau. More derisive of authority than ever, they organised an illegal procession and, to test the resolution of the Administration, placed a well-known criminal, wanted by the police, in the brass band that led the way.

Colonel Allen was entirely the wrong man to flout. The police obviously had to act. Six police, led by a respected New Zealand police officer, went into the procession to arrest the criminal. Resistance led to a serious scuffle, police were injured and firing broke out. The police retired to their barracks where they had to resist a full-scale attack by the Mau. In the struggle Tamasese, endeavouring it seems to restore order, and some other Samoans were fatally shot.

This was in every way a deeply regrettable affair for which New Zealand was vilified throughout the world. Legitimately one could not find fault with the police for doing their duty. Certainly wiser heads in the Mau might have prevented such deplorable bloodshed.

Recalled from a holiday on the Milford Track, my wife and I genuinely grieved over the death of this promising young man just as time was beginning to ease the contest with the Mau. With Tamasese's brother elected to the title and the titular leadership of the Mau, both sides had to wait for the election of the Labour Government in 1935 to restore amicable relations.

That was the time when I first came in contact with one of the ablest and most attractive members of the Labour Party, John A. Lee. A man of many parts, tall, rangy and handsome, he moved with the grace of a wild animal. Lee was without doubt the best orator I ever heard in our Parliament. He had a beautiful, full and resonant voice. He spoke with logic of thought and argument, and emotion of mind and speech, in almost perfect English. It was a political tragedy that he was not given Ministerial rank in the first Labour Government. Though burning with resentment at being overlooked for Cabinet, he now took an interest not only in the Under Secretary's Housing portfolio, of which he made such a success, but also in Western Samoa.

The situation was interesting. Lee had been an unmerciful critic of the previous Government. Now he sat down and studied the problem. In all my experience this was the first time I saw a responsible politician do this. Lee went into the matter exhaustively. With the results of Lee's studies the MP Frank Langstone went to Samoa and effected a generous settlement. This met many of the demands of the malcontents. Salaries for Tamasese Me'ole and Malietoa Tanumafili I helped link to the Administration the two highest Samoan leaders with the capacity to lead Western Samoa to self-government and ultimately – though it seemed difficult to contemplate for so little a land, with or without American Samoa – independence.

CHAPTER 3

DEPRESSION AND DICTATORS

Before then we had to endure the terrible years of the Great Depression and the rise of the Dictators. The seeds of trouble were laid in that seventy-million-pound election which saw Coates replaced by that kindly old gentlemen, Sir Joseph Ward, who was by no means the feisty leader of earlier times when he purloined power in 1928.

Coates was in many ways a sad loss as a leader. Why then did his Administration fail? Possibly a sustained campaign of adulation led the public to expect too much from this young and comparatively untrained man. Like every Prime Minister he then had to control and contend with difficult colleagues in Cabinet and party. He became the victim of oceans of advice from people, among them pests of the highest order. Coates was not adept, as Fraser later proved to be, in shaking off such parasites, many of whom created widespread criticism. Sometimes too the military bearing of a senior army officer jarred and was misunderstood, and even resented, in the democratic atmosphere of New Zealand.

This was all probably less important than a widespread, long-running whispering campaign that Coates was frequently under the influence of alcohol. It was claimed that he was such a deep and heavy drinker that he was frequently unable to transact public business. This was undoubtedly a factor in the loss of public confidence, but it was most unjust and foully untrue. No one worked more closely with Coates than I day by day and hour by hour. And I never saw Coates at any time under the influence of alcohol; indeed he was a very abstemious man. These malicious rumours, which deeply distressed him, played some part in his fall from popular favour.

Despite all this, the main cause of the defeat of the Coates Administration, which did small credit to those who swallowed it, was the absurd vote-catching proposal of the Liberal Party to borrow seventy million pounds. This was forty-odd pounds for every man woman and child in the country. Many believed in this preposterous proposal, which may have been due to a typist's error in adding an extra nought. Needless to say the sum was never borrowed.

In any case when we arrived back in New Zealand Ward's administration was in office and welcomed with open arms the very adverse report we had brought back on the conduct of affairs in the Mandated Territory. They used it with some effect to belabour the Reform Party, though that was the party that, feeling all was not well, had sent us to inquire.

As loyal civil servants in the high traditions of an unbiased civil service, we transferred our allegiance with complete fidelity to Ward, whom I had never met. On being called to his office I found the old gentleman delighted with our report on Samoa. Clearly he felt that it would give him a lash with which to whip the defeated Administration. I found him busily striking out any mark of praise and running phrases and sentences together regardless of context. We were able to steer him away from the worst of his indiscretions, but it was a sign of how far disease had worsened his judgement. He even tried to correct me on the date in Samoa, a day behind because of the international dateline.

I found Sir Joseph delighted beyond measure at his rehabilitation in public esteem. But he was a shell of the man he once had been. He was not only old and in very bad health, but already somewhat childish in his actions and reactions. As a result those who cared for him had to protect him from all labour. In my experience he did no administrative work of any kind.

For political reasons this was concealed from the public. His son Vincent, with a super Oxford accent, but an astonishing amount of commonsense and business acumen, took charge of the Prime Minister's office and basically of the Government's activities. Replies to letters were prepared in the usual way. Hundreds and thousands of them I found out later were signed in the Prime Minister's name by Frank Thomson, who showed a capacity for forgery which deceived New Zealand until Sir Joseph passed away, still a figure of contention and argument.

Ward's passing was a great loss to his party, and to his colleagues, the oddest set of men imaginable. There were a few sensible and experienced Ministers, but for the most part they were the queerest set of dullards and incompetents I have ever come across in comparable positions. I have no great admiration for politicians generally, and most of the Governments I have served have been inefficient to a greater or lesser degree, mostly greater, but this was the worst.

The ignorance and incompetence of some Ministers was outstanding. One of the new Ministers came to offer me assistance in weighing tenders for a large contract. Later, as we walked out of the room with the dying Prime Minister's signature attached, he said to me 'I think I should tell you that I have a third interest in that contract.' I could not believe that I had heard correctly. In the end, as it was undoubtedly the best contract, Frank Thomson and I, both shaken, simply left a note on file.

Another of this remarkable group established in his office a young lady who accompanied him on his travels. Although he described her as his niece, she was a cause of much gossip. Yet another Minister was given to the use of a 'dickey' that made him an object of ribald comment on his walks on the waterfront, the last place to be impressed by a false front. One, a Seventh Day Adventist Minister, established for his staff a rule of no work on Saturday, perhaps the forerunner of the long weekend, but an astonishing innovation at the time.

The Ward Government, with a leader so incapacitated and a group of such ignorant, inexperienced, incompetent and hesitant Ministers, was exceedingly inefficient, but knowing so little perhaps meant that no one was seriously hurt, nor was the country. A few sensible and experienced Ministers were able to carry the heavy burden of national administration until Ward passed away in 1929.

On Ward's death, the Government devolved on George Forbes, a Prime Minister of an unusual type. 'Farmer George' in the strictest accuracy, he never aimed to be anything else. Devoid of ambition, he was a man of the people, distinguished for his good plain qualities. A talented Canterbury halfback, he had had the good fortune to take up land under the closer settlement schemes and become a successful farmer. He was an upstanding citizen who was probably surprised to become a Member of Parliament, and astonished to find himself Prime Minister.

Forbes was a man of good sense, likeable, but with no special qualifications to govern the country. But then how few do. Despite acquiring some familiarity with legislative affairs in his long apprenticeship as an MP, he had no experience in administration of any kind, let alone

Berendsen graduating with LLB, 1914. *Berendsen Family Collection*

Berendsen's wife, Nellie, and their sons, Ian and Keith. *Berendsen Family Collection*

Carl and Nellie Berendsen dressed for the coronation of King George VI, London, 1937. *Berendsen Family Collection*

International

NEW ZEALAND'S BERENDSEN
Offered, a right hand.

Sir Carl Berendsen made the pages of *Time* magazine in 1949 when he announced, regarding the United Nations resolution that the Great Powers voluntarily curb their veto powers in the Security Council, 'I would give my right hand for the success of this organisation.' He remained passionately against the veto throughout his career. *Time Magazine, 25 April 1949, p. 16.*
Image provided by the Alexander Turnbull Library.

UNITE
UNITED
AIR LINES

UNITED
AIR LINES

Above: Carl and Nellie Berendsen in the early years of their marriage. *Berendsen Family Collection*

Facing page: Members of the Allied Far Eastern Commission arrive on the USS *Mount McKinley* in Yokohama, Japan, 9 January 1946. Sir Carl Berendsen is at the bottom right of the photograph, sharing a step with Major General Frank McCoy (United States). Just behind Berendsen is Sir George Sansom (United Kingdom). At the top left of the photograph are Major Jim Plimsoll (Australia) and Nelson T. Johnson (United States), Secretary of the Commission. *SC 228546, Berendsen Family Collection*

Previous page (top): Carl and Nellie Berendsen on their diplomatic travels. *Berendsen Family Collection*

Previous page (bottom): Carl and Nellie Berendsen greeting British diplomat Sir Ronald Campbell. *Berendsen Family Collection*

Carl and Nellie Berendsen. *Photograph by Peter Basch, New York, Berendsen Family Collection*

the special administration involved in national government. Forbes was logical enough, if pedestrian. He could make a case with reasonable cogency and, because of his simplicity and directness, handled his Cabinet well. In all his political and administrative problems he was fortunate to have the important support of a shrewd and able man, Robert Master. This experienced businessman took control of Forbes, and acted as his link with Cabinet, the party and the people.

In 1930 Forbes had to go to London for the Imperial Conference. He selected quite a team, including Sir Thomas Sidey, a tough, wiry little politician, famous for his untiring, persevering campaign to establish daylight saving in New Zealand. In Dunedin, with family wealth and commitment to public service, he held something of the position of a squire in the Old Country. A lawyer by training, he took the keenest of interests in the affairs of Dunedin and the whole country. Though he was no more than a sensible, logical, workmanlike speaker, Sidey's reputation and courage always earned him a respectful hearing.

The team also included the High Commissioner, Sir Thomas Wilford, a leading Liberal politician. Wilford was a man of many parts, a leading criminal lawyer and outstanding advocate with a national reputation for defending murder cases. A set speech by Wilford was a thing to remember. He had a wonderfully picturesque use of words and imagery, and I would rate him one of the finest of our parliamentary orators. During the Great War he had set up as an expert in world affairs, and it was no surprise when Ward sent him to London, where he represented New Zealand with credit at the League.

Frank Thomson and I as officials were joined for the 1930 Conference by Dr Val Armstrong of the Department of Scientific and Industrial Research and Dr George Craig of Customs, whose three daughters were later taken by the Japanese in Singapore and tragically never heard of again.

Forbes, like Fraser later, was a very poor speaker, and most painful to listen to, but in Britain his personal qualities carried him through. He never pretended to be anything but transparently honest and sincere and he got through that conference with credit. In the countryside and the provincial cities as well as the capital he was well liked.

At the conference and travelling back, Forbes also got on well with his Australian colleague. J.H. Scullin was of the same friendly, gentlemanly type as Michael Joseph Savage. He was free of that bombast and ruthlessness characteristic of Labour politicians, especially Australian ones. It was difficult to understand how Scullin ever rose from the ranks of Labour to become the titular Head of that combatant group. Ultimately I suspect he became Prime Minister for the same reason as Savage did. The people as a whole liked him, were not afraid of what he might do, and trusted him to do his best with his admittedly limited abilities.

On this visit I must confess my Prime Minister was part of one of the most terrible experiences of my life. On one day on the official visit to Edinburgh we were afflicted with twenty-three speeches. Nine of them were by Dominion Prime Ministers, none of whom was a good speaker. The last agony of a cruel day saw the official dinner, with all the visitors in the last stages of exhaustion and boredom, drag on until after midnight. At that point poor Forbes was buttonholed by some professional patriot who insisted upon 'a most important interview' then and there. Forbes, exhausted as he was, was too polite to thrust him off. I left him to his unhappy fate.

The 1930 conference was again focussed on the constitutional issue of Dominion status. The Balfour formula of 1926 proved useless so far as Ireland was concerned. The whole question was referred to the Sankey committee. Judge Sankey, a Labour supporter, was slow and pedestrian and the Irish were round him like gadflies, quick, witty and implacable in their contempt for their Chairman. Kevin O'Higgins, a man of the people, later to die tragically; Desmond Fitzgerald, dark, handsome and debonair, but as fiercely patriotic and Irish as O'Higgins; and Patrick McGilligan, perhaps the wittiest, quickest and most vehement of them all, ran rings round the incompetent Sankey.

Sankey's performance remains linked in my mind with muddled pomposity. The silly creature became an object of derision with his constant repetition of a Chairman's catch phrase: 'I don't say you're wrong, and I don't say you're right; I'm merely thinking aloud.' This he repeated again and again, until under our voices we all repeated it with him. If anything that followed was, in Sankey's view, thinking, it was profoundly ineffective in that atmosphere.

Sankey's exhibition was painful for us, who in our hearts held the same position as the British and distrusted both the brilliance and the cause of the Irish. The Irish had achieved the same degree of complete independence as all the other Dominions. Why could they not content themselves with utilising their untrammelled freedom to legislate as they willed? Why raise these questions of theoretical principle and dogma that were to lead Ireland to become a foreign country? Any attempt to convince these bitter, but intelligent and witty men to the contrary was doomed to failure. Eire soon came into being; neutral, inimical, and resentful of Ulster's opposition to being included in the new state.

While at the conference, my wife and I met the Rudyard Kiplings at Buckingham Palace and to make conversation quoted from his reference to the gorse-swept hills of Wellington and his description of Auckland as the last, loneliest and loveliest. 'Have they got a better pub there yet?' he asked and I had to admit that they had not. At 10 Downing Street, where most of the meetings of the Imperial Conference were held, we met the Ramsay MacDonalds at home. We also put to sea with the navy for manoeuvres in the Channel, and took part in the opening of telephonic communications between London and New Zealand.

With the High Commissioner, Sir Thomas Wilford, I then went with Nellie to Geneva as a member of the New Zealand Delegation to the League of Nations for a meeting of the Permanent Mandates Commission. This was a competent, if somewhat cynical body of experts, much more fitted to its task than the really very stupid Trusteeship Council of the United Nations.

In explaining our troubles in Western Samoa, I found the members knowledgeable and understanding. Most like Lord Lugard had been Administrators themselves, so they understood the odd turns that affairs may take. Sir Eric Drummond, the Secretary General, was a good but weak man. His Deputy, M. Avenol, was one of the poorest class of formal civil servants. He had risen to high standing by never taking a risk and by always doing the popular thing. Avenol's distinct leanings towards appeasement made him a less than useful servant of the ill-fated organisation at this critical time.

So we left for home, Nellie and I visiting Venice, Rome and Naples, with which Wellington more than stands comparison, as well as seeing something of the misery of Port Said and the beauty of Ceylon, and its ancient capital of Kandy. Back home, in order to be nearer Parliament, we sold our Island Bay home to move first to the Glen, just beyond the

Botanical Gardens, and then to Central Terrace in Kelburn, close to the university.

On return I found myself exceedingly busy with my own foreign affairs, and someone else's Pacific Island problems. Now mine by inheritance, they were still a nasty mess. In 1932 they required me to return to Samoa with Paul Verschaffelt, whose eccentricities were getting worse, to ascertain how our reshaping of the local Administration was coming along.

In Samoa Colonel Allen had seen the worst of the troubles through and then handed over to General Hart. Things were by no means settled, but were improving under an efficient Secretary to the Administration in Alfred Turnbull, later Administrator. This visit required us to travel all over the country. Nellie and I became somewhat bored and worn by the extent of the traditional ceremonies, gift making, entertainment and lengthy feasting required. General Richardson's attempt to halt these time consuming and costly Samoan customs had given great offence and helped in the alienation of local feeling that had sustained the Mau.

By the time we returned to Wellington, touching at Niue on the way to pick up bananas, the balance of my attention had shifted from the comparatively minor tasks of the Pacific Islands to the growing tension of the international situation. The British telegrams so freely made available to Dominion Governments helped me form a most gloomy picture.

By 1934 indeed the situation loomed so seriously that I warned the Government in a written memorandum that the nations of the world 'were selecting their partners' for the next world war. New Zealand would do well to prepare against a war that seemed certain. No particular notice was taken of that warning. The forces of evil gathered themselves unchecked, indeed encouraged by popular apathy and the appeasement of good but simple people.

About this time Frank Thomson passed away. This led to my appointment as Permanent Secretary of the Prime Minister's Department, a nomination that made no difference to my duties and functions, but left me with official responsibility for the three Departments of the Prime Minister, External Affairs, and the Cook Islands.

In my short term of responsibility, I was unable to do much for the Cooks, except to provide every inhabited island with a means of radio communication. In the hurricane zone I felt it essential for the people to have cheap, reliable radio sets to keep in touch during what were regular emergencies.

In 1935 New Zealand faced the totally unexpected defeat of the Forbes–Coates Government. Forbes had had the misfortune to be Prime Minister during the Great Depression. The policies he chose to meet its distressing impact earned him undeserved unpopularity, fomented of course by the political opponents who hoped to succeed him.

Forbes was by no means a great man, but he was a good man with much common sense and native wisdom, a simple man of real, if quiet humour, and direct and uncomplicated thinking processes. As a farmer and citizen he had learned that to spend more than he earned was to court bankruptcy and disaster. With the drastic fall in national income Forbes concluded that national expenditure must be substantially reduced. Despite the contrary views of many economists, Forbes decided to cut the national coat according to the national cloth. This meant reducing staff and adding to unemployment.

As the economists advocated, he and Coates in coalition altered the exchange rate. This lost the country the services of William Downie Stewart as Minister of Finance. Another of the old school of gentlemen and scholars in politics, a man of wide reading and culture, he brought to the task of government an equipment rare in New Zealand history. Of the strictest probity and integrity, a moderate Conservative of inflexible principle, this powerful guide for many years to our Conservative leaders refused to follow the Socialistic experiments which beguiled Coates.

So when the planners proposed the lowering of the exchange rate, Downie Stewart refused to depart from the straight and narrow path of financial orthodoxy. Unusually, he resigned. New Zealand shows few such examples of politicians sufficiently honest to abandon the honours and emoluments of office because of principle.

The Forbes–Coates Coalition also instituted widespread public works with a deliberately low remuneration. This policy naturally helped the Labour Opposition. They had adopted the most popular of all political theories; to spend, and to spend irrespective of the effect, as a cure to the human suffering that was common not only to New Zealand, but also to the world at large.

This showed up in Savage sponsoring the idea that it was no longer necessary for anyone to save money. With a Labour Government to see to it, the future of all would be assured. Savage and his colleagues would see to the contingencies of sickness, accident or old age. So stupidly they helped build an undue dependence on the State at the expense of the plain self-reliance of free people.

For the Great Depression the Forbes–Coates Administration of course had no tittle of responsibility. I know how deeply concerned Forbes and his colleagues were, and how earnestly in perplexing circumstances they strove to do the right thing, and to alleviate suffering. To a considerable degree, they did minimise the worst of the distress for New Zealand, compared with the USA.

Any Liberal Government may have been doomed at a time when old fashioned liberalism was falling behind in the great struggle between right and left, when economists were preaching new fangled ideas of priming the pump, and when ideologues talked of costless credit as a road to prosperity. There is of course no such thing as costless credit but the outburst of expenditure under the Forbes–Coates coalition eventually did prime the pump of industry and business and the Depression, as preparations for war mounted, did pass away.

I should note that the priming of the pump, which Coates adopted on the advice of his brilliant young adviser, Dr R.M. Campbell, ruined his relations with his own Reform Party. Planning and spending were highly unpopular with that section of the community that supported Coates and Reform, people with whom I associated myself. I am not a planner. After watching their muddled efforts over twenty-five years, I suspect the Do-gooders and New Dealers. Be that as it may, Coates's appearance in the guise of a Socialist convert, heading a conservative party and usurping their belief in private enterprise, was a potent cause of his second downfall, along with Forbes, at the hands of Labour and the electorate.

CHAPTER 4

THE SAVAGE GOVERNMENT

To me the installation of the first Labour Government under Michael Joseph Savage was an astonishing result. Labour had been slowly improving its position in the country, but the passionately bitter leadership of Harry Holland had limited the Party's chances. After Holland's death in 1933, Savage's charm and balance changed all that.

After the too prudent approach of the Forbes Government, everybody instinctively trusted this sympathetic, kindly man to deal with the Great Depression. His broad and Christian tolerance calmed the fears and apprehensions of the people. He came into office, as he said repeatedly, as a friend, who thought well of his fellow men. Under Savage's leadership, Labour was able to offer dramatic but sane and appealing solutions to the problems of the country.

Never a violent political partisan, I was somewhat apprehensive in face of the threatening cheers and hoots of the horny handed as they welcomed their new masters and excoriated the old. After so many years of Liberal and Conservative Governments, we were about to explore a new world under Socialistic theorists, largely untrained and uneducated, and fanatical in their hatred of the governing classes.

Although I had never met Savage until he had been sworn in, I had no personal qualms. He knew that the higher echelons of the civil service were of a different political philosophy but this did not seem to discomfort him, as it did his colleagues like Peter Fraser and nearly every other member of the Labour Party. Savage knew and liked men and accepted that our duty as civil servants was to serve the legitimately elected Government to the best of our abilities.

Savage had no apparent qualifications for his high office and its onerous and complex responsibilities. He had earned his living in modest employment in Australia and New Zealand, but neither his experience in the Labour movement nor in Parliament, could assist in the daily burden of administration that so taxes the industry, the intelligence, the judgement and the application of a Prime Minister.

The surprising thing was how quickly Savage settled down as Prime Minister, and with his new Administration proceeded to alter the face of the country and to remove many injustices. He had a much larger view of things than any other Prime Minister I have served, yet proved to be an excellent administrator. Of course he saw too many people, as do all our Prime Ministers. He signed too many letters. But while the others burdened themselves to the point of inefficiency, Savage would delegate.

The Prime Minister made an admirable leader and Chairman of Cabinet, which, despite a number of heavy-handed characters, he kept firmly in order. He even brought the most overbearing of his colleagues, Peter Fraser, into line. He focussed on dealing with his own responsibilities, chose good men in general, and then saw to it that Ministers and officials each carried their fair share of the load. This was indeed heavy when so much was being altered and reshaped. Nor did he fall into the error of working day and night. He rationed out his time, instituted orderly methods of business, and at the end of the day, left his desk clear.

Almost immediately after the election I was sent to London and Geneva. As an experienced official acquainted with the matters with which he would be dealing, I was to help install W.J. Jordan as New Zealand High Commissioner in London and our representative at the League in Geneva. The general idea was that this kind of thing was out of Jordan's experience. As he would be obliged constantly to deal with such duties in his High Commissioner role, it was thought prudent for an experienced official to be at his side when he first assumed the new duties, both in London and Geneva in 1936.

My wife and I as a result joined Jordan and his wife and daughter on the *Niagara*, which was to meet such an unhappy fate a few years later in that war which Jordan, completely blind to the realities of the time, repeatedly and heatedly affirmed could never occur. Never did we have a happier voyage, or more congenial travelling companions. Mrs Jordan and Gwen were charming and genuine, and Jordan in such circumstances showed all the best of his many-sided personality. He was friendly and gay, and the small table we shared in the dining saloon was full of chatter, laughter and good cheer. Indeed Jordan was one of the most popular figures on the ship.

Jordan was one of the most unusual characters I have known, a mixture of the good, the silly and the unpleasant. With little (I almost said no) formal education, he had raised himself by the way of Labour officialdom to dignified heights, while remaining proud of his original start in life as a London policeman. There was nothing he enjoyed more than reminiscing over those old days, as in taking us to his old haunts in the poor quarters of London and introducing us to his relatives – good simple folk, poorly endowed with the goods of this world, but richly endowed for the next.

One of the most striking of Jordan's qualities, and certainly one of the most enjoyable, was his high and puckish sense of humour. Jordan was one of the wittiest men I have ever known – indeed I am not sure I should not say quite the wittiest. He was full of fun, could tell a story as well as anyone, and was full of yarns and quips and jokes, and adept at coining names for people. No one went to sleep in Jordan's company, and one had to be quick witted to keep up with him.

Jordan was another who had, as most of his party did, a profound suspicion of the Senior Civil Servant. Once I had his confidence, he did not conceal from me his fear that his work in London and Geneva would be sabotaged by this treacherous class. Jordan never lost this quite unreasoning and unjustified suspicion of officials. One distinguished New Zealand civil servant, who had been bombed out of his post in Europe at the opening of the war, who deserved well of his country, and who was to rise to high office, was met with a barrage of abuse when he called on the High Commissioner.

Another official for whom Jordan developed a high degree of hatred was Dr R.M. Campbell, one of the most distinguished of all New Zealand civil servants.[1] I have a shrewd suspicion that Jordan became jealous of Campbell's reputation, and the advice and guidance he gave him, in Geneva and London. Presumably he felt that Campbell took some of the limelight and lustre from him as High Commissioner. As a result we eventually had to transfer Campbell, a close personal friend of Peter Fraser, who held the highest opinion of his abilities and character, back to a most unsuitable post as Public Service Commissioner in New Zealand.

---

1 Frequently on mission in London as a key economic adviser in the 1930s, Dr Campbell served as official Secretary at the High Commission (in effect Deputy High Commissioner) 1940–46 and again 1953–58. See *Dictionary of New Zealand Biography*, Vol. 5, p. 91.

After the long journey to London, our party went off to Geneva. There we met a range of New Zealanders attached to the League Secretariat: J.V. Wilson, John Condliffe, J.H. Chapman and E.J. Riches of the International Labour Organization. I was particularly pleased to see John Condliffe, with whom I had played cricket at Victoria University. He had then become a notable Professor of Economics at Canterbury before joining the League and authoring the highly regarded World Economic Survey. Subsequently he made his career at Berkeley in California as one of the world's foremost economists and New Zealand's greater expatriate sons.

At Geneva I discovered that Jordan had many unpleasant traits. On a superficial acquaintance he might prove charming, but his overbearing temper, and arrogant and combative spirit often overcame his better social qualities. In my case they showed up in a gross error on his part. The weakness that immediately shattered our good relations after our arrival in Geneva was his marked disinclination to take instructions from his Government. He showed the most violent resentment of my efforts to keep him to his brief. Jordan had no academic skills and was ignorant of the highly technical and complicated subjects before us. What was worse he simply refused to study the papers. At variance with Savage and Fraser he went out of his way to scout the possibility of war. 'There'll be no war,' Jordan screamed in his high falsetto, and with the utmost contempt for those who prudently held the opposite view. 'All this talk of war is just moonshine.'

This fixed and almost maniacal disbelief in the possibility of war led him, as I say, into serious error. Jordan proposed to disregard our detailed and strong opening statement about the threat of war and the stupidity of meeting aggression with appeasement. He now decided to use his discretion. He would act the plenipotentiary.

The problem was that our statement had the specific approval of Cabinet and Jordan knew this. There was no way I could allow him to sell the soft soap of appeasement on New Zealand's behalf. I argued with him, not only on the merits of the line he preferred, but as to the impossibility of departing, without consultation with Wellington, from the instructions with which he had left New Zealand. Jordan would have none of it. What was he? A mere clerk? I cannot convey the disgust and contempt he put into that word. I now had to tell him that if he persisted, I had an inescapable responsibility to tell Wellington. Jordan was only at last persuaded to make a watered down version of the statement approved by his own Government. He did so, and when he came back to the hotel, there were tears in his eyes – I suppose from mixed emotions of doubt, humiliation and anger. My stand had drawn me into a violent, long drawn out, unsought and undeserved quarrel.

In any case, and naturally enough perhaps, Jordan soon visited his indignation on me. I showed him a letter to my Department in which, though I made no reference to our struggle, I did comment on the hard work and strain of the conference. This was a red rag to a bull for Jordan, who as I have said, never looked at a document, had seen no hard work, or indeed any work at all. He turned on me with a ferocity which I have never before experienced. It was almost boundless in its rage and hatred.

In this debate, I was no match for a Labour politician brought up on a diet of dissension and struggle. His onslaught was violent in the extreme. It left me shaken for weeks. All I could do was tell Savage the whole story when I got home. The Prime Minister gave me all the sympathy, encouragement and approval any man could wish. As a result it was made clear to, and in the end accepted by Jordan that he was in fact the servant, not the master of the Government, the instrument of its policy, and not its founder.

Besides my difficulties with Jordan, I also had to handle a delicate situation at Geneva with the previous High Commissioner. Sir James Parr, a reserved and stiffish man, remained a member of the Delegation. Now, not the most congenial of colleagues, he had to serve under Jordan. Later Parr was to earn some notoriety in the thunderstorm that so seriously disrupted the schedule for departure from Westminster Abbey after the coronation of King George V. To overcome the bottleneck, Parr 'threw a fit' and was driven home comfortably and rapidly in an ambulance.

For the League these were the days of Abyssinia. I was shocked by the levity and unreality of the endless discussions, the evasion of the issues, and the search for an encompassing formula. Worse was the crude pretence that the passing of a resolution would provide a solution for the first real and inescapable test of the system of collective security. The manoeuvres to avoid taking a firm position on this vital matter were appalling. The relevant Committee spent its time looking for some way to disqualify Abyssinia from participation. Anthony Eden, the Foreign Secretary, and William Strang, the Permanent Under-Secretary of State in the Foreign Office, were not at their best, and the French Minister Yvon Delbos shuffled and evaded the issue.

For the first time in my life in a matter of primary moment, I took a firm and critical stand. It was the only thing I said in this Committee and it was enough. I asked for the floor. I then enquired whether there was anyone in the Committee or at the Assembly who denied the right of the victim to be represented at the enquiry into that aggression. There was no answer. So the Committee went on to approve Abyssinia's representation.

This irresolution of the League filled me with apprehension. I had been dismayed by the failure to do anything when Japan invaded Manchuria in 1932. Now the floundering of the League over the last chance to avert World War II was even more disturbing. The scoundrelly booing and catcalls from the Italians that greeted the Abyssinian Emperor Haile Selassie were a disgrace to humanity.

Worse was to come with the wretched Hoare–Laval proposals for settling the Abyssinian conflict.[2] These called for the appeasement of the aggressor, Italy, by the dismemberment of Ethiopia, the victim. This perfectly shocking initiative, produced with satisfaction by a fool and a knave, seemed to meet with approval as a divinely inspired solution.

In the first serious business in foreign affairs with which the new Government had to deal, Savage stood firm. A map of the area to be handed over to Italy roused the indignation of Cabinet. Calmly and moderately we drafted a telegram making it clear to London that New Zealand would have no part in such a plan. New Zealand's message was the first wave in the storm of indignation that swept the world, threw Hoare out of office, and wholly destroyed that sinister plan.

---

2 The Hoare–Laval Pact 1935 was negotiated in Paris to end the war in Abyssinia. Ceding much of Ethiopia to Italy, it destroyed the authority of the League of Nations, and, in rewarding aggression, led to the resignation of Sir Samuel Hoare, the British Foreign Secretary, and his replacement by Anthony Eden, and the dismissal of Pierre Laval, the French Premier, himself later executed at the end of World War II for supporting the Nazis. Hoare served as Ambassador to Spain 1940–44. His book, *Ambassador on Special Mission* (London: Collins, 1946), tells of his work in securing the neutrality of Franco Spain.

But the damage had been done. The League did no more than pass pious resolutions while refusing the sanctions that would have denied Italy oil and the use of the Suez Canal. Ill-placed fear of the Italian fleet enabled Mussolini's hordes to continue their attack. Eventually they broke the unorganised levies of Ethiopia with poison gas. Through the poltroonery of the Great Powers the aggressor carried through the conquest of Ethiopia. Most of the nations then recognised Italy's imperium – but not New Zealand.

The League's cynical abandonment of all principles in the face of determined evil was a low point in the history of civilisation and particularly of Britain – though we were to fall lower in the foul abandonment of Czechoslovakia. In Geneva I felt ashamed listening to the vapourings of the Organization for Intellectual Cooperation – the League's UNESCO – when the whole world was about to go up in flames.

This session convinced me that the League would do nothing effective to prevent the colossal conflict that was looming. My gloomy forebodings were reinforced travelling home. In Germany we experienced the menace of a police state. No one smiled, many swaggered, most whispered, and all frowned. Nellie and I had a particular fright when we failed to record the currency we had brought with us. The German officials were so threatening that we virtually held our breath until we crossed the border into Holland (where incidentally we saw television for the first time). In that free land we knew we were safe – and infinitely relieved to be out of Germany.

On our way homeward, at Gibraltar we heard the firing and listened to the most lurid tales of the cruelty and ferocity of the Spanish Civil War. At every port, mailbags from my Department kept me up with the affairs of the world, though not of Wallis Simpson and the decision of Edward VIII to abdicate. En route through the Suez Canal we passed shiploads of Italian 'heroes' being given every facility, even priority, while they jeered and catcalled at us.

After talks in Canberra, in Wellington I expounded to the Government and the public my fears and indeed certainties of the evils to come. I had come back sure that another world conflict was imminent. In a complacent little backwater like New Zealand I was either ridiculed or condemned as a warmonger. In speaking up as publicly as I could, I made not a ripple on the magnificent self-satisfaction of New Zealand and its confidence that nothing in the world could possibly affect us. The view prevailed that being friendly would either ensure that a dangerous crocodile would eat someone else, or get him to change his ways.

Let no one believe that wars come on people without notice. There is always notice. The question is whether people act. Let no one believe that the thousands of things that need to be done can be improvised on the spur of the moment. Prolonged thought and preparation must be given to such major issues. To this end I got our Prime Minister and his Cabinet, many of them pacifists like him, to authorise preparation of a 'War Book'. My Prime Minister's Department took charge of the work, which fell to Colonel Stevens, on secondment from the army. Hundreds of others from dozens of Departments met in innumerable committees, from defence of harbours to the provision of arms, from the management of the national economy and its trade, to censorship and internment. We had to examine all contingencies for the welfare of the nation, and some were not cheerful.

No sooner had I got this work under way than we had to leave with the Prime Minister for the Imperial Conference of 1937 and the coronation of the new King. Our little family were left with my mother, with the help of friends. In England, the High Commissioner and Walter Nash, already there, joined us for the coronation and the conference. No man alive got around more than Walter Nash; and none took a more exuberant pleasure in the good things of life than this exponent of the equality of man. Savage on the other hand, in his distaste for pomp and ceremony, reacted violently and unfavourably to Jordan's news that he had to wear Court dress and that this involved knee breeches. He was not a man for uniform. But everybody would be in uniform, Jordan informed him. Indeed he himself had already purchased his.

'How much?' said asked Savage. 'About three hundred pounds.' 'No three hundred pounds for me,' said Savage, to whom the expenditure of such a sum for such a purpose was revolting. 'You don't have to buy one; everyone hires them, but I'll have to wear mine often,' said Jordan. 'Where from?' asked the disgruntled Prime Minister. 'From Moss Brothers,' replied Jordan.

At the time Savage could not be persuaded and retired undefeated to ponder on his fate. Only when Nash and Jordan persuaded him that as New Zealand's representative he had to be seen to do the right thing did Savage give way and agree to wear his uniform – though he hated it, and shrank from public sight, in case he should be thought to be an exhibitionist, or some ill-disposed person should laugh at him. The rest of us, who certainly wished to attend the coronation, gathered next day at Moss Brothers. Of course we were very late, and naturally Moss Brothers' large stock had pretty much been picked over.

My own experience was embarrassing in the extreme. I have always hated the rigmarole of being fitted by a tailor. This was worse, much worse. I was taken into a corner, which I assumed to be part of the fitting room. There were pumps – black pumps with gold buckles. There was only one pair anywhere near my size, and they were too small and very painful. But no better could be found and I took them. Next day at the Abbey I had to kick them off and go through the whole ceremony like a Moslem, in my silk – golden – stockings. Then came a pair of white silk knee breeches; then a black coat covered with white lace, then a cocked hat, with long white feathers, and finally a sword of gold. I was told to put the things on and proceeded to do so.

Obviously I had to remove my outer garments for this purpose, and I did so. I was standing modestly but decently in my underwear when I heard loud and unmistakeable sounds of popular amusement close at hand. To my horror I found I was in one of the shop windows, and half London was enjoying the spectacle. I shouted to the representative of Moss Brothers to pull down the blind, which he did, but this displeased the great British public, which had apparently grown to expect this exhibition as part of the coronation festivities. To jeers and groans from outside, I proceeded to fit myself, with shame and haste, and quickly took my choice.

Next morning we were up at four, for we were to be at the Abbey by six, and there was much to do. With the assistance of one of the hotel's maids, my wife had no difficulties, but I was soon floundering. I tried on my shoes, very tight, and then I started to put on my stockings, and came at once to a problem as insoluble as it was unexpected. I tried all sorts of expedients but every time I moved those stockings fell down. Neither my wife nor the valet could help me. So with some resentment against those who might have been expected to help, I had to solve the difficulty with a couple of safety pins fastening the top of each stocking to the bottom of my singlet.

Then I got into my breeches and something was obviously wrong there too. I called out that I had been given elephant's breeches that were far too long and wide. Fortunately Jeffrey in the next room discovered that he had been issued with what he was pleased to call canary's breeches. So we happily exchanged garments. Then I got into the coat, the only simple thing in all these strange garments. But I could do nothing with the sword. I did not know how it went on and I could not find out and Jeffrey did not know, and the valet did not know.

Never particularly bright at 4.30 in the morning I tried this way and that. Finally I hit on what appeared to be the solution. The shoulder strap which I assumed was meant to go over the right shoulder was intended to go under the coat, and the sword stuck through a slit. So there you were, or rather there was I, to all appearances ready for the road.

Then a thought occurred to me, as thoughts, often embarrassing, have a habit of occurring to me. 'Nellie,' I said, 'do you realise that we are going to be in the Abbey from six in the morning till well on in the afternoon? What do we eat?' She conceded the validity of the point, and suggested sandwiches. So we ordered some chicken sandwiches. 'Who carries these?' I asked. 'You do. In your hat.' And so I did. And it was all worth it for the coronation, the sort of pageant which the British do better than any one else.

The 1937 conference began after the coronation with Stanley Baldwin and Ramsay MacDonald representing Britain, Mackenzie King Canada, Lyons Australia, Savage, Nash and Jordan New Zealand, Hertzog South Africa, and Ireland not represented at all.

These were dangerous days as I had reported to first the Forbes, and then the Savage Government. Another world war was looming and the conference had to face an ugly international situation. What policies should the Commonwealth adopt to meet the position in the days of appeasement when men seemed unable to think clearly on fundamental matters?

Baldwin in an emotional little speech warned the conference that Germany meant ill and handed over the Chair to the egregious Neville Chamberlain. The most deluded figure of the times then pressed ahead with his policy of appeasement, admittedly with the support of the other Dominions, that was to lead to the betrayal of Czechoslovakia.

My Prime Minister would have nothing to do with the policy of appeasement. Savage was not a good speaker, though easily the best of the New Zealand Prime Ministers of my time. His patent honesty showed in simple plain words and, short sentences, clearly connected and delivered slowly, with emphasis and at times with emotion, often with a challenging pause, after a promise or a threat, with and a provocative 'Now then'. He did not orate; he talked to his audience.

Now with the utmost courage and determination Savage laid bare the nakedness and wickedness of appeasement. His very lack of all those qualities that were apt to impress such a superficially glittering gathering, his earnestness, and his simplicity shattered a somewhat shameful debate. His fidelity to the highest ideals made a great, though in many quarters, a bitter impression. He stood alone for right and justice.

Not even Joe Lyons from Australia helped. He was a delightful teddy bear of a man, rounded and lethargic, and without much of the get-up-and-go one associated with someone who had risen to the top of the Australian Labour movement. 'Is your policy peace at any price?' Savage indignantly asked. 'If it is so, I cannot accept it.' Eden, embarrassed, rose to answer. 'No. Not at any price, but peace at almost any price.' To this Savage replied, 'You can pay too high a price even for peace.'

Savage was particularly upset when Lady Astor commented adversely on his attitude in *The Times*. He was already uncomfortable with all the pomp and ceremony and irked by the high life of the Savoy Hotel. Now he refused to make the customary tour of the UK. I felt this would have been good for Savage and the Commonwealth. But his anger at being held up to public ridicule and contumely led him to return home immediately. On the voyage, every now and then he endured great pain. Of this he made light, so that none of us knew that there was anything seriously wrong.

CHAPTER 5

WORLD WAR II

Once home I set myself to expedite in every way the preparations for imminent war. We did make substantial progress. This included vital measures for the expansion of the New Zealand Air Force. On a personal level my wife and I had real satisfaction during these testing times in building another home in Kelburn. Late in 1938 too, our son Ian was selected as one of the two New Zealand Rhodes Scholars for 1939. In the event he actually left Auckland for Oxford on the day Hitler invaded Poland. Caught up in the war, after service in the Pacific, he ended up as a Captain in the famous New Zealand Division that fought with the Eighth Army in the Italian campaign. After the war, he took up his scholarship at Merton, and then made his career in the UN Secretariat.

Neither the New Zealand Government nor I were taken by surprise by the outbreak of war. The scales had fallen from Chamberlain's eyes and once Hitler attacked Poland on 1 September 1939, New Zealand was informed of the British Ultimatum. The Labour Administration were in no doubt as to their policy or their duty. We had prepared telegrams and messages for this eventuality well beforehand.

That September night at the Cabinet offices in Wellington was the testing time for all our preparations and for the hundreds of regulations, appointments and actions we had arranged. Everyone who might be wanted gathered in my office. We had a group of a hundred or more in my anteroom while Cabinet went through our proposals. Until then they were known only to the Prime Minister or to Peter Fraser.

As the Orders in Council came on the agenda, I called the appropriate officials into the Cabinet, the matter was discussed and disposed of, and I sent them off on their business. We worked all through the night to turn our peaceful and carefree little country into a nation, small indeed, but resolute and prepared for war, so far as preparation lay within our power or resources.

So our Dominion formally went to war. The necessary legislation was passed and gazetted; steps were taken to raise the armed forces of the country; all vital points were protected against sabotage; the ports were protected; a system of reporting ships and aircraft was arranged; a system of censorship was established; all dangerous aliens were rounded up and interned in camps; special bodies to handle individual problems were at work; communications were moved from Government House to the Prime Minister's Office; and good men who had been earmarked moved there from other Departments.

That night neither Peter Fraser nor I got any sleep. He then took me for breakfast to Bellamy's, the first and last time I ate there. I had been working for thirty-six hours without rest and went home sadly, knowing that our world would never be the same again, that millions would die, and millions more would mourn.

Full credit should be given to the Labour Administration for a most commendable piece of work, and for the responsibility with which Peter Fraser and his colleagues took on the task of organising New Zealand's war effort. They deserve particular credit for developing a War Cabinet. This consisted of three members of the Labour Government: Fraser, Nash, and Fred Jones, the Minister of Defence. Adam Hamilton, the first leader of the National Party, and Gordon Coates joined from the Opposition. This ensured the full cooperation of all political parties. Coates in particular contributed the whole of his strength and judgement.

As Secretary of the War Cabinet, I could never have imagined the incredible disorder we were to face in the higher direction of the war. We were indeed fortunate not to be put to the test of battle on our shores. Although it was devoted and intelligent, the War Cabinet proved to be incredibly inefficient. It provoked agonies of frustration in trying to extract decisions. If the same lack of procedure were applied to a commercial enterprise, we would have succumbed to bankruptcy.

Here, as elsewhere, Fraser bore the brunt of the work. His contribution to New Zealand's war effort was greater than that of any other man. He was intelligent and quick but also honest and courageous. The problem lay with his methods; they were impossible. Things got decided in spite of him rather than because of him. Fortunately Coates provided some balance. His strength and judgement, his drive and demand for decisions, with help from Jones, gave some modest amount of business-like order to the War Cabinet. His personal influence also helped bury the intense political differences between the main parties.

What was to be New Zealand's part in larger operations at the centre of the conflict? As in the previous war the plan was, in collaboration with Britain, to send troops to the Middle East. Preparations were made to recruit a Division, during which Fraser, as Savage was so unwell, went to London. This was my first wartime mission and I left with the gloomy certainty that I would not survive the journey.

We flew by flying boat under the command of the well known Captain Burgess to Sydney and then by the Imperial flying boat service, by short hops, to Townsville and so onto Darwin, the East Indies and Singapore, to Bangkok, across India to Basra and Baghdad, on to the Sea of Galilee, Alexandria, Suda Bay in Crete, and Piraeus thence to Corfu, Brindisi and Rome; and then onto Marseilles where we took the train to England. The long slow flight showed something of Fraser's courage and constancy. He never got sick, tired or discomposed; he was quite the best traveller I have known.

From London Fraser and the Australian representative, R.G. Casey, went to visit the Western front. They both came back severely dissatisfied with Allied preparations. Our main task then was to select General Freyberg to command the New Zealand Division. I had known Freyberg, though not as well as his two brothers, Paul and Claude, when we were young men together in Wellington, and where Freyberg had won fame as a long distance swimmer.

When Fraser raised the matter with the Chief of General Staff, General Ironside's warm approval of Freyberg was the deciding factor. Soon Freyberg was on his way to Cairo to make arrangements for the encampments at Maadi and the reception there of our men. On our way home, via Cairo, Freyberg then showed the Deputy Prime Minister what he was doing before joining us for the flight to New Zealand. It was in Cairo that Fraser formed his high opinion of Freyberg. Despite the chances and adversities of the war his confidence was never to be shaken.

Back in New Zealand Freyberg selected his officers. Before departure he held a dinner party for his senior officers and their wives and asked Nellie to act as his hostess. The launches then set out to the transports waiting in Wellington Harbour. Nellie and I were far from unmoved as, early in 1940, the ships moved silently and darkly out to sea with the first echelon of the soon-to-become-famous Second New Zealand Division.

Not long after Freyberg's summer visit, in April 1940, Savage died and Peter Fraser became Prime Minister. He was tougher and sterner than his predecessor. We were fortunate, as toughness and resolution was what the war demanded. Fraser had both in quantity.

A rugged looking individual, Fraser had a massive face, a huge nose and the largest hands I have ever seen. A serious cast in one eye forced this omnivorous and unceasing reader to place the document two inches from his good eye. Altogether he was a big man, physically, morally and mentally. Tall and straight, heavily built, he gave an impression of great power. Indeed power was his principal characteristic.

This self-educated man did not always know what he did not know, but his range of knowledge was enormous, if somewhat mottled. Fraser had an astonishing mastery of newspapers, had read widely in the literature of Socialism, enjoyed music and ballet, and indeed displayed some judgement of art and the theatre. Despite gaps in his knowledge, Fraser was surprisingly well equipped for his role as a wartime leader.

Fraser was above all a consummate politician. His control of his Party and of Parliament – as distinct from his management of Cabinet and his workload – was skilful in the extreme. He had an uncanny sense of anticipation and could, and did, prepare for difficulties before they arose. A poor judge of individuals, he knew how to deal with men in the mass. Inheriting a turbulent team, he strode calmly and confidently over intrigue, using, as occasion required, the velvet glove or the mailed fist.

Highly skilled in tempering the wind, or in soothing injured susceptibilities, Fraser must rank high among our Parliamentary and political leaders. He was gifted with the finest perception and the nicest appreciation of shades of meaning and implication. In sheer ability, and in his capacity to think quickly and accurately, Peter Fraser was easily supreme among the New Zealand Prime Ministers I have known.

Fraser became Prime Minister just before the fall of France. One of my first tasks under Fraser's leadership involved the French colonies in the Pacific. In the New Hebrides, a gallant Frenchman named Henri

Sautot brought his countrymen over to the side of de Gaulle, and after some considerable hesitation and comic opera coups, New Caledonia followed, largely because of Sautot. The Society Group, however, with its harbours of Papeete and Bora Bora, remained poised in doubt and uncertainty. The British Navy were anxious to be assured of the fine and sheltered anchorage of Bora Bora, and of denying it and Papeete to a possible adversary, by establishing a Gaullist administration.

The New Zealand Government now entrusted me with the task of endeavouring to bring this about. To fulfil this mission I was sent in the cruiser *Achilles* – just back from the Battle of the River Plate, and still wearing the honourable scars of that historic conflict[1] – with a shipload of flour following, to help establish a Gaullist administration. The *Achilles* arrived with the White Ensign flying, and a launch, with the Free French flag and the Union Jack hoist, came out to our vessel. Sautot, the Resident Commissioner in the New Hebrides, with the support of the Committee of de Gaulle, led by Raymon Pognon, and an Australian war ship, successfully challenged the Vichyites and took over the administration. The Free French supporters and a Revolutionary Committee had ousted the Petainist Governor and had formed a new Government. After some shifts and changes, and a resounding plebiscite – 5324 for de Gaulle and only 18 for Petain – the General finally appointed the distinguished Admiral d'Argenlieu as French High Commissioner in the Pacific. Throughout the war we were in close and friendly touch and later met frequently in the United States and elsewhere. The arrangements I had made for funds and supply for the French, and the use of Bora Bora and Papeete for the Allies, endured satisfactorily until the end of the war. France then repaid our loans, with New Zealand using some of the money to purchase our fine Legation in Paris.

That year of 1940 too we made arrangements, of some importance in the light of later events, for Pan American Airways to fly into

1 *Achilles*, the more famous of two Leander class six-inch-gun cruisers seconded in the 1930s to the New Zealand Navy from the Royal Navy, earned fame in the classic Battle of the River Plate. An outgunned British force – the eight-inch-gunned *Exeter* and the six-inch-gunned light cruisers *Ajax* and *Achilles* outfought one of the three famous German pocket battleships, the eleven-inch-gunned *Admiral Graf Spee* (an ironic footnote on the Battle of the Falkland Islands in 1914). New Zealand eventually sold the *Achilles* to India where she served in the Indian Navy as the *Delhi*. When the *Achilles* was due to be scrapped, New Zealand failed to accept the return of our 'HMS *Victory*' as a naval museum; not even of a gun turret, as offered through the present writer, as a Minister visiting New Delhi in 1978.

Auckland. That required me to go with Nash to Auckland to welcome the first flight of one of the famous Clippers. Strangely at that time the Labour Cabinet gave credence to some self-professed experts in security, and even brought one from England.[2] They took up our time for some months until Fraser, who was always slow to move, got onto the matter. More important, the New Zealand Department of Scientific and Industrial Research, after the British sent an officer to advise us on radar, began to produce our own radar sets, an invaluable and little known contribution to our war effort.

After the fall of France in June and the miracle of Dunkirk,[3] Britain narrowly saved itself in the close-run Battle of Britain.[4] As we moved into 1941 Britain was still under sustained attack, and I left with the Prime Minister for further consultation. This was the most interesting and adventurous of all my travels. On the flight over we faced real difficulties and risks as we passed through Iraq where, after the rebellion of Rashid Ali, we flew over the British forces moving over the desert to re-establish control.

In Cairo, staying with Ambassador Sir Miles Lampson, the Prime Minister spent day after day in the heat visiting the New Zealand troops, inspecting their camps, hospitals, recreational facilities and outposts, all over northern Egypt, and as far south as Suez. Not one unit was missed, and if I thought his handshaking and heavy pleasantries a little overdone, the Prime Minister's attentions seemed to be appreciated.

---

2 The Security Intelligence Bureau was established in 1940 under Major Kenneth Folkes. For an account, see *Nordy: Arnold Nordmeyer – A Political Biography* by Mary Logan (Wellington: Steele Roberts, 2008), p. 163.

3 In May 1940 the German army broke through the Ardennes, bypassed the Maginot line and broke the French and British armies apart. The German blitzkrieg drove the British army back to the beaches of Dunkirk. Inexplicably, Hitler held back his forces, enabling the Royal Navy to mobilise a fleet of small boats and secure evacuation. 'The Miracle of Dunkirk' saved the British army – some 330,000 men – and despite the fall of France, altered the course of the war.

4 Before invading Britain, Hitler had to secure mastery of the air. In the summer of 1940 the Royal Air Force, under Air Marshalls Hugh Dowding and Keith Park, a New Zealander ('one of the few brilliant Air Marshalls of the war') over southern England fought Goering's Luftwaffe to a standstill. It was the closest of close-run things. 'Never in the field of human conflict has so much been owed by so many to so few.' Of the two- to three thousand-odd pilots, some two hundred, including some of the best, were New Zealanders. One of the decisive battles of history, the Battle of Britain led Hitler into the two-front war his Generals feared. See *The Man Who Won the Battle of Britain (Hugh C.T. Dowding)* (New York: Charles Scribner's Sons, 1969) by Robert Wright.

Travelling by car, I found the Prime Minister's preferred motoring speed to be between seventy and eighty miles an hour. This nearly led to disaster on the military road from Alexandria to Cairo. The car blew a tyre, swung off the road and turned over four times. As were going over I realised what had happened and that in all probability this was the end. Most certainly the lives of all of us were saved by the steel roof. Four of the six passengers, including C.A. Jeffrey, the Prime Minister's Private Secretary, were badly injured. The Prime Minister, with a huge lump on his forehead, and I were badly shaken. But he seemed quite composed, and, as always in a crisis, at his best.

The Prime Minister had arrived in Egypt in March 1941, at the end of the German attack on Greece and just as the Battle for Crete was about to begin. General Wavell was frank, telling us that limitations on arms, supplies and transport would make the coming campaign hard and difficult. Fraser wanted to fly to Crete to support Freyberg, who had had no input into the decision to send the Division to Greece, but was now in command of the forlorn hope in Crete.

The German attack prevented a visit. Fraser had to content himself each day in going to Wavell's HQ. At first the General was almost hopeful but one unhappy morning he told the Prime Minister that the end was near. Despite the failure of their naval attack, and the decimation of their parachutists, the Germans overwhelmed our forces. Courage alone was not enough. The Battle for Crete was lost; but not honour.

In such a crisis Fraser was at his best. Was there no hope of victory? He then set to work to satisfy himself on the means of evacuation. Every single man should if possible be brought back. For some days the evacuation proceeded with substantial success. One morning a New Zealand Colonel came to plead for more help. He had just been ordered off the beaches and was dirty and unshaven. 'You're not leaving us, Sir,' his troops had pleaded. So I took him to Wavell, where he gave the staff full details of his detachment. Back home with me this gallant officer put his head in his hands and cried.

Under attack in the desert, the British forces were strained on all sides. Wavell still did all he could to meet the demands of my Prime Minister, so heavily on his back at such a critical time. At lunch on the great wounded battleship *Warspite* Admiral Cunningham showed Fraser his crippled ships. Still the Prime Minister asked Cunningham to make a last try to save the doomed men. The Admiral pointed to his orders and declined. Fraser persisted in his request. It was almost a demand, for Fraser was not a man of light touch. He wanted one last try and he wore down Wavell and Cunningham. 'If the *Phoebe* comes in safely tonight, I'll send her back.' When she did, I heard Cunningham say, 'I want you to go straight back, Captain; do you think you can?' 'Of course . . . but we must give some of the men a rest.' And the *Phoebe* did get to Crete and back with hundreds of men, perhaps with my Colonel's men.[5]

After the *Phoebe* left, we went to Aboukir to meet Freyberg and his staff after their evacuation. We all had to begin to plan for the future. As British planes could no longer fly across Italy, we were to fly down the Nile to Khartoum, and thence across Africa to Lagos by the route established to ferry American aircraft from West Africa to Cairo and the Middle East.

About five in the morning I picked Fraser up at the Embassy. It was extraordinary how such a dilatory and unpunctual man was always ready for trains, ships and planes. It was a bumpy flight. It was surprising how high the swirling air of the desert actually rose. Even at 12,000 feet the flying was very rough and uncomfortable. We were fascinated by the sight from the air of the mighty Nile, of Omdurman and then of Khartoum. The city itself, where in a balmy climate we slept delightfully on the rooftop with just the stars above us, was a green and pleasant place. To fill in the time the Consul General took us to the battlefields and General Gordon's stairs, as well as a dairy farm where the cattle fed on bulrushes. While we were picnicking on the Nile, the censorship on our movements set rumours to work at home that we had met with some disaster.

From Khartoum we eventually left for El Fasha, still in the Sudan, a large and wide area. We were much impressed with the excellence of the Administration and the high calibre of the local British officials. It is

5 The greatest of our citizen soldiers, Howard Kippenberger, recorded the results of the Prime Minister's pressure and the importance for 2 NZEF of the last-gasp trip of the appropriately named *Phoebe*, the Moon Goddess: 'I went down and saw the *Orion* with grim faced soldiers unloading the bodies of hundreds of the Black Watch killed by a single bomb – and the *Perth* with both her fore turrets blackened wrecks – and then saw the *Phoebe* come in. Troops streamed off her, and then I saw Grooby, and then Fraser, Dave Kirk and little Vincent, and the rest of them, and then Jim (Burroughs) and met them openly crying.' Quoted in *Howard Kippenberger: Dauntless Spirit* by Denis McLean (Auckland: Random House, 2008).

a wry thought that these devoted colonial officials should now be held up to public obloquy, particularly at the Trusteeship Council, where so much that is ignorant and irresponsible passes for enlightened wisdom. Today Sudan is well on the way to self-government, and I will venture the opinion that whatever the joys of freedom, the Sudanese will be worse and not better off under a government of their own people or of the Egyptians. An illiterate people cannot judge its own rulers, even if allowed to do so. Independence then usually means anything but independence for the bulk of emancipated people, who merely find themselves changing masters, and not always or often for the better.[6]

At El Fasha, I was attacked at siesta by a host of bed bugs before we flew over Chad, came down for lunch in Nigeria at Maiduguri, and then flew on to Kano, a great city of some hundred thousand people, the centre of the indigo industry, and a place of great antiquity and historic traditions. There our British colleague presented us to the Emir with some pomp.

From Kano we flew low down the Niger, over dark and impenetrable forest, on a flight so turbulent the crockery was smashed. In Lagos we stayed another week and visited Abeokuta where the Alaki astonished me and impressed the Prime Minister when he took one look at me, and said 'Know your wife'. And so he did. He had sat with my wife at the 1937 coronation dinner. 'Nice woman,' he added. I agreed with him and this meeting of old friends was an occasion he felt should be marked in the traditional way. Iced champagne was produced – in darkest Africa – and we all drank thankfully of the Alaki's hospitality. The Alaki's daughter had just returned from a nursing course in England and the state actually had a Karitane clinic. Who could have imagined that the ideals of Truby King would have taken root in these distant parts? On the other hand, when the Alaki drove off everybody had to fall flat on their faces and stay there as long as his vehicle was in sight. Fraser was greatly impressed. He thought this procedure might be adopted with some advantage in New Zealand.

In Lagos, rather than wait for the Imperial flying boat detailed to pick us up, we hitched a ride on a Catalina, via Freetown and Bathurst in Gambia, to Lisbon. On the Tagus River our flying boat was moored

6 Sir Carl's comment is worth noting, given the situation in 2005 in the Sudan; that nation, once upon a time, of 'blacks run by blues'.

next to a German one. We then flew to Britain along the route on which the famous actor and film star Leslie Howard's flying boat was later shot down under the misapprehension that it was carrying Winston Churchill.

At Poole we were met by the Dominions Secretary, Lord Cranborne, one of the famous Cecil family. After a weekend at Cranborne, we went to the Dorchester in London and were allocated offices in the War Cabinet rooms in Whitehall. There Fraser lost no time in berating Clement Attlee for appointing a Labour member who was being dropped from the wartime Government as High Commissioner to New Zealand. Attlee sleepily promised to attend to the matter in the morning and the protested appointment was not made.

Attlee in turn woke us up one night to review the draft of the Atlantic Charter and its famous Four Freedoms.[7] Fraser was invited to be at the War Cabinet offices at 2.30 a.m. I woke him. We dressed, and made our way there. Some alterations were made to the draft – one, actually included, being made by Fraser himself. In later years it was a great shock and disillusionment to me to find that the great Charter never had any corporeal existence No one can ever see a copy of the Atlantic Charter for no document was ever formally executed. Whatever the intentions of its authors, the Atlantic Charter never was an effective piece of international machinery. It remains only as a beacon, a dream and an inspiration.

During this visit I had my first experience of enemy bombing – and I did not like it. Fraser himself was in the provinces and instead of being grateful was intensely disappointed, until on one of his later visits he was present during the worst period of the V.1 and V.2 attacks. His demeanour under this kind of fire was as cool and unflurried as my experience of him would have indicated.

As I lay in my bed in the Dorchester while the bombs fell all about and the anti aircraft guns played their devilish piano I felt as if it were

7 At sea, before American entry into the war, President Roosevelt (a member of President Wilson's Democratic Cabinet at the time of the Fourteen Points) and Prime Minister Winston Churchill idealistically defined the purposes of World War II in the Atlantic Charter (July 1941): Peoples should enjoy the freedom to choose their governments, to work for their economic prosperity, to co-operate for their well being, and to maintain peace in freedom from fear and want, and to abandon the use of force pending the 'establishment of a wider and permanent system of general security'. This joint declaration of international policy foreshadowed the formation of the United Nations as the successor to the League of Nations. See James MacGregor Burns, *Roosevelt: The soldier of freedom* (New York: Harcourt Brace Jovanovich, 1970).

my own person that was the objective of the raiders. Still I stayed firmly in bed. No German was going to drive me to the shelter, not when I could hear from the street below: 'What ho Bill. A bit more 'ell.' . . . and in reply: 'To 'ell with them. Let's go and have a pint of beer.' As soon as the all clear sounded, every toilet in the hotel was flushed. The sound of rushing water was most impressive, and must have been a great drain on the water reserves.

The blackout conditions also created problems for me. Once while I was walking back from the Cabinet offices to the Dorchester by some means or other I got lost in the very dark street and stumbled into a trench at the side of the road. I was an unprepossessing sight when at last I found our doorway and made my way through the sandbags and light trap at the entrance.

There were great difficulties in moving by car at night-time. The car lights had been almost entirely eliminated. All that was left was a mere slit cross that peeped out from the blinding obscuring the lights. It was almost impossible to observe the approach of another car until it was right on one, and yet the cars moved in numbers and with confidence.

London was now vastly different from the city we had visited in 1939. Much of London, particularly around St Paul's, was in ruins. The sight was infuriating but inspiring. We visited the other main cities that had been attacked, and in hard-hit Portsmouth at an admiral's HQ we heard on radio the matchless rolling voice of Churchill: 'Let them do their worst . . . we will do our best.'

In Britain Fraser devoted much of his time to visiting New Zealanders and – his weakness – accepting the Freedom of city after city. Fraser liked the life of a visiting potentate and could scarcely be persuaded to return to his more immediate duties in New Zealand. We had no sooner finished planning his complicated itinerary than he insisted, to the annoyance of the British Admiral in charge, on visiting one small unit of New Zealanders. By chance that delay saved our lives. Those on board our original flight were all killed.

On the way home we were entertained in Dublin by the remarkable Irish leader Eamon de Valera and then in Adare in the West before leaving from Foynes via Gandar for Chesapeake Bay and Baltimore. In our huge 160-foot wingspan Boeing Clipper with its eleven cabins we flew with pilots going home from ferrying American aircraft to Britain.

'Neutral is it?' said one Irishman. 'But tell me who we are being neutral against?'

After the Prime Minister inspected our people in camp in Canada we finally left on the long Pacific flight home, via Honolulu, Canton Island, Fiji, Noumea and Auckland. After all that we had been through Nellie was not admitted to the welcoming party within the Customs barrier in Auckland. I made plain to Nash how very badly I felt about this snub.

CHAPTER 6

THE WAR IN THE PACIFIC

In December 1941 the war changed dramatically. Japan attacked Pearl Harbour. Oddly, the signal to alert British forces in Malaya, who were soon in action against the advancing Japanese, went not to the Government in Wellington but to the Services. They could not decode it; one of those inexplicable errors which may carry large consequences. Fortunately in this case there was no ill effect.

The immediate impact of facing another powerful and ruthless foe was depressing in the extreme, as we saw the Japanese hordes moving rapidly, and apparently triumphantly, down the Pacific and into southern Asia. But of course Pearl Harbour was not an unmitigated tragedy. The Japanese attack brought the decisive power of America into the struggle. Not even Roosevelt could have made his country do this voluntarily.

Still New Zealand faced the question: Would America be able to save us from invasion? This was moot after the loss of the two British battleships and the fall of the famous fortress of Singapore on which such great hopes had been built, and to which New Zealand had contributed so substantially. Facing this prospect of invasion, on top of events in Europe, the country entered 1942 on 'a new high in lows'.

The rapid and startling successes of the Japanese severely shocked the people and especially the Government of New Zealand. Criticism was directed at the value that we had all placed on Singapore and its defenders. Certainly when we had met him in Singapore, Fraser and I had not been impressed by the drawling, effeminate General Percival.

On the Singapore failure I can provide no good answer. Our Imperial Conferences had all directed our attention to the chances of world conflict. Despite Chamberlain's policy of appeasement, and the pompous and stupid Inskip being in charge, the Committee of Imperial Defence had warned us of the danger from Asia. Now New Zealand began a long series of demands for men, arms and munitions for its own defence. These I thought somewhat unreasonable. Indeed they seem humorous in the light of what did happen, but not then, in the light of what might happen.

The New Zealand Chiefs of Staff, all professional fighting men of some competence and experience, were of the opinion that nothing more than a hit-and-run raid need be anticipated. Anything like a full scale invasion was out of the question, at least until the Japanese had the use of bases much nearer New Zealand, probably not until they had taken Fiji. Its importance to the defence of New Zealand was early recognised and throughout the war New Zealand had troops stationed on the island. We also sent coast watchers to many of the Pacific Islands.

Assuming responsibility for Fiji, we then sent our anti-aircraft guns there, all six of them. With the rest of our forces in the Middle East, New Zealand was in effect defenceless. So there was a logic in our cries for help, mainly to the United States. Our telegrams grew more and more insistent and we took with poor grace President Roosevelt's intimation that global considerations had to take first place. This meant placing priority on the European theatre and holding on in the Pacific until the defeat of Germany.

Within a month or two, however, we were thrilled to receive a Division of the United States Marines, the First Division, under General Vandegrift. This force was only incidentally sent to protect us; it was the very beginning of that offensive, the assault on Guadalcanal, that was to push the Japanese back, and ultimately to defeat them. With their presence we all felt safer, but nothing was left to chance. Likely beaches were wired and guarded, harbour defences improved, trenches and shelters dug, a blackout enforced, and a Home Guard of considerable numbers developed.

At this time the United States appointed General Patrick Hurley as Minister to New Zealand. Hurley, who had been Secretary of War to President Hoover, appeared as a harbinger of hope and confidence. With a repertoire of good stories, he came to some extent to hypnotise Fraser, who almost seemed to worship this rambunctious character.

In reciprocation we appointed Walter Nash as Minister in Washington. Sitting on the main war planning bodies he performed invaluable work. He agreed at once with the allocation of New Zealand to the South Pacific Naval Command under Admiral Nimitz,with Admiral Ghormley coming to New Zealand.[1] Not appreciating the extent to which it would be a naval war, the Government had had some preference for coming under General MacArthur's command in Australia.

Ghormley soon transferred his HQ to Noumea, nearer the actual seat of war. Flying on a Sunderland, which could just reach Noumea in one hop, Coates and I were actually there with our party to see him at the time of the disastrous naval defeat in the Battle of Guadalcanal. The loss of four Allied cruisers and the withdrawal of naval support for the US Marines allowed the Japanese to send in reinforcements and led Nimitz to replace Ghormley with Admiral Halsey.

The Prime Minister was then invited to Washington for talks with the President. By this stage the building Frank Langstone had bought on Observatory Circle was being used by Nash as a Legation and Chancery. Only when we managed to secure the building next door could we, by providing for the separation of office and residence, make the arrangements work.[2]

Nash had wanted me to go with him as Counsellor but I could not work with him and told him so. I said to him and Fraser that I would not go unless ordered. They kept pressing me and I finally told them that I would if I was guaranteed the succession. This horrified Nash and the Prime Minister, and I heard nothing more until the time came to select a successor to Nash.

During Fraser's visit Nash was in his element. He loved showing the Prime Minister the extent of his contacts and his place in the counsels of the Administration. Nash had in fact done admirably in Washington, but he did not invite Fraser to stay with him during his visit, and Fraser

1 The United States Naval Command comprised Fleet Admiral Chester W. Nimitz, Commander of the United States Pacific Fleet after Pearl Harbour and during World War II, and director of the US victories of Midway, Iwo Jima and Okinawa; Admiral Robert Lee Ghormley, Commander South Pacific Area and Force June–October 1942 during the early stages of the Guadalcanal campaign; and Fleet Admiral William Halsey, Admiral in Command of the United States Third Fleet during much of the Pacific War. With much experience in naval aviation and aircraft carriers, Halsey was at sea in the USS *Enterprise* during the attack on Pearl Harbour. He replaced Ghormley mid-October 1942, in the critical stages of the Guadalcanal campaign. He then led the Third Fleet for the rest of the war, taking the Japanese surrender on its flagship, USS *Missouri*, on 2 September 1945. See E.B. Potter and Chester W. Nimitz (eds.), *Sea Power: A Naval History* (Englewood Cliffs, N.J.: Prentice-Hall, 1960).

2 Observatory Circle was a strategic site for the New Zealand Embassy. Langstone had bought a building across the road from the Vice President's residence, and Berendsen's purchase then added the British Embassy as our next-door neighbour.

was a little cool as a result. So was I, when I found myself invited to Nash's dinner for the Prime Minister, but only for after-dinner coffee.

Nash was another complex character. Like Fraser he had a first rate intellect. But some of its higher features were balanced by the less redeeming qualities of a short plump man of high moral worth carrying around an emblem of his religious beliefs on his watch chain. His staff as a result knew him, not for this sign, but for his admiration of himself, as 'Little Jesus'.

For my part I wished that his good intentions had not rested on his egregious inability to organise his work. As with Fraser, time meant nothing to Nash. As a Minister he boasted that he never went home on the day he left it. This meant that he fiddled from eight on one morning until one or two the next morning.

Nash could not bear to make a decision. Papers piled up in his office. They stayed there for days and weeks, or months or years, and sometimes for ever. He then devoted a great deal of time and care to 'going over' these papers. Once he invited me to assist in this monumental and completely fatuous task, but I declined on religious grounds. He even carried these heirlooms with him to Washington. This habit of holding papers caused serious dislocation of public business. While the wheels of God might grind slow, we would have been happy if Nash's wheels had ground at all. But Nash, like Fraser, kept people waiting. This was more than a sign of muddlement and a lack of administrative training. Having got to the top he exercised his power in the littlest possible way.

In Washington on this visit he actually asked me what people were saying about him in New Zealand. Honestly I replied that people were saying that he talked too much. Fraser later asked with some indignation who had been telling Nash that he talked too much. All he could do was smile when I emphasised that I had told Nash what he had asked, not about my opinion, but opinion in New Zealand.

Back in New Zealand a few weeks later Coates and I, as Secretary to the War Cabinet, set off with General Puttick and Air Marshal Goddard for talks with the Americans in New Caledonia. We then went on to inspect the New Zealand forces, as well as the Fijian troops being raised, in Fiji.

Fraser was making good use of Coates's military reputation and experience to manage the Pacific war. Coates took on the important tasks of consulting on the many problems arising with the Americans and in managing the New Zealand forces stationed in the area. In this complex and demanding job Coates's gifts and personality were invaluable. He never shirked or postponed a duty, and remained focussed until we had achieved the main object.

Working closely again with Coates, I grew very fond of this straight, handsome, lovable man. He may not have been a great man, but he was an able man, honest and good and loyal, a sensible and successful administrator, and a worthy New Zealander. His sudden death in 1943 was a serious loss to Fraser personally and to the New Zealand war effort.

My last expedition with Coates was to inspect the shaking down of the New Zealand Third Division in Fiji under General Barrowclough. While I was there I was able to see something of my son Ian, who oddly enough, despite his flair for mathematics and languages, and never having driven a car, had been placed in motor transport, before being commissioned in the Artillery.

Barrowclough was a man of reserved manners but his distinguished military and legal record had won him command of the new Division. In the face of inadequate resources for his task, he pressed the Government hard. In some measure this secured him the additional men, artillery, armour, transport and training needed before the Division was transported to New Caledonia, the key staging point for the South Pacific theatre. So quietly and efficiently were the affairs of the Division conducted that one formed the opinion that this was a business rather than an army.

In the event the Third Division never did fight as a whole, being used as smaller combat teams in small, isolated island campaigns in Vella Lavella, Treasury Island and Green Island. With the improving position in the Pacific, the bulk of the Division was then transferred to the Middle East. There they bolstered the New Zealand forces for the campaign in Italy.

Our party then inspected the New Zealand troops in Tonga and called at Norfolk Island, where New Zealanders were just completing an airstrip and where Coates needed to talk to the Australian Administrator.

Prior to our departure for Fiji, Fraser had confided to me that we had to have representation in Canberra. Serious divergences in policy had in fact emerged in our two countries as a result of the Japanese onslaught. Prime Minister Curtin was insisting in the crudest way, irrespective of conditions elsewhere, on the immediate return of their forces to Australia.

Fraser, one of the soundest thinkers on world problems, did not want to recall the New Zealand Division from the Middle East. He did feel the urgency of the need for Australia and New Zealand as far as possible to follow the same policies. If this were not possible, he realised that each country should be aware of the reasons for any divergences. To attain such a result New Zealand had to have a voice and an ear in Canberra, where Australian policy was made and implemented. Fraser told me that he intended to appoint me to the post. As was usual with him, nothing happened for some time.

BOOK III

DIPLOMATIC AFFAIRS

1943–1952

In 1949, during the resumed session of the Third General Assembly, Peter Fraser, who had been in London, was expected to fly in to New York at seven o'clock in the morning. Careful preparations had been made for two cars to go to the airport. One of these, in the care of Hunter, Berendsen's driver, was to pick me up, then pick up the Berendsens, and then proceed.

At about four o'clock, acting on a premonition, I rang the airport and was told that Peter Fraser's flight was due at six, not seven, o'clock.

I rang Sir Carl.

His reaction was volcanic: 'You're mad!' he said. 'You're spoiling everything! You've got the time zones mixed! You'll answer for this!'

'Yes,' I said, 'but I'm coming in a taxi and would you and Lady Berendsen please get ready.'

When we arrived, he was ready but Nellie was not. As in the words of the old song 'she had her shoes and stockings in her hand, and her feet all over the floor.'

In the taxi, Berendsen went on the attack. He repeated that I was mad. He excoriated Nellie, who was putting on her shoes and stockings in a profusion of waving legs and underwear. And he told the driver that he didn't seem to understand that he wanted to get to the airport as soon as possible.

I kept my head down. Nellie made the sort of soothing chirrupings at which she was so adept, and the driver suddenly said, in a deadly quiet voice: 'Listen bud, unless you want to walk you'd better keep quiet. And I'll get you there, nice and pretty.'

Berendsen immediately changed tack: 'Oh no!' he said. 'Don't take any notice of what I said. I'm an old man (he was 58) and I sometimes say things I don't mean. You're driving splendidly. So please go on!'

Quiet prevailed.

We reached the airport and Berendsen was able, as though there were nothing untoward, to meet Peter Fraser and his party in his usual noisy way.

But as we all walked out together, he tapped me on the shoulder: 'Saved the ship, boy!' he said. 'Saved the ship!'

Tom Larkin

CHAPTER 1

CANBERRA AND THE ANZAC PACT

While I was away on tour in the South Pacific with Coates, the Prime Minister announced my appointment as New Zealand High Commissioner to Australia. There was no criticism, except that of Sid Holland. The Leader of the Opposition claimed that I was too valuable to New Zealand to be sent abroad!

For my part I was not sorry to give up the labours and responsibilities of the War Cabinet. The toil, worry and long hours had taken a toll of my strength and my health, now at risk from a duodenal ulcer. I did dislike the idea of living abroad and leaving our sons behind, but my mother at least felt she was going home to Australia.

Fraser wished us to get to our new post as quickly as possible. We left within two weeks of my return from the Islands and arrived in Sydney on St Patrick's Day, 17 March 1943. The press took some friendly and encouraging notice of our arrival, particularly in the maiden flight of my eighty-two-year-old mother.

I had some qualifications for my appointment. I happened to have been born in Australia. That gave me a warm and sympathetic interest in everything Australian. I could never return to that appealing land without an emotional reaction to the sights and sounds and scents of my childhood. Australia was very dear to me and my heart.

Once in Sydney we plunged into a round of calls and then left for Canberra. There we made makeshift arrangements. It was very cold. The adventure of going to bed on a winter's night in Canberra is something to remember. Office space and houses were of course hard to find in wartime.

My first task was to press for a meeting with the Prime Minister, John Curtin, so that I could start my round of calls. He finally deigned to look out for a few minutes from discussions with his chief adviser, the uncooperative and unpleasant Shedden.

I never did get on decent terms with Curtin or Shedden. Curtin's health was very bad and this, together with the magnitude of his war efforts, without doubt contributed to his ill humour. I had to operate with a dying Prime Minister who, worse, never forgave Fraser for his Government's decision, after Japan came into the war, to leave the New Zealand Division in the Middle East. The Australians, after careful assessment, had decided to bring their troops back to defend the homeland. In substance they were right.

Curtin intensely resented New Zealand's independent policy. Because of that fundamental difference, he did not like Fraser. That in turn did not dispose him favourably to the new High Commissioner. He never did like me, and I did not like him. Nevertheless I had to press on with making the best contacts possible with politicians, officials, and civilians. The High Commission's task was to build the relationship between the two countries. In particular we had to help procure supplies for New Zealand.

Each week, as we worked at developing our High Commission, I reported on what was happening in Australia. Quickly we became engaged in a huge range of activities from the simple to the bizarre. On occasion, such as when we assisted with the urgent supply of penicillin, then a new wonder drug, we helped save a life.

At my official lunch the Prime Minister unbent and said some pleasant things. My reply was one of the most apt and suitable I have ever made. As a result I found myself on the end of too many invitations to speak. In war one might have expected less socialising. This did not happen. In Canberra, as I found later in Washington, war actually increased the number and display of such functions.

Although Curtin had now welcomed me formally, I never felt on real terms of confidence with him. Only when the Frasers were in Canberra did I ever enter the Prime Minister's residence. Differences continued as a result of the two countries being included in separate defence areas. New Zealand lay in the South Pacific Naval Command of Admirals Ghormley and Halsey, and Australia came under General MacArthur's Army Command.

Curtin had quickly and completely succumbed to the theatrical brilliance of MacArthur, and this may have influenced his attitude towards New Zealand. It did not help when Fraser used confidential information about Australian policies in secret session in Parliament.

Curtin was furious: 'He's blabbed the whole bloody thing.' My interview with him was stormy and unpleasant.

Canberra is a very specialised place and far from typical of Australia. So we had to go frequently to Sydney, where there were no fewer than four New Zealand societies. On one visit to Melbourne I found myself speaking at seven different functions, often to the same people! There and in other parts of Australia we got on well with Australians. Under the outer rind of rough, tough manners for which the country is properly noted, we learned to recognise the sterling qualities and the distinct character of Australia and Australians. The country and the people have a thrusting, hustling, forceful nature, quite individual – more individual indeed than the national characteristics of any other land, or people, that I have experienced. This is to be seen especially in sport, which lies at the centre of the Australian character.

The Australians are determined to make themselves heard and felt. They seek their objectives with a single-mindedness, and often a ruthlessness, that at times astonishes and dismays the beholder. There is no softness in the manners of this great country in the making. Australians are a virile and ambitious, as well as a courageous and a generous people.

This virility and ambition is mirrored more manifestly in the Australian Parliaments. I could never have imagined the language used at times in the Commonwealth Parliament. Bad tempered and ill intentioned, the two parties warred without restraint. No holds were barred, no words were too crude. Australian Parliaments were not, as in Wellington, dull. The leading politicians were loud-mouthed and illogical grotesques, a combination of the bright and depressing, the scintillating and nauseating.

One of the best examples of an Australian politician was the fascinating former Prime Minister, that great Australian patriot, the forceful and pushy Billy Hughes. Only Australia could have produced a waterfront unionist who could impact so forcibly, and for so long, on his country. As a speaker he was fluent, mischievous, impish, venomous and barbed, quick of mind and bitter of wit. He was such a wonderful raconteur and conversationalist that my wife Nellie loved to have this still active political leader as her dinner partner.

Of course we had difficulties in our work. In 1944 I had a stand up row with a stupid Protocol Officer over the Anzac Day ceremony. As the latest diplomat accredited in 1943 I had had to lay my wreath last of all the Heads of Missions. As New Zealand was the joint heir of Anzac, in 1944 I made representations for a change. When this drawing room admiral ruled against me, I told the Department of External Affairs that I expected New Zealand to be given its proper place in every respect alongside Australia. Unless this happened I would publicly resign and go home and make the reason clear.

Fortunately I had the support of the Head of the Department of External Affairs. Nobody ever explained how a military officer like Colonel Hodgson had secured this post over the objections of serving officers. Hodgson was a combative man; indeed he was the most violent person I had ever met. But he was at all times helpful to me once I learnt to avoid any conventions and make my approach without any side or affectation. In the event Hodgson, as one who had served in Gallipoli alongside the New Zealand troops, needed no great urging from me. He took the matter to the Governor General, who arranged for me to be placed alongside Australia in all respects. So I laid my wreath jointly with the Australian representative. 'Good on you,' Fraser backed me up with a grin.

Nor was the top level of the Administration more courteous than its Protocol Officer. After a long search for a house, in which I had taken every step to secure the necessary authorities, I found that the Prime Minister had himself proscribed the deal because the lady selling the house was making a profit! We needed the house badly and I was committed to the purchase. Now, without a word to me, and with the rudeness characteristic of Curtin, I heard that the sale was to be disallowed.

I was thoroughly aroused, the more so as the vendor reproached me for trying to escape the bargain. So I went to Hodgson and made it perfectly clear that if an approved purchase were to be disallowed, I should immediately and publicly resign my office and return to New Zealand. Hodgson took the matter to Dr Bert Evatt, Minister for External Affairs, and the Australians changed their minds. Hodgson told me this, but not Curtin. He continued to be rude and discourteous to me. In any case the sale was approved, and we moved in just before Christmas.

Another difficulty was that visitors were inclined to assume one had nothing to do and that they should stay with us. The Frasers were no trouble as houseguests but Walter Nash was another type altogether. Under the worst possible circumstances for such a fussy and demanding little man, he insisted on coming at Christmas. We had just moved into our house, and were still really camping. We had neither furniture nor equipment – not even a stove – let alone staff. Worse still, an opossum or two managed that night to come down the chimney and desecrate our bathroom. Who cleaned up the mess? My wife was prostrate, so it had to be me. Nash never knew the trouble he and the possums had caused us. We lost our holiday, our temper and our love for our great New Zealand statesman. How gladly we handed him over to the tender mercies of Bert Evatt.

I was unable through Curtin, whose treatment of Fraser and bad manners I resented, to establish any cooperation between the Australian and New Zealand war machines. Instead I came to rely for action on the Minister of External Affairs, the extraordinary Dr Evatt. It was he who proposed the ANZAC Pact to lay the framework for a system of detailed and continuous consultation between our two countries.[1] Its negotiation and signature was the principal achievement of my time in Canberra.

I am entitled to take some of the credit for the ANZAC Pact of 1944 as I had some responsibility for recording formally what was inescapable. The two countries now faced common perils without the protection of the United Kingdom. We had the assistance of a mighty ally in the United States. But our first imperative was to recognise the similarity of interests of the two British Dominions in the South Pacific.

The simple fact was that Australians and New Zealanders were not only the same people, but we were also in the same boat. The priority was to assure ourselves of the closest cooperation between our two countries. Though small, together we must be stronger. That was the basis of the ANZAC Pact. In formal language, facing our common peril, we accepted our common destiny and we recognised the common benefit in working together.

---

1 For more information on the ANZAC or Canberra Pact (21 January 1944), see Robin Kay (ed.) *Documents on New Zealand External Relations, vol. 1, The Australian–New Zealand Agreement 1944* (Wellington: Department of Internal Affairs, 1972).

The text of the ANZAC Pact was largely the work of the Australians. With Evatt the moving spirit, they suggested the Pact and largely did the drafting. I told my Government that the proposals were sensible, and suggested some modifications which Fraser approved. By the time he came to Canberra for the final negotiations Evatt had given me a full copy of the Australian case, so finalisation and signature was quick and easy.

Then without warning I received a telegram from the Prime Minister. Walter Nash was to leave Washington to resume his work as Deputy Prime Minister and Minister of Finance, and the Government had selected me for the post. My wife and I were astonished. Washington was a key post in wartime, the most important in the gift of the Government, and they were offering it to me – an official. What a struggle they must have had in Cabinet!

It meant problems for Nellie and me. We would have to leave our two sons. What were we to do with my mother? In the event she passed away before we left Australia. We concluded that it was our duty to accept the posting to Washington. The ANZAC Pact made a fitting apex to my work in Australia, as did the signing of the ANZUS Pact to finalise my service in the United States seven years later.

CHAPTER 2

WASHINGTON

On our return from Australia we were met in Wellington by two Ministers, one of whom was the acting Prime Minister, the Hon D.G. Sullivan. Marvelling at the Government allotting me the same salary and perquisites that Nash had enjoyed, I received my instructions.

Before leaving we had a week or two in the Bays with our son Keith and his fiancée. We then flew to New Caledonia, where Admiral Halsey arranged for Ian to meet us, before we boarded a US military transport to take us to San Francisco. On that voyage no one was allowed to move anywhere without a life jacket. This was wartime.

In Honolulu I saw Admiral Chester Nimitz and then went onto San Francisco. Hundreds of relatives were there to meet the returning veterans on our ship. A band ashore struck up 'God Save the King' and 'God Defend New Zealand' to welcome us formally into our new life.

With many stops, we then flew to Washington, where the State Department and the senior officers of the New Zealand Legation met us. Starting up I installed myself in the office Walter Nash had used. I then put in train the kind of routine I hoped to establish. The day after that, the Frasers arrived on their way back from the United Kingdom and, though we were so new, they stayed with us. Fortunately they were easy visitors in a house.

Walter Nash had not left the country, as he was attending the Bretton Woods Conference.[1] He pressed me to come up to New Hampshire to gain the benefit of his experience. Fraser advised me against going. Nash, he said, would snub me. I went anyway, and basically that was what this odd little man did.

Once back from New Hampshire I moved to improve the running of the office. Nash was one of the poorest administrators one could find, so I wanted to bring our organisation more into accord with modern

1 The Bretton Woods Conference (1944) was a 44-nation meeting in New Hampshire that formulated rules for international monetary cooperation, the International Monetary Fund, and the International Bank for Reconstruction and Development (the World Bank).

practice. I then set off on the exhausting round of the calls required in Washington, one of the most protocol-ridden capitals in the world.

Naturally these calls started with the President. I had first met Franklin Roosevelt with Peter Fraser in 1942. He had received me then in a tone of confidential intimacy. Now, while exchanging copies of our speeches, and handing him my Letters of Credence, we entered into easy and informal conversation.

The President raised one issue of some interest. In Washington after each meeting of the Pacific War Council,[2] which Roosevelt chaired, Nash had got into habit of announcing to the press as much of the transactions as he felt he could disclose. Much comment had been created by this quite unusual procedure in respect of secret meetings. In New Zealand we had assumed that Nash, a most competent public speaker, had been authorised to act as the Council's public relations officer. Nothing of the kind. President Roosevelt now asked me point blank: 'What are we to do for someone to tell the press about the Pacific War Council?' I replied, 'Why we always assumed the Council had appointed Nash to see the press on the Council's behalf.' The President smiled and winked.

Despite his paralysis, Roosevelt was an imposing figure. A large and handsome head, tossed back from time to time in a characteristic gesture; a long, long cigarette holder; and a desk littered with photographs and curiosities stood out. His voice was full and round – it was one of his principal assets. Roosevelt's manner too, was easy and friendly. He possessed the rare gift of making those who met him feel that they gave

2 The Pacific War Council was a Washington-based advisory body of the Allies engaged in the Pacific War, which met from 1 April 1942, with President Roosevelt as Chair, until September 1943, when it lapsed. Walter Nash, as Ambassador, was the New Zealand representative. In his absence, Geoffrey Cox, a New Zealand Rhodes Scholar, then on secondment from the New Zealand Division as First Secretary to the New Zealand Embassy, sat eight times, including the one meeting attended by Churchill. On his arrival from the Middle East, Nash had taken Cox in field dress to meet FDR, and, when asked, Cox told FDR that General Freyberg thought the Eighth Army with its better field guns would, as the front narrowed, defeat the Germans. 'I'm glad to hear that,' the President commented. 'Over the opposition of my Generals, I've just sent eighty Sherman tanks to help.' Cox, who thought highly of Berendsen, has written many valuable books, inter alia *A Tale of Two Battles* (London: W. Kimber, 1987), *The Road to Trieste* (London: Heinemann, 1947) and *The Race for Trieste* (London: W. Kimber, 1977) on the famous New Zealand Division, in his terms 'the Xth Legion, of the 8th Army', as well as the unique *Defence of Madrid* (London: Victor Gollancz, 1937), now translated into Spanish, and *The Red Army Moves* (London: Victor Gollancz, 1941), which Nikita Khruschev had translated into Russian.

him genuine pleasure. I never met a man who more instantly captured the interest and sympathetic regard of all to whom he spoke. He radiated charm, a charm which he even transmitted in his formal speeches and over the radio. The President was well aware of this faculty and utilised it without mercy. Of course the charm did not always last, but many were carried away into a lifetime of devotion to their leader, who had won such an extraordinary victory over a paralysis that would have severely limited a lesser man.

In his struggle with polio, FDR had made use of Warm Springs in Georgia and this led to the establishment there of the National Foundation for Infantile Paralysis. Roosevelt took a warm interest in the Foundation and was a regular visitor to Warm Springs for his own health and to support the Foundation. He was to die in the little cottage he established there, and many years later I presented a gift from New Zealand to the Foundation Museum and made a public broadcast at what had become a monument to a great and good American.

Roosevelt's voice was one of the most musical and appealing I have ever heard, and he knew well how to make the best use of that asset. He kept in touch with the electorate throughout the whole country by regular and frequent talks over the radio. FDR's 'fireside chats' were easy and friendly, even intimate in tone, and he did indeed know how to gain and to hold the interest and attention of all his hearers. Some adored, others burned. FDR's invariable opening remark, oozing goodwill, was delightful or infuriating, according to whether the listener was an admirer or hater. 'My friends,' he would coo to establish the tone which the ladies especially loved. Roosevelt was a really magnificent speaker – one of the best I have ever heard. He was such a master that I came to value highly the opportunities I had to hear him.

These fireside chats were of course most carefully prepared and edited by a group of writers who produced draft after draft for consideration and final approval by the President. What was apparently no more than a comfortable and cosy chat by one simple man opening his heart to his friends was in fact a most meticulously calculated and crafty utilisation of the President's right to address the nation by radio as a means of spreading party propaganda. There was no attempt to deny the political intent, such was the conviction of Roosevelt's followers that his retention in office was essential to the well being of the State.

Much of Roosevelt's remarkable appeal to the electorate was due to his talent for public speaking. There were many other reasons. He had the support of a wide section of the population during the Depression, which called for drastic steps to eliminate the widespread want and misery that was unprecedented in American memory. He and his party, and the political principles they developed after, rather than before his election, stood for the underdog, just as the Labour Party did in New Zealand. And that is always and inevitably a popular cause and rallying cry. There are of course far more underdogs, and it is easier to take from those that have and give to those who have not. The role of Robin Hood has always been popular.

It was not only to his faultless technique in his public speeches, and to his programme of distribution of money and goods, that Roosevelt owed his constant and flexible command of public support. He was absolutely magnificent in his relations with the press. Regularly, once a week and frequently more often, he held a formal press conference. Something like a hundred of the best pressmen in the land, most of them unfriendly to him, would interrogate the Head of State with a freedom and, at times, venom that would be incomprehensible in our more sober community.

With the press, Roosevelt was very much at home. His quick mind enabled him at all times to retain command, and if he occasionally slipped, his mistakes were astoundingly few. He used the occasion to the utmost advantage to achieve his primary objectives – publicity and mastery of the electorate. The system he laid down for public cross-examination of the Chief Executive by accredited pressmen was carried on, almost necessarily, by his successors.

Roosevelt was not only dependent on his appeal to the ignorant and the dispossessed. His long-standing and decisive support throughout the whole country depended on his political sense. He was the consummate politician, always moving warily with an ear to the ground, ready to follow or lead, as the occasion seemed to require. He knew superlatively well how to appeal to the man in the street or on the farm.

Roosevelt had the capacity too, to change his character and appearance to meet the demands of the moment. The squire of Hyde Park – wealthy, aristocratic and fastidious – could disappear and he could relate to the locality of the moment. In the South he wore a wide-brimmed hat and affected a local accent, greeting all and sundry with the local 'Howdy'. This proved highly successful and was adapted wherever he went.

After the President, my wife and I had to call on Mrs Roosevelt, and then I alone had to meet the Vice President and the Chief Justice, and with my wife meet their wives. After that I called on all the members of Cabinet, the Supreme Court Judges, the Dean and all the other seventy members of the Diplomatic Corps. This was a formidable task. It took several months. At the same time we were trying to assess who must be known in Washington, and here the staff were worse than useless. We had to fall back on the Social Register in establishing what I would call diplomatic contacts. I knew we would have no time for personal social relations.

During Fraser's visit we more than once went to visit the Secretary of State. Cordell Hull, competent and earnest, was at that time at the height of his popularity. There was much in his personality to warrant public liking and confidence. His origins were of the West, and he possessed all the traditional fire of the frontier. A rather small, dark man, of a choleric disposition, Hull's language, when he was roused, was reputed to be of the highest Australian standard. Hull's term in office was marked by a long, but relatively unsuccessful attempt to lower the US tariff, such an imposing barrier to world trade. But the key issue was the growing and fundamental differences of the United States with Japan.

Hull's principal assistant was Sumner Welles, a man of greater intellectual power and unbridled ambition. Their relations were bad, with President Roosevelt, according to his custom, playing these ill-assorted colleagues off against one another. On occasion Hull would not know of actions being taken by Roosevelt and Welles behind his back.

Hull will be remembered for the dramatic break with Japan. He never appeared to greater advantage than in the courage and fidelity to the principles of liberty, order and justice that he showed in the long negotiations with Japan, and then in the blistering comments he made to the Japanese representatives at the final fateful interview after Pearl Harbour.

The tragic unpreparedness of the American forces at Pearl Harbour has been the subject of many enquiries. Hull can have had no doubt of the inevitable results of his negotiations, but, as I saw it, no responsibility for the tragedy fell on him. It was, incidentally, later in Hull's office that I learned of the arrangement under which Russia was to make war on Japan within ninety days of the struggle ending against Germany.

Among the members of the Cabinet on whom I called was Henry Stimson, the Secretary of War. Stimson was a man of culture and education, a patriot of character and honour, if a trifle dour and cold, a Republican who regarded his acceptance of office in a Democratic Administration as a duty. I made a point of telling Stimson how impressed I had been by the sympathetic treatment accorded a large group of shell-shocked veterans, as well as the thousand wounded men, and exhausted nurses, on the military transport on which we had travelled to San Francisco.

Stimson was a very able Secretary of War, but his principal claim to fame was the support he allegedly offered the League, on behalf of the United States, against Japanese aggression in Manchuria in 1932. As I read it at the time, and I was in a position to do that, his statement fell short of a concrete offer of America's armed support if the League had taken a stand. Nor do I believe, if such an offer had been made, that the American people would have tolerated such a marked departure from their public position. But if it had been possible, its historic importance is that collective security might have become a reality and World War II averted.

Roosevelt was a masterly and particularly uninhibited politician – a realist in the most positive sense. So he was by no means punctilious as to the means or the methods of the people he used or adopted for his purposes. He let little or nothing stand in his way. Conspicuously, Roosevelt as President had no sense of personal loyalty. If the occasion required, he had no hesitation in jettisoning his closest colleagues, and without explanation. In general an offender would wake up one morning to find another organisation established and ready, with the President's approval, to take over. Such was Roosevelt's contempt for money – the people's money – that the bitter pill was usually wrapped up in the continuation of salary and perquisites. So few of those bypassed made any loud clamour. This was done dozens of times as the plethora of initialised Government undertakings grew, and with them inexplicable and unexplained sinecures.

Roosevelt's methods were seen most clearly at the 1944 Democratic Convention. At that gathering he had no hesitation in abandoning his Vice President, Henry Wallace. At the same convention he created something of a record in jettisoning another of his closest associates. James Byrnes was one of the most trusted and respected political figures in America. He had wielded so much power so well, and had been engaged in so many capacities in the administration of the country, that he was generally known as the Assistant President.

Roosevelt in fact promised Byrnes the Vice Presidency, but in Chicago, without a word, he simply abandoned him. At a time when Roosevelt was not expected to outlive his term, the Convention was choosing the next but one President of the United States. When Sidney 'the Kingmaker' Hillman chose Harry Truman ahead of him as Roosevelt's running mate, Byrnes never forgot, nor forgave this trickery.

Byrnes had been used in many different posts as a reliable and trustworthy workhorse of the Administration. Would he, if selected as Vice President, have done as well as Truman? No one will ever know. In my view Byrnes would have done good work in any post, even in the Presidency. Yet with all Truman's faults and weaknesses, I doubt if anyone could have done better in the essentials than the Senator from Missouri.

Byrnes was important in my view in the tentative initiation, during his period as Secretary of State, of the American reaction to Communist expansion. I saw him come to the correct decision that there was nothing to be gained by attempting to placate the implacable, by seeking to talk reason to the unreasonable, by assuming that the dictators in the Kremlin were guided by moral principles, or by imagining that any trustworthy agreement could be made with tyrants. Byrnes decided the line had to be held against Communist expansion. Later this would become known as the Containment Policy. When he left office, I told him that history would record him as one who had served well and deserved well of his country and the free world.

FDR was an extraordinary President, but as Byrnes learnt, he was indeed tricky. Not even his intimates knew where Roosevelt stood today and where he would stand tomorrow. He was a creature of the moment. Nor was he above threats to ensure support from waverers in the face of reckless experiments. And he did not hesitate to put these threats into effect. Those who did not vote correctly were met with implacable opposition at their next election, with the whole Democratic Party, and often with the President himself, intervening. So Roosevelt worked with great success to maintain his personal control of the country.

History will not fail to record, and with disfavour, Roosevelt's open attempt to override the Supreme Court of the United States. This was meddling with the power of the most sacred and fundamental of all American institutions to override the acts of Congress and of the President. Roosevelt's complaint was that the crusted old Tory Justices were not alive to the necessities of the day. His programme was being balked by the Court declaring that his executive acts and statutes were contrary to the Constitution. So he set out to remedy a situation intolerable to a man of his nature. For once in his long and triumphant career his attempt to pack the Court forced Roosevelt to go back on his tracks. Not for years did he cease to seek opportunities to wreak his vengeance on those who had deserted him in this battle.

There should be no misunderstanding of Roosevelt's services to America and to the rest of the world in World War II. No one else could possibly have done what he did, and have achieved so much and so rapidly to aid the fighting democracies. Let me be clear. I lived through the experience in the closest possible contact with the issues. Without Roosevelt, there was no possibility at all of the British Commonwealth alone holding out against the triumphant hordes of despotism. It needed this leader's clear understanding of what was at stake. It required his careful and painstaking education of public opinion in the United States and throughout the Americas. It depended on his courageous and farseeing plans to assist Britain and its allies, in the first place, by all means short of war. In the great and fundamental struggle between despotism and freedom, Roosevelt deserved the gratitude of the world for what he did before the Japanese catapulted the United States into the conflict.

In war Roosevelt proved himself a leader not less potent, and not less inspiring, than in peace. His qualities, in some degree dictatorial for a democratic leader, were admirably adapted for the conduct of a great war. He knew to a hair's breadth the dividing line between the political control essential for the application of national power, and the military direction of the armed struggle, which political interference can confuse. Roosevelt was indeed the Churchill of the Americas. Between them, the two great leaders, at the exact moment of desperate need, supplied the inspired and practical leadership the democracies required.

The usual White House programme was largely suspended during the war, and I saw little of Roosevelt until the swearing-in at his fourth inauguration. It was a bitterly cold day, with snow and sleet, and the ceremony was restricted to the principal American officers of state, the heads of diplomatic missions and the Roosevelt families. The only protection from the weather was a tarpaulin laid on the snow. The swearing-in ceremony itself was short. The President made a desperate effort to get upon his feet to take the oath, and stood there at last, upright and alone, depending on his own strength, and his own resolution, to keep him upright for the oath. This he took in a firm and resonant voice. He was then borne inside to rest. Numb with cold, we followed into the White House to join the political guests for a lunch on a paper plate that would not have graced a Sunday school picnic.

One of my first special assignments as Ambassador was to represent New Zealand on the Council of UNRRA at a conference in Montreal.[3] I found UNRRA both inspiring and exasperating, effective and frustrating; a curious mixture of mushy goodness and practical help. The work of UNRRA will live on, but there was much that was fustian in its transactions, and much that was ineffective in its operations.

Largely run by the major contributors, the Great Powers, the conference contributed to the spate of talk typical of both the Social, and Humanitarian and Cultural Committee of the United Nations and of UNESCO.[4] Here there were too many naïve, woolly-minded, starry-eyed visionaries with no desire to put a foot to the ground. I am indeed doubtful about all these high-flown optimistic plans for the good of mankind. The shortcuts, shibboleths and formulas for which this meeting was a sounding board will not achieve this. Soon I came

3 The United Nations Relief and Rehabilitation Agency (UNRRA) was formed in 1943 to provide relief at the end of World War II. Its effective work, in seventeen countries, extended from 1945 to 1947.

4 The United Nations Educational, Scientific and Cultural Organization (UNESCO), a Specialised Agency of the United Nations, was established in 1946 to promote collaboration through education, science and culture in order to further universal respect for justice, for the rule of law, and for human rights and fundamental freedoms.

to doubt the commonsense of a meeting which discussed preposterous proposals to treat everyone in the world in exactly the same way, proposals that would simply allow the strong and the ruthless to submerge the innocent and meek.

It was at this conference that I first met Dean Acheson, the leader of the American Delegation. Over time he became the member of the United States Cabinet with whom I had most to do. I was associated with him for a very long period. In the early period of the Democratic Administration he had been associated with the Treasury, but had been relieved of this post because of a difference of opinion with Roosevelt over the pricing of gold.

From the time of my arrival in Washington I was fortunate to work closely with someone of such ability. The Secretary of State, of all men, looked a diplomat. Tall, handsome and distinguished in appearance, calm and confident, Acheson, the son of an Episcopalian bishop, carried at all times the stamp of a patrician origin and upbringing, and a Groton and Harvard education. His abilities as a lawyer had then carried him to a prominent place in the profession and a large income.

Acheson was not really political. No doubt he belonged to the Democratic Party, but he took little part in political campaigns. I never recall him making a political speech. Yet he was an excellent speaker, with a fine rounded voice, a Harvard accent, a marked capacity for logical and cogent presentation, an apt choice of words, and the most priceless of all gifts – a sense of humour. He was at his very best when delivering a case extemporaneously, though he was also a good reader and could deliver a speech without making himself appear to be a puppet.

At the Montreal UNRRA Conference, Acheson led the American Delegation admirably. As the major contributors, the Americans were concerned to ensure that the maximum possible aid got to the suffering with the least abuse and waste. Acheson was to play a substantial part in UNRRA's success under two outstanding American Directors, Governor Lehman and Mayor La Guardia, in 1944.

The UNRRA Conference also led me into a radio debate with the Chair, Governor Lehman, and a Czech representative. This debate was to prove vital in establishing me as an American radio performer. It opened up a free and almost constant access to the very best platform in the United States. Radio audiences were numbered in the millions and I assess must have been of immense benefit to me as Ambassador.

Soon after the conference I was billed to speak at Worcester, Massachusetts, with Eleanor Roosevelt, whom we had first met in Canberra during an extensive wartime tour. I saw then how eloquently she spoke without notes. She is easily the best woman speaker I have ever heard. Her thin, high-pitched voice was capable of extraordinary modulation, with a precise and pedantic, almost prissy enunciation. She had an outstanding power of logical presentation. This was matched by a patent honesty and open human sympathy that led her to support a mass of humanitarian and charitable causes.

None was more important to the First Lady than the cause of the American Negro. This she championed with a courage and pertinacity beyond all praise. Resolutely she set her face against any degree of discrimination and pressed for the bare implementation of the American Constitution's claim that 'all men are created equal'. When the Daughters of the American Revolution refused the use of their hall for Marian Anderson, Mrs Roosevelt asked her to perform at the White House and organised a huge concert for her at the foot of the Lincoln Memorial.

A complicated and bewildering personality, this great woman would be as difficult to describe with fidelity and understanding as her husband. The First Lady's merits and qualities placed her among the greatest of Americans, and incomparably she was the greatest woman I ever met. While FDR was engrossed in his political career, Eleanor Roosevelt had had to make her way out of the shade of an interfering and domineering mother-in-law, Sara Roosevelt. She then had had to build her own career, fighting with conscience and courage for the causes she espoused.

In many ways Roosevelt's wife must have been a thorn in her husband's politics. The most politically minded of men, he was always weighing one cause against another, and then adopting that most calculated to carry with it the weight of public opinion. Of course he also supported the underdog, if only to win the preponderance of the nation's suffrages.

After Eleanor Roosevelt became engrossed in her own external interests, she was to suffer much from the activities of her turbulent Roosevelt children. James took to politics and became a leading figure in the political life of California, just failing to attain a predominant position. When I met him in Cairo he seemed a typical Roosevelt, well-mannered but showy and assertive, and out of his element at the headquarters of an army fighting for its existence. Franklin also entered politics, in New York City. At the heterogeneous gatherings of the extended Roosevelt family at the White House, or when their children noisily interrupted our official call on the First Lady, I marvelled how Eleanor Roosevelt carried on with such skill and equanimity.

The proposed radio broadcast that I was to undertake with her was eventually left to me to carry out on my own. The First Lady could not come because of the ill health of the President. Soon after, while I was in London with the Prime Minister, this great man died, and I had to fly back with Anthony Eden to Washington for the funeral. In the preceding months I had had the opportunity of observing the President closely. My own estimate, and the hints of others better informed, had led me to conclude that he was not long for this world. On his return from the ill-fated talks at Yalta, I came to the definite conclusion that the President was dying – and I told my Prime Minister so.

Despite the warnings we had had, Roosevelt's passing in April 1945 came as surprise in its suddenness. My memories are of Roosevelt as I personally knew him: gay, witty, courageous, nobly intentioned, bearing intolerable burdens with a light and jaunty confidence, leading his country steadily and conscientiously where in his opinion it should go, earning deservedly an honoured place in the history of his time, and for all time. The world would have been demonstratively a poorer and more tragic place without him. No other man, or group of men, could have achieved what Roosevelt did, and the world should remember this.

My radio debate after the UNRRA meeting in Canada then led to an invitation to speak to a huge audience at the Metropolitan Opera House on a favourite subject, 'The Moral Factor in World Affairs'. From that time on, I was able to command a choice of platforms. This was an enormous advantage in my work as Ambassador in a post like Washington, where publicity is the breath of life, and on my Ambassadorial visits throughout the US.

DOVES OF ALL NATIONS
"Now then, off you go—and mind, no quarrelling!"

After the UNRRA conference, Nellie and I set off on an Ambassadorial tour of the Midwest. I had declined the request of our Minister of Industries, Commerce, Supply and Munitions, Dan Sullivan, to attend the great Chicago conference on civil aviation as his assistant.[5] I knew nothing of the problems to be considered at this conference but did, as he asked, write his opening address. This he delivered in its entirety but things were not comfortable between us. Sullivan felt I had failed to get him an audience with the President, but since he was neither a Prime Minister nor a Foreign Minister, he did not in American practice qualify. Nor was there any room for him as a visitor to attend the formal opening of Congress. Worse, the British Consul General in Chicago invited me to dinner with the British delegate, Lord Swinton, and left Sullivan to come in after dinner. Sullivan was furious at being upstaged.

5 The International Civil Aviation (Chicago) Conference (November–December 1944) was a 54-state conference to develop conventions for international civil aviation in the post-war world and to approve the establishment of the International Civil Aviation Organization; ICAO came into being in 1947.

CHAPTER 3

SAN FRANCISCO AND THE UNITED NATIONS

Early in 1945, just before the death of the President, Prime Minister Fraser took me with him to London. We flew in a Liberator with a British crew and stayed as guests of the British Government at the Savoy. The principal subject for discussion in London was the forthcoming San Francisco Conference. This was to bring together an international organisation to replace the League of Nations, killed on the outbreak of the Second Great War, which it had had such ample opportunity to prevent, but which it had ignored until the war was upon the world.

It was of course not the League that had failed, but its individual members. This applied specially to the Great Powers, who persistently declined to act when action was plainly and urgently needed. They preferred to shut their eyes to the hurricane clouds on the horizon, and to do nothing to prepare for a catastrophe. The Big Three had already had significant negotiations about the League's replacement, but neither Fraser nor I were satisfied with the proposals that the US, the UK and the USSR were to present to the San Francisco Conference.

In the London discussions in 1945 we found ourselves in a minority of two. Australia and New Zealand took roughly the same line. We sought to inject a sense of reality, which was had been lacking in the League, into the new organisation. We argued specially that the new body must not be shackled with the vetoes that the three Great Powers had demanded individually for themselves. They wanted a veto over everything but talk, and even over some of the talk. Such an organisation, designed to keep and, if necessary, enforce the peace, would obviously be inadequate for that purpose if a veto were included. For keeping the peace internationally we pressed for the same machinery as in the national field – legislation, judicial process and, in the last resort, enforcement. This was the ultimate means of repressing crime and aggression, both international and national. Force clearly could not be applied with an essential promptness and certainty in the face of a Great Power veto.

If they could not agree among themselves, the Great Powers appeared to feel that that the peace was lost anyway. In face of this argument, it was our contention, subsequently shared by most of the small powers, that if the three Great Powers were agreed, there would be no global conflict. But the facts were that the three Great Powers never had agreed for long, and probably never would agree for long. The new organisation therefore had to prepare for the contingency that one of the Great Powers might be, or might support an aggressor. In short, without one of the Great Powers involved, there could be no conflict that would require the intervention of the new organisation!

Fraser was completely sound, and utterly courageous in such matters. He argued strongly and incessantly and fruitlessly against the veto. Although frank enough, the London discussions were useless. We found ourselves being treated with that kind of friendly and patronising tolerance that adults show to a fractious child. We were told that we were unrealistic and that we were not facing the facts of international life. As subsequent events were to show, it was of course the Great Powers who were not facing the facts. We were urged in the nicest ways to be good children, and not to rock the boat. It was all senseless and reminded me so tragically of some of the discussions before the Great War. For too long I had been watching ostriches in this business of foreign affairs.

The San Francisco Conference to establish a new peace organisation was called together in June 1945, soon after my return from London for Roosevelt's funeral. Fraser himself came to this meeting to lead the New Zealand Delegation, and I was appointed the only other New Zealand delegate. The other senior member of a large New Zealand party was the Chief Justice, Sir Michael Myers. Though not a delegate, my old friend came to handle the complex and important legal questions involved in creating a new international organisation.

Myers was one of the great lawyers of my own day. I knew him well as a man of wide reading and general erudition. He had a brilliant mind and a decisive and instant intelligence. In achieving a leading position at the New Zealand bar, his name, on one side or the other, had been seen in most of the great legal contests of his time. So quick was Myers's mind that, trusting to his acute perceptions, he was at times inclined to pay too little attention to detail. He had, for example, been baffled by O.F. Nelson, a curiously complex character himself. In cross-examining Nelson for the Crown, I saw Myers take Nelson too lightly. But when Myers was on his toes in a cause he considered worthy of his mettle, he was a man to be feared, as his record showed.

A man of wide charity and warm friendships, and proud of his Jewish descent and self-made success, Myers had taken a vivid and responsible interest in the affairs of our country, and indeed of the Commonwealth, and the whole world. As I knew well, Myers was thoroughly versed in my own speciality of foreign affairs. For a long period he had joined me on my morning walk to the office. Never did I fail to gather some interesting fact or point of view from such conversations. In discussing the ills of the world, one could never sleep while talking to such a brisk mental agitator. At San Francisco Myers's dignity and skill gained him the highest respect among the legal representatives from all over the world.

The great San Francisco Conference on the West Coast of America was to last for two months. It was wonderfully staged and managed by our American hosts. San Francisco is of course one of the most beautiful cities of the world, and probably the most beautiful in America. Its people were helpful and hospitable. Fully organised by the Big Three at the Dumbarton Oaks Conference in 1944,[1] we met in commissions, steering committees, working committees and plenary sessions.

The conference took up the Dumbarton Oaks drafts and set to work under the chairmanship of the Secretary of State, Edward Stettinius. Some changes were made but the original and fundamental defect remained. The Great Powers would not alter or delete the individual veto. In effect this meant the Great Powers declined to accept any real system of collective security, for no system of collective security can operate effectively if any one of its members can exercise a veto. Here we had our most powerful members reserve to themselves the right not only to refuse to take action against an offending aggressor, but actually to prevent any action at all.

1 The Dumbarton Oaks Conference (21 August–7 October 1944) was a four-power (China, Britain, USA and USSR) preparatory conference to establish the purposes and principles of a new international organisation and its charter, which were finalised at the San Francisco Conference in May 1945.

A SLIGHT DIFFERENCE IN PLATFORMS

So even if every other member wished to take action, any single one of the Big Three – extended at San Francisco to the Big Five – could veto any action for any reason, however capricious. This was a negation of the concept of effectively and automatically utilising force against an aggressor. Without force, any system of collective security would prove a farce; and a dangerous farce, for the illusion of safety that the existence of the organisation fostered, in the minds of the simple and the good, would prove a dangerous sedative.

Fraser, as I have said, was most clear-minded over such things, and he agonised to see the chances of our generation being frittered away by those who would not see, and who would belittle and patronise those who did see. Working with Evatt of Australia, Fraser conducted a magnificent campaign for reality and commonsense in a charter intended to preserve, and if necessary enforce, the peace of the world.

These two leaders of the small nations took on themselves the right to demand the floor whenever and as often as they felt desirable. This was despite a rule, accepted without question by more reasonable men, that speakers were to be called upon only in the order in which they sought the floor. Frequently and indefensibly they insisted on speaking out of turn. As a result, at an international meeting attended by many hundred delegates, each of whom would have made speeches, Evatt and Fraser between them accounted for one fifth of the documentation!

Evatt's procedure was to move from room to room in the City Hall to check on the dozen or so committee meetings. Stalking like a lion looking for prey, his great tousled head hanging low, he would march up the middle of the room, oust the current Australian representative from his seat, and immediately demand the floor. If this privilege was not immediately granted, he would despatch a myrmidon to explain that his presence was urgently needed elsewhere, and that the Chair should not deprive Australia in this democratic convention of its right to express its view! Too often Evatt got his way, and having spoken, would strut off to his next pitch.

Evatt had a large, somewhat pallid, and quite individual countenance with irregular and puckish features. They gave the impression of a man asleep and lethargic, when nothing was farther from the truth. He dressed badly in wrinkled and untidy clothes, and did not improve his general appearance by his habit of rumpling his already untidy hair as he spoke – and he was almost always speaking. Evatt might indeed be said to have been unhappy whenever he was not holding the platform, and conspicuously so when somebody else was. Yet Evatt was, like Fraser, a very poor speaker, one of the worst it has been my misfortune to hear. He made his points clearly enough but he was so prolix, his sentences so confused and unfinished, and his voice and accent so unpleasant, that to listen to him was a penance. His voice was thin, lean and whining, and his accent the worst Australian one could possibly shudder to hear. I speak as the possessor of a pure Australian accent that filled me with revulsion when I listened to a recording. Yet our dreadful Australian accents were popular in the United States, where they were thought to be cute. Evatt in any case took this disability, which might have crippled the political career of most, in his stride, and overrode it with ease.

Evatt was a man of quite exceptional ability. His mind was one of the finest, if not the finest, I have ever met. It was linked to an unbridled ambition, outrivalled in my experience only by that of General MacArthur. A boy wonder, who had made a phenomenal career at the bar, he had written extensively on the Australian Constitution and produced an excellent book in defence of Captain Bligh. After becoming a judge at an astoundingly early age, he had thrown over a great career in the law for politics. There all the walls in the Labour Party fell to his trumpet as he climbed surely and rapidly in the political councils of Australia. His special interest in foreign affairs soon led to his appointment as Minister of External Affairs.

As Minister, Evatt rapidly made an international reputation for himself and for his country. In my considered opinion, in the many matters in which I saw him involved, Evatt was, on the whole, right in almost every case. On all large issues Evatt's own judgement was unerring and his courage inspiring. On matters of real principle I never saw him in obvious error. I liked him too for his wide and catholic interests in the arts, the theatre and sport. Despite his defects Dr Herbert Evatt was in my opinion the greatest Australian of his time.

On occasion Evatt might be perplexed by local Australian considerations and I did see him misled by hope when he accepted at face value Edward Stettinius's statement that either Australia or New Zealand would always be members of the Security Council.

As Secretary of State in Roosevelt's last Administration, Stettinius was a complete nonentity, a shirtfront, whose appointment must have been a quirk of Rooseveltian logic. He might have done good work on Lend-Lease; that was in accord with his good-natured disposition to act as a glorified Santa Claus. And although I often doubted whether he was aware of what it was all about, as was true of many of the delegates, he did preside adequately over the San Francisco Conference.

The problem Stettinius faced was that he had little if any knowledge of the vast and intricate web of foreign policy and the complex of international interests with which he had to deal. FDR's appointment of him as Secretary of State seemed to me as inept as that of Inskip as Coordinator of Defence for the United Kingdom in the critical time before the war. In the end, as I told Fraser, who had a high opinion of Stettinius, the Secretary of State was not only about to be removed from his post but could not make any offer of Security Council membership to Australia and New Zealand. That after all was to be decided by secret ballot.

As the two leaders of the small nations at San Francisco, it was the veto that was the principal object of the attack of Evatt and Fraser. Fraser as I have said was a shockingly poor speaker, the worst of all my Prime Ministers. Nevertheless at San Francisco, where his enthusiasm was engaged, he rose to great heights. Since he was an even worse reader than a speaker it was still a great trial to be obliged to listen to some of his efforts. Early in his career Fraser had had his important speeches written for him, but he was too large and honest a character to accept this method for long. By San Francisco he was drafting statements with his own hand. With his near-sightedness neither he, nor anyone else, could really use his hotchpotch of notes with confidence.

Going once to the rostrum for a plenary meeting with a large public gallery, our Prime Minister held a squashy and amorphous mass of papers in his hand. On the rostrum he dropped his notes and they fell to the floor in a loose mess. In no way put out, Fraser stopped, got down, and slowly, to applause, calmly gathered them up. But he could not see well enough to place them in order. So he read each page as it came to hand. The whole thing of course made nonsense. That was an exquisitely painful experience for his team.

THE ONE-MAN BAND

On balance, however, at San Francisco Fraser did the very best of his work. In their joint efforts the future was to show that Fraser and Evatt were right. They at least could not be accused of stupidity and of shutting their eyes to the facts. At the end of the Conference there was much rising in homage to this country and that country for its contribution. This was to forget that the Great Powers, by their insistence on the veto, had emasculated the United Nations, while the small powers had allowed themselves to be overborne by the Great Powers. This basic error made somewhat futile the call to the conference to pay homage to Evatt as the leader of the small nations, however well deserved the compliment.

At San Francisco the Russians of course had no intention of allowing any effective system of collective security to come into being. They were to create many difficulties as the conference struggled on week after week. They were certainly clear-minded enough to realise that the veto in the hands of the Soviet Union could only be to their advantage. While the organisation itself would provide an admirable sounding board for their incessant propaganda, it would be unable to prevent their nefarious plans.

To me it was frustrating and infuriating in a high degree. People would not think. They preferred to ape the ostrich in the hope that the unpleasant things, that they would not allow themselves to see, would thereby disappear. As we were to learn all over again, they did not disappear. Evildoers did not become like the good folks and sit down in friendship. History has proven this over and over again. Evil exists and, in using force, will be dangerous as far ahead as man can see. At San Francisco the nations lacked the sense of realism to recognise this basic fact of international life.

The popular reception given to the Russians and their satellites was particularly disturbing to me. At this meeting the Soviets insisted on three votes. The conference simply shut its eyes to reality and pretended that the Ukraine and Byelorussia were independent countries. Such nonsense should have warned us where we were going.

Sooner or later even the most optimistic delegates realised that it was useless to try further. More than half of the small nations were aware of the fragility and ineffectiveness of what was to come out of San Francisco. But we eventually decided to take what we could get.

We had to admit that the Great Powers were totally unwilling to accept an effective system of collective security. Such effectiveness required third party judgement with automatic enforcement. Instead the Big Three insisted on their right to remain judges in their own case; and in everyone else's case.

So the choice became clear. It was not between a real system and a sham system of security. It was between a Great Power veto system and no system at all. Plainly indeed we had no choice. Better a truncated system than none. So after nine weeks we signed. Peter Fraser and I signed the United Nations Charter on behalf of New Zealand. At the time I thought it right to sign, and I still think it was right. But I saw – and said so frequently and publicly – that in essence it would not do. The United Nations Charter could not do what the world expected, and was entitled to expect, of its drafters.

What was the result? Effective collective security had to be effected outside the United Nations. The member states had to turn to the regional pacts for which the charter fortunately made allowance: NATO, the Rio Pact, the ANZUS Pact, the US–Philippine Pact, and the US–Japanese Pact.[2] Such regional security pacts were all very good in their own way. They were, however, fragmentary substitutes for the worldwide system we might have achieved at San Francisco. Such a system we should never achieve when enemies of civilisation could stultify action to maintain the 'international peace and security' the Charter enjoined on member states. It was as simple as that – and few could be made to see the obvious.

Outside of the conference, the New Zealand group enjoyed San Francisco. Fraser was always at his best in his lightest or his sternest vein. He ate two of his meals each day with Nellie and me and took a great interest in the extracurricular activities of the Delegation. He always consulted on what we might all do in our spare time. Every weekend the Delegation took an expedition into the lovely countryside, with its rich Spanish names, history and architecture; such a joy to a New Zealander accustomed to the dismal architecture of our own land. He was particularly keen to visit the Yosemite Valley and the sequoia forest giants.

---

2 Chapter VIII, Article 52 of the United Nations Charter deals with regional arrangements for 'the maintenance of international peace and security'.

While we were at San Francisco, Senator Connally, the Chair of the powerful Senate Foreign Affairs Relations Committee, and as simple and essentially ignorant a man as ever got into a position of world power, came bursting into a conference session with the claim that the Germans had surrendered. His report was not true, but the Germans did surrender soon after.

So with renewed hope we all turned to the war in the Pacific. This was a time when one yard in San Francisco was launching a ship a day. Many of the wives were asked to officiate, and Nellie would have liked to have been among them, but not, I was delighted to hear, when suggestions of bribery in the giving of launching gifts surfaced.

At last the Conference broke up, having done – or slummed – its work; at any rate it was finished – what could be done had been done, and what could not be done was represented to the world as negligible. This was sadly a dishonest, deceptive and dangerous piece of publicity. The public was led to believe that the San Francisco Conference had been eminently successful. World peace was allegedly now safe, for all time, through the establishment of our new organisation.

Looking back the vast number of well-meaning men and women still consider the San Francisco Conference as having succeeded up to the highest hopes of mankind. In fact in the essentials San Francisco failed. It did not establish a system of collective security that would work. The successful efforts to hide that unpalatable fact anger me.

Let me assert that in the United Nations we have something that is infinitely precious to mankind. But in honesty, and in prudence, people should recognise that the United Nations as we have established it – and because of the veto there is no practical means of altering it – is completely incapable of fulfilling its primary, fundamental purpose: the protection and preservation of the peace of the world, if necessary by force – and force will certainly be a necessity at times. It cannot do this, and it is senseless and dangerous to pretend to the contrary. The fact, quite undeniable and demonstrable, is that an effective system of collective security cannot be established in an organisation stultified by a veto.

If sensible people recognise that fact, why then did we not eliminate the veto? A majority after all dislike and distrust this provision. The answer is simple and twofold: it cannot be done – there is no way to do it; and if it could be done, none of the Great Powers would allow it. The fault goes back to the insertion of the veto clause at our conference in San Francisco. At the time I characterised the clause as a monumental and crowning piece of human folly. When the Great Powers insisted on the veto, we lost the chance to alter any portion of the United Nations Charter, even one word, without the consent of each one of the five Great Powers.

Nor, when one examines the situation further, would any one of the Great Powers agree to eliminate the veto when it would mean subjecting themselves to decisions made under the present voting system of the General Assembly. There of course there is no veto, and each member has one vote. This sounds democratic until one weighs up the vote of an Iceland or a Liberia, or even a New Zealand, alongside that of the largest, most powerful, and most responsible states. This equality of voting power is abused by blocs and by bargains which disgrace the Assembly and ensure that the Great Powers are unlikely to subject themselves to such irresponsibility.

The removal of the veto, even if we could achieve it, would not automatically establish an effective system of collective security. To operate effectively and automatically such a system must be a thing of the spirit, and the spirit is not there. So in this era the member states have had to approach such a system through regional arrangements, outside the United Nations, but consonant with the spirit of the Charter. There is a long, long way to go before we will internationally possess a reliable system of collective security, such as every democratic member of the United Nations – and there are not so many – has established in the national sphere. But the deed is done; we cannot alter its terms, and we must make the best of its shortcomings.

The UN can do, and it does, many things of the utmost value to mankind. We must never lose sight of what the United Nations can achieve. Even in its present form, with all its defects, even with all the frustrations and inadequacies of its operations, the United Nations is still indubitably and unquestionably the noblest adventure of mankind today.

The United Nations provides first a constant meeting place for the free nations of the world. It is a forum where these peoples can express their ideas and their ideals. It is a round table at which they can discuss their differences and their hopes and their fears. The UN also provides a body constantly available for mediation, arbitration and conciliation in international disputes, a process which has already and unquestionably prevented many armed conflicts. We can say the UN is the town meeting of the free world, though it is worth noting that it was not, as is the common belief, conceived of as a universal body. The founding members deliberately restricted membership in the Charter to peace-loving nations. This is what makes it difficult to admit a country like Red China, which made war on the United Nations.

In lesser matters the United Nations does invaluable work. What has been done for the many millions of refugees is beyond all praise, and would alone justify its existence. Amidst much that is visionary, the Economic and Social Council has done good and lasting work for the physical and economic well being of the world's peoples. The Trusteeship Council too, watching over the progress towards self-government of dependent peoples, has proven to be an invaluable factor in international life. Among the various specialised agencies, the International Labour Organization has striven to improve the conditions of the workers of the world, while the World Health Organization has succeeded in improving health all over the globe. Let us not forget how many of these activities, so often taken for granted, warrant the existence and the cost of the United Nations and its family of organisations. With all its shortcomings, we can now see the organisation we created as a great and mighty factor for good in this sad old world.

In this sense I can maintain the United Nations deserves the support of all right thinking people. If it is not better, as it should have been, it is our own fault, and should not detract from what is being done. So long as we do not deceive ourselves, as so many do, that it secures the world against aggression, it is a grand and beneficent enterprise. Of course it might have been so much better. But the United Nations is still very, very good. The tragedy behind the facade is that when we had the chance – which may not recur in these times – we did not do better.

CHAPTER 4

THE DIPLOMATIC ROUND

An Ambassador's work is never done. On my way home from San Francisco, Fraser asked me to fulfil a speaking engagement he had made at Portland, one of the garden cities in Oregon in the Northwest. This lush green state's climate is very like our own country. Later I found my address being enshrined in the congressional record by the local Senator, a curious man called Wayne Morse.

Back in Washington, after Evatt stood up the organisers, I had to speak as part of a panel to a large forum in Constitution Hall on the United Nations Charter, which we had just signed. My views were much those of Evatt's, and I put them strongly, without much contradiction from my principal opponent, Senator Fulbright. Indeed I found he held much the same point of view. The panel basically agreed that while San Francisco had achieved the maximum possible, it was inadequate. The battle for peace had not been won.

The life of an Ambassador is full and demanding. His duty is in general to watch over the interests of his country in the land where he is accredited, and to keep his own Government informed, fully, immediately and in detail, of all developments there in which they may be interested.

His first responsibility then is for him personally, and as intimately as possible, to know all the people from which information may come, and to keep closely in touch with affairs as they arise. He conducts all the business transactions between the two countries, and he is the channel for all communications from one to the other. He must interpret the country to which he is posted to his own land, and his own country to the land of his accreditation.

In Washington this involved me, as the direct servant and agent of the New Zealand Government, early on in the Pacific War Council directing the conflict in the Pacific, in the Far Eastern Commission[1] to

1 The Far Eastern Commission (1946–52) was an eleven-nation commission, including New Zealand, established to supervise the Japanese surrender until after the peace treaty of 1951. Its operative arm was the Four Power Allied Council for Japan, attached to the Supreme Commander, General Douglas MacArthur, in Tokyo.

supervise the occupation of Japan, and in the membership of the British Commonwealth Committee. Later I was to be involved in the Korean Committee, and in negotiation of key treaties with the United States and with Japan.

The Ambassador was also responsible for the work of the significant New Zealand military, scientific, commercial and supply missions, as well as all the consular offices in the United States, and then that of the United Nations in New York.

A large part of the day-to-day work of the Embassy focussed on information. Scores of reports on policies and developments covering every field of American endeavour flowed out each week, with matters of urgency dealt with by telegram. In turn we interpreted events in New Zealand to the US Administration.

The Ambassador to such a large country was committed to constant travel to get to know America and to create goodwill and understanding about such a small and isolated country as New Zealand. In my term my wife and I visited every state in the Union except Arkansas. Americans, we found, had a taste for speeches and would gather in considerable numbers for such purposes. In all I made something like five hundred separate public addresses in thirty-four separate states and in nearly a hundred cities. One also became known through the columns of newspapers, radio and television, and a huge inflow of correspondence. After a series of addresses to teachers in New Jersey, I was given an honorary degree at Rutgers, the state university.

An Embassy had to handle a lot of enquiries from our own Government and the Departments in Wellington while responding to those from the American Administration. At the same time we had to look after our own nationals who wanted advice and assistance. In our time we had to deal with a host of marital problems arising from wartime marriages.

As I have indicated, the Ambassador was expected to represent New Zealand at innumerable international meetings. UNRRA and the Food and Agriculture Organization flowed on to the UN and its various organs. These UN meetings, including the General Assembly and Trusteeship Council, came to take up two thirds of my time, and much of the time of my colleagues. On top of such official work, the Ambassadorship meant a host of formal duties, from national functions such as the inaugurations, to the opening of Congress, White House dinners and receptions, a huge range of National Days, including our own, and a mass of Embassy calls.

The Ambassador was even responsible for New Zealand investitures. These were quite large functions. Each might cover forty or fifty to be honoured. The most moving of all my investitures occurred in 1948 when the dying Admiral Nimitz, one of the heroes of the Pacific war, asked me on my way to New Zealand to present his British order in his home in San Francisco, a month before he died.

On top of official and formal duties, any Ambassador in Washington faced a killing social round. There were so many functions one simply had to attend; in all say three National Days a week. Then there were the local charities. On top of that an Ambassador had to make friends.

While on a speaking tour to the Midwest I was recalled to Washington for the first meeting of the Far Eastern Commission. The US Government had established the Commission with its allies in the Pacific War to enable all the nations involved to share in establishing the principles for the occupation of Japan. At the beginning Lord Halifax represented Britain, and Dr Evatt Australia. We had representatives from France, India, the Netherlands, and the Philippines. As I was the New Zealand representative I felt I had to be there.

I was wrong. Nothing happened except the egregious effort of Evatt to secure the Chair. This quite properly went to an American but the Commission itself never was to get off the ground. Its sabotage in Tokyo by Douglas MacArthur, as he did with the Allied Council there, was not necessarily a bad thing. The interference of well meaning but irresponsible bodies might have interfered with the admirable task MacArthur performed in Japan.

That summer while we were sailing in Chesapeake Bay we learned of the explosion of the first atomic bomb at Hiroshima in August 1945. I had no inkling of such a development but it did not take much thought to indicate that we were on the threshold of a new and foreboding chapter of human life, one that could mean the end of the current war and the end of an era in history. The world would never be the same again.

To learn more of this historic development we hurried back to Washington from holiday. About this time I was advised of my forthcoming knighthood. I had never contemplated such a thing. It was unheard of for a New Zealand public servant to receive such an honour, and I had certainly never sought such preferment.

Towards the end of 1945 the first organisational meeting of the United Nations was to be held in London. Fraser, who was in Washington on the way there, agreed that there was no need for me to be with him, and that it was better that I joined the Far Eastern Commission for its meeting in Japan. When my knighthood was announced on 1 January 1946 we were actually sailing on the *Mount McKinley* on the way to Japan. I found Americans, while professing to despise such distinctions, deeply impressed by a title.

Although the Far Eastern Commission was to prove a failure, our journey to Japan proved remarkably interesting and informative. In Honolulu we were joined by Colonel Guy Powles, who was to come back with me as Counsellor at the Legation; Frank Corner, brilliant, competent, responsible and likeable; and a young intellectual James Bertram, a New Zealand Rhodes Scholar who had lived for several years in China, travelled with the Communist armies and spent the war in a Japanese prisoner-of-war camp after the capture of Hong Kong in 1941.

After ten days we sailed into Tokyo Bay and I was met by Captain Bard, who had accompanied us from Noumea to San Francisco in the *President Johnson*. He was now naval officer in charge of Yokosuka and the Tokyo–Yokohama harbour area. A visit ashore left us contemplating the impact of firebombing on Japanese cities, especially in the industrial areas.

Later visits to other cities like Kure and Hiroshima confirmed the scale of destruction the Japanese had brought on their people. With only a quarter of its former inhabitants, Hiroshima had just disappeared from the earth. The Bomb had had the effect of destroying everything, living or dead, within an area about half a mile in diameter. No building or any part of a building survived except two or three walls of ferro-concrete structures; the rest was just fused slag on the ground. The heat of the explosion had had left the image of a man and his donkey outlined on the pavement, as in a photograph. Solemnly we wondered at the fate to which mankind might be heading.

At Hiroshima we met the Mayor and members of the City Council. Even then they were thinking of establishing their city, which had suffered so cruelly from the first impact of the atomic age, as an international memorial to peace. We were impressed with the honesty of this group, in contrast to some of the other local authorities who filled us with apprehension. Who could be sure of the future of this warlike people, who had waged a great war with unparalleled ferocity and a high degree of atrocity? I for one found it hard to believe that the Occupation could achieve such a radical transformation and build a democracy in a hardworking people with a tradition of slavish obedience to the State. Much would depend on the efforts of the West to develop cooperation and trade with a Japan, which was so close geographically to the Soviet Union and to China.

After our arrival the Heads of Delegations to the Commission began work by lunching with the MacArthurs. By good staff work I suspect, MacArthur affected to remember me from Australia. No one but the General was expected to say a word. He talked incessantly, and one wondered how he could keep a sense of proportion and sanity in such an atmosphere of reverential worship. In Tokyo the General of the Armies lived and was treated like a Great Proconsul. Human nature can stand just so much of that before it taints.

The Commission then met with occupation officers to hear about their problems. These earnest, intelligent and knowledgeable people were bent on getting the defeated nation back on its feet. By improving the health and education and social conditions of the people, they were to put them on the way to becoming a nation of self-respecting, self-supporting and peaceful citizens. All of us on the Commission were immensely impressed by the calibre of the officers actually undertaking this monumental work. So we were too by MacArthur himself, if not by some of the time-servers surrounding the great man.

Our visits into the countryside gave us some idea of Japan. We were impressed by the excellent Japanese railways and constantly struck by the politeness of the people. Most of all we were delighted by the beauties of this island country. The Japan we saw was a lovely country by nature and by art. Its landscape, with its roads and walls, its hedges and thatched villages, paddy fields, terraces, and rural walks, its gardens and warm springs, had great range and depth. Its simple but meaningful temples exuded a sense of peace and strength. I was spellbound by the simplicity and economy of Japanese art.

Before our departure, the Supreme Commander came to lunch on the *Mount McKinley*. He talked brilliantly and incessantly while we listened. He was indeed a fascinating conversationalist, with a wise and judicious choice of words. MacArthur might be egotistical, but he was always compelling. Among his topics MacArthur told us of Japanese war plans. Some were ill conceived and others badly implemented but he was loud in his praise of that 'honey' of a campaign in Malaya.

So Colonel Powles and I left for Washington and Frank Corner for Wellington, with Rex Cunninghame, who had joined us as a translator. James Bertram, only after the approval of our Government, as I would not approve it myself, went to China to see Madam Sun Yat Sen.

Back home from Japan, work resumed with speaking tours in Texas and Louisiana. The latter was the state where the egregious Huey Long, before he was assassinated, had acted like a dictator in the land of the free. His name was still venerated in New Orleans. Many of the most responsible citizens felt that Long had done much with his public works programme for the state. If he and his associates had taken a cut of ten per cent out of all public loans and taxes, with their great bridges and roads, and an excellent hospital system, they had added something of lasting value. This man with real Presidential ambitions had left his monuments, even if he did not aid the cause of human liberty.

In Florida we saw something of its famous attractions, like the Everglades and Daytona Beach, but, despite their beauty, we were less attracted by the ostentatious display of wealth in places like Palm Beach and Miami, where I went to speak at the university. In Atlanta I spoke to the English-Speaking Union and went to all of the historic battlefields before going back to Washington for the second UNRRA Convention at Atlantic City. It was here that Governor Lehman transferred authority as Director General to that hurricane of a man, Mayor La Guardia, and that I was elected Chair of one of the two main committees. This proved useful experience for a task that was to fall on me on many more occasions.

At this time, as New Zealand's representative, I entered into discussions to clear the Lend-Lease accounts between the United States and New Zealand. Of course there had been reverse Lend-Lease from New Zealand, mainly with the supply of provisions and foodstuffs, and materials, including ships, to the American forces in the Pacific.

This was a long and detailed business, in which the New Zealand authorities, urged on by Walter Nash, were, I felt, taking a biased and ungenerous attitude. This was in contrast to the inspiring generosity of the American Government. In confidence I expressed my views as strongly as possible to my own Government. I knew that, while our friends in America were behaving well, we were behaving badly in this matter. I do not think that my representations had much effect. Nash and the Treasury officials finally came to the United States and in the end agreed that each side had received almost identical assistance. So the slate was wiped clean. We could have attained exactly the same result without unnecessary and unworthy haggling.

The Americans also let us take over a large amount of American surplus material. They then applied those funds to student exchange, the germ of what became the Fulbright Scholarships, called after the distinguished Senator, himself a Rhodes Scholar, who put the scheme through Congress. We were all glad to get the Lend-Lease negotiations out of the way. They had presented a long and wearisome problem, full of detail and concerning many millions of pounds. I was quite satisfied with my own intervention in the matter. I am by no means sure that Nash was equally satisfied with his. Even when we signed the agreement he came back to the Embassy moaning that he ought to have got another 600,000 pounds. In my view the Americans had offered one of the most generous settlements in the annals of our history. Truly, I told him, there was no limit to his insatiability. He took this as a great compliment, which was not what I meant at all.

In the summer Nellie and I went to Maine, the customary holiday state of some of our colleagues in the Embassy. We enjoyed a peaceful holiday with little social life in Belfast, with our son, Ian, who met his future wife there at Pitcher Pond, where some of the Legation staff were staying. Then it was back to duty at the UN General Assembly in New York.

Peter Fraser had of course attended the preliminary meeting in London at which Trygve Lie had been appointed Secretary-General. The Norwegian was an excellent choice for a post of great authority and great responsibility. He was a compromise between Lester Pearson of Canada, whom I would have preferred, and Paul-Henri Spaak of Belgium, who was vetoed by the Soviet Union. Lie was the best man acceptable to them, but he was to disappoint them in their hopes of using him for their nefarious purposes.

When the Assembly adjourned to New York, Fraser did not attend, and I led the New Zealand Delegation in 1946, as I was to do for each Assembly, apart from 1948 and 1952 when in the US Presidential Election year they were held in Paris, until I retired in 1952. Until a permanent home was prepared, the Assembly met at Lake Success, some twenty miles out of the city. I now found myself tied to New York for the greater part of the year, a great interference with the work in Washington.

At the London conference Fraser had been elected Chairman of the Social, Humanitarian and Cultural Committee, also called the Third Committee, a post in which, to my surprise and consternation, I was expected to succeed him. I was in no way nervous about controlling such a body. What sobered me was the Committee itself. It was concerned with the most insubstantial, visionary and dreamy of the subjects that any crank in the world could think up. I would not be believed if I recorded some of the more absurd ideas.

Now I do not want to dismiss the possibility of usefulness, but I do hate nonsense. Many of these proceedings seemed to be nonsense. While so many vital and urgent things needed to be done to save the world from war and slavery, I could scarcely tolerate it with patience. But there is a type that pays primary attention to such childish stupidities, and it was this type that I was destined to lead and guide in some of their infantile preoccupations.

Do I overstress this aspect of the United Nations? If I do so, remember I had witnessed the old League of Nations dying, because it had been led astray on such wild goose chases. Now here they were on my platter. As leader of the New Zealand Delegation, I must perforce, so I was informed, inherit the post Fraser had been allotted in London. So at the United Nations I began this additional activity that was to absorb most of my time for the whole of my Ambassadorship in Washington. The General Assembly met for three months – and what they could talk about, without doing anything, for such a period, is a question I could never answer. The shame of it all was of course that the question was never asked. The spate of talk at the United Nations seemed to be taken for granted. It should be sternly reduced if sense is to be made of this fundamentally very sensible organisation. Without Christmas arriving, the Assemblies might well have carried on indefinitely.

In addition to the General Assemblies, there were occasional Special Assemblies, and the Trusteeship Council, on which I was the New Zealand representative. So I found myself spending about eight months of the year in New York, leaving only four months for Washington and the rest of my constituency. The situation was impossible, and I told the Government in Wellington that the situation called for two separate officials.

At this first meeting in New York, David Wilson, our High Commissioner in Canada, and Mrs McIntosh and J.V. Wilson from New Zealand were also delegates. I had to distribute the work as best I could, taking account of the fact that delegates are often ignorant of the subjects to be discussed, and that I was immobilised as Chair of the Third Committee. With some considerable effort our Delegation managed to handle the assignment with credit. Indeed my general debate speech[2] was included in the authoritative 'Vital Speeches of the Day', and we played our part in all of the more important discussions.

As Chair of the Third Committee I found myself busily engaged in establishing an organisation to handle the vital and moving problem of the refugees from World War II. Millions of them were suffering intensely, if not dying of starvation and exposure. This was a most difficult affair, requiring long and detailed measures. The Soviet Union in particular added exasperatingly to our difficulties. They insisted that every single Russian refugee should at once be returned to Russia, whether they desired repatriation or not. The refugees who were opponents of that cruel and oppressive dictatorship knew this meant execution or, at the best, the Siberian camps. Fortunately the British and the American representative, Eleanor Roosevelt, stood squarely against the Soviet machinations. In the event none was sent home unless he or she asked for repatriation.[3]

---

2 General Debate Speech, First United Nations General Assembly 1946 – Statement by Sir Carl Berendsen 28 October 1946. See Appendix, and *New Zealand Foreign Policy: Statements and Documents 1943–57* (Wellington: Government Printer, 1972).

3 Berendsen would have been unaware of the forced repatriation of the Cossacks in the British zone in Carinthia in May 1945 and the involvement of New Zealand's General Weir of the British 46th Division. See *Victims of Yalta* (London: Hodder and Stoughton, 1977) and *The Minister and the Massacres* (London: Century Hutchison, 1986) by Nicolai Tolstoi, and *Firebird* by Natasha Templeton (London: Hodder and Stoughton, 1994).

THE RIVAL BUSES

I dare not speak at length of the mass of visionary proposals that occupied so much of the time of the Third Committee. The calendar has still not been altered as a result of our deliberations. Nor can I bear to think of the Arab delegate, a great advocate for human rights provided that they did not include rights for women, hammering away at a proposal to translate all of the classics into all of the languages of the world. The Committee did usefully debate a long list of human rights that were to emerge later in Declarations and Conventions of Human Rights. Sadly they provided no balancing emphasis on human duties. Nor did they dwell on the means of implementation and enforcement. Yet these are basic to the most fundamental of all rights: the right to peace.

At this first General Assembly in 1946, chaired by Paul-Henri Spaak, Dr Evatt made his first cast for the Presidency. On this occasion he was opposed by another and trickier Evatt in Aranha of Brazil. We heard the most fantastic stories of the Brazilian's potentialities and achievements. Aranha became President for the first Special Assembly on Palestine in April 1947 and then for the second General Assembly in the autumn of 1947. Evatt simply found himself outclassed by this wily Latin American. It was an outstanding lesson for our statesman from Australia. He then had to wait until the third Regular Assembly in 1948–49 to win and add to the international reputation of Dr Evatt and of Australia. Evatt made an intriguing and talkative but not particularly distinguished President.

These early Assemblies were studded with social engagements of the most trying kind. It became a scandal. More time and energy was being wasted on useless things than on the meetings themselves. The huge and costly Presidential receptions held each year were particularly useless. On the other hand the Secretary-General's lunches and dinners were always interesting. Yet at one I can remember the egregious Sulzberger of the *New York Times* bolting with the conversation. He kept telling all and sundry where they had gone wrong, and what they should do, and what he had seen, and what he had thought, and what he now thought, to our infinite boredom.

All in all I have to record that the United Nations began very much as the League of Nations had left off. Words were the real objective; the formula was the end sought. When they had passed a resolution members felt they had done something. There can be no greater fallacy. Many resolutions I have to record were idiotic. Most were simply meaningless and without effect. I was always grateful that there was just sufficient residual sense to persuade even scatterbrained delegates not to vote for some of the more criminal Soviet resolutions. With the international situation shrieking for responsible and practical steps to protect our liberty and sustain order and justice, I found it exasperating to spend so much effort on nonsensical debate. The United Nations was simply not dealing with the world's problems. The international system was in particular failing to preserve and enforce the peace of the world.

CHAPTER 5

BITTER BATTLES

Early in 1947 I was in New York for the first meeting of the newly established Trusteeship Council.[1] This was the body established to replace the Mandates Commission of the League of Nations. Its constitution, as laid down in the Charter, and to be reinforced by experience, was a bad one. The Council, a political organisation, was much inferior to the former expert body, which behaved as experts are accustomed to do:, with sense and discretion, founded on long experience.

The Trusteeship Council was deliberately made up of an equal number of administering and non-administering country members. Two camps developed and the division between the experienced and the inexperienced, with the lure of the headlines, was necessarily bad. On the one hand, the administering powers naturally tended to hold together even when there was real ground for criticism. All were vulnerable to the carping misrepresentation and mischief of the Soviet representatives. The Council did some good work, but this was despite its constitution. Properly organised, it could have done much better work.

Let me be frank and admit that there was much in the record of the colonial powers of which they, and humanity in general, could not be proud. In the past there had been much injustice, exploitation and oppression. In recent years, however, personal experience and observation told me that there had been an enormous change, in substance, rather than form, for the better. Old ideas had been discarded and a new spirit had emerged in the administration of dependent peoples. The interests of the local inhabitants had become primary.

The results were clear. The imperial powers were now contributing to the colonies. Colonialism and imperialism had become dying aspects of a world that was rapidly changing, not always for the better. Gradually, dependent peoples were moving to self-government. My view was that this laudable movement should proceed sensibly but slowly, for haste

1 Charter of the United Nations: Chapter XII International Trusteeship System. Chapter XIII The Trusteeship Council.

could be destructive in such matters. Regrettably haste was more likely to predominate than discretion, and I feared some of the inevitable results.

I was able to speak as one who had seen most of the colonies of all nations in all parts of the world. In my own small way I had assisted in the administration of New Zealand's dependent areas. I knew with certainty that there did exist in most of the colonial powers an entirely new spirit of humanity, generosity and responsibility. What was more I knew that those who criticised these powers so bitterly often themselves lived in glass houses. They were vulnerable to equal or greater criticism. But of course when I pointed this out, I was told that the United Nations did not exist for the control or the criticism of the domestic affairs of sovereign states.

This showed up first in the difficulties experienced in transferring the Mandates to the Trusteeship system. The Charter provided for agreements between the 'countries concerned'. The Soviet group tried to insist that they were concerned countries. Once we had got past their attempt at a veto we had to secure the approval of the United Nations to each of our agreements. The very nature of the problem presented difficulties. These were exacerbated by the malevolence of the Soviet bloc, and the stupidity of others. So the colonial powers asked New Zealand to take the first shock.

If I had realised the venom and violence of the discussion I doubt if I would have asked Wellington to agree to New Zealand taking the lead. Unjustified heat and unbridled offence came not only from the Soviet Union and its satellites, but also from India, (led by the able, but somewhat sinister Krishna Menon), Nationalist China, and some of the sillier Asian and Latin American countries.

These critics seemed to assume the administering powers were evil and selfish in seeking to bring Trust Territories gradually to self-government. Now there was nothing Machiavellian about the motives of New Zealand. All we wanted to do was assist the small territory of some fifty thousand Samoans living in an area of about a thousand square miles. Our hands were clean but we were in the front line. The malcontents wished to attack the others, but to do that successfully, they first had to attack New Zealand.

Our critics made the most outrageous suggestions. To suit their taste they assumed the right to redraft our agreement. Vehemently they sought to lay down a fixed term for self-government and the end of the Trusteeship, irrespective of progress made or the wishes of the Trust peoples. I sat as quietly as possible through days of exasperating debate as absurdity after absurdity was put on record. The matter would have dribbled on for a month but I lost all patience. I told them that they had no right or power to alter or amend the New Zealand agreement.

My argument was clear. I stressed that it was entirely within the judgement of the administering country to transfer its Mandate to the Trusteeship system. New Zealand had carefully prescribed reasonable and explicable conditions under which we were willing – indeed anxious – to transfer to the new system. We were not, however, criminals in the dock, and we had no intention of accepting that role. So I took our stand. I objected and I objected 'with indignation to any aspersion on the good name of New Zealand'. If our critics maintained their attitude, I made it clear, New Zealand, with the utmost regret would feel obliged to deprive itself of the privilege of United Nations supervision. In this situation New Zealand and its friends in Western Samoa would just have to make their own arrangements irrespective of the Trusteeship Council. I had no doubt, I made plain, that we would do very well. Nor did I refrain from expressing my astonishment that the representatives of India and China had made such unjustified and uncalled for attacks on my country and our proposals. These attacks would be carefully noted in New Zealand.

My bad tempered and vigorous protest had the desired effect. Our critics awoke to the fact that what the administering powers were proposing was a voluntary act. With a few trifling alterations our agreement was forthwith approved and the first of the new Trusteeships was established for Western Samoa. The proof of its success followed in the consistently complimentary comments of the Trusteeship Council – apart from that of the Soviet representative of course. No doubt he would have lost his head if he had approved anything we did on the movement towards self-government. My only concern was lest progress was pushed ahead too fast, and whether such a tiny country as Samoa, divided it was, could be independent.

At the end of the first meeting of the Trusteeship Council, I spoke to the American Society of International Law on the United Nations and international law. When I was asked to repeat that address in

Washington, I was one of two speakers at the District of Columbia Society. The other was Alger Hiss. Even after Whittaker Chambers accused him of being a Communist, like Dean Acheson I declined to wash my hands of Hiss. It was not until I read the evidence that I had to accept the guilt of this unfortunate and most brilliant man with his fine intellect but morbid mind.

Speaking engagements followed at a string of universities including Princeton, New York City, Columbia and George Washington University. Here one was sure of an understanding – if critical and argumentative – hearing. Following Walter Nash I also addressed the annual Socialist Convention at Tamiment, Pennsylvania, on Trusteeship. Norman Thomas, the Socialist leader, was a convincing and polished orator, and a good and earnest man. This was a large and very intelligent gathering which gave us the opportunity to visit the remarkable holiday resort of the powerful International Ladies' Garment Workers' Union, led by the masterful and able Dubinsky.

Soon it was time again to leave for the 1947 General Assembly in New York. We were joined by David Wilson, Mrs Roberts and J.V. Wilson as delegates. Little was accomplished in the next three months. The New Zealand Delegation simply took its part in the work of the Assembly, where I was again Chair of a committee, on Trusteeship. This Assembly saw the beginnings for the United Nations of the long drawn out and entirely unsatisfactory discussions on Palestine.[2]

At that time the infinitely complicated and bitterly contested disputes between Jew and Arab were coming to a painful and bloody head. The British, who had for so long borne the troubles of the arbitrator, found themselves in an impossible situation, trying to carry out an impossible task. Perhaps no nation on earth could have reconciled the irreconcilable, but the British had striven hard. Now in handling this intricate question, they were suffering grievously, and by 1947 they were at the end of their patience and, more important, their resources. The British Government had therefore decided to hand this problem over to an appropriate international body. Clearly the United Nations had to assume responsibility.

---

2 General Debate Speech, Second United Nations General Assembly 1947, Statement by Sir Carl Berendsen, 20 September 1947. See Appendix and *New Zealand Foreign Policy: Statements and Documents 1943–57* (Wellington: Government Printer, 1972).

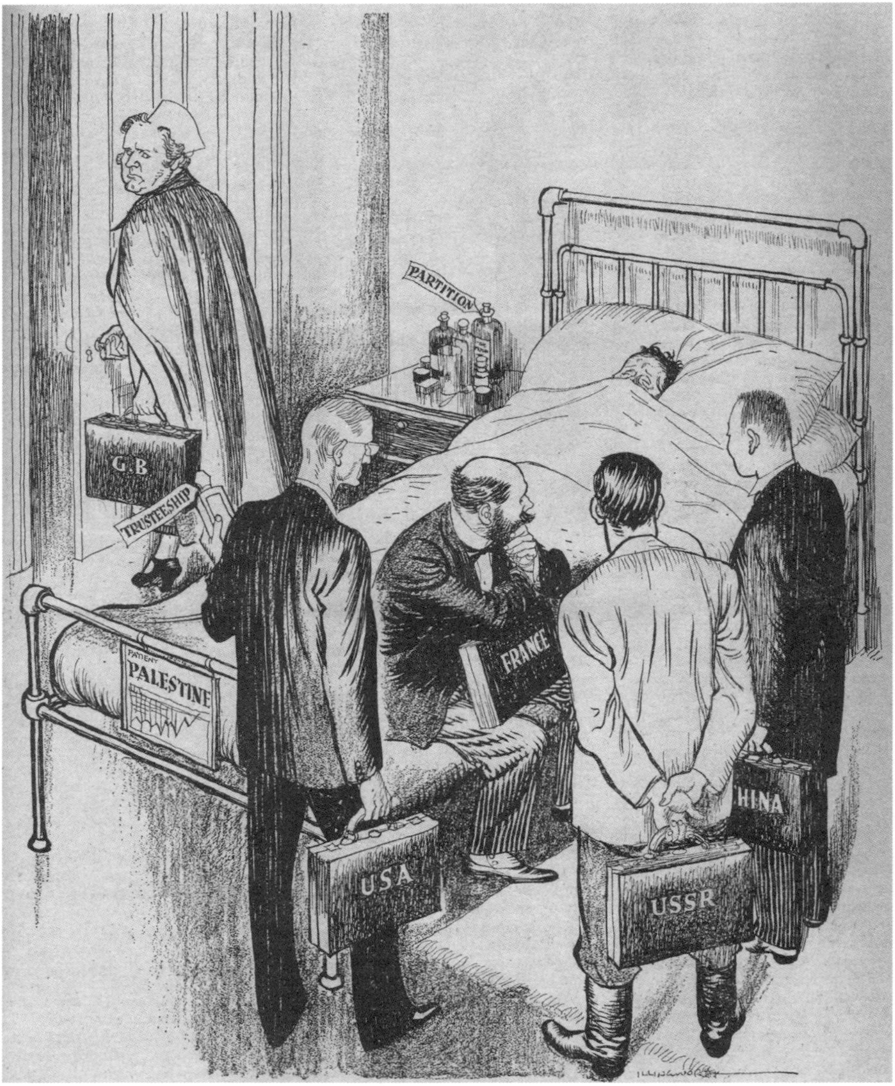

NURSE GIVES NOTICE
"And now, gentlemen, we shall have to get something done ourselves, instead of telling *her* what to do."

The Palestine issue was made intractable by the bitter animosities of the two protagonists. I saw much of both sides. Each point of view was natural enough and defensible enough. The problem was that each was completely antagonistic and exclusive. The Arab thesis was that Palestine was an Arab country in which the Jews had possessed no foothold for a thousand years. A Jewish home there was not particularly objectionable so long as their numbers and powers were kept within strict limits. What was morally wrong, and impossible in practice, was to cut off from this country a large slice of territory, and many thousands of protesting Arabs, to make a a new sovereign state. On the Jewish side was the Balfour Declaration.[3] This envisaged a Jewish State of Palestine. Logically and historically the Jewish case was a strong one. From this position Arab opposition was contumacious and irreconcilable.

For a long time no one could see on balance where the right and wrong lay. This arose from the actual nature of foreign affairs. There my experience taught me that everything was a mixture of black and white, and that nothing was ever entirely right or wrong. Inevitably one had to deal with a conflict of wrongs. Out of this one had to seek and, usually sooner rather than later, arrive at a proper balance, with the scales of justice falling between one side and the other. That was all we could hope for in this imperfect world.

Having said this, I have to confess that the Palestine question was more difficult and complicated than most. Both sides were rigid and inflexible in the highest degree. The Jews, difficult enough in all conscience, showed some signs of being more reasonable and accommodating. The Arabs, badly led at this meeting in the autumn of 1947, refused to budge an inch. They began shouting the word 'war'.

The best we could achieve was a compromise. In general I am not in favour of compromises. They often entail a surrender of principle. Nevertheless they are not always unwise. In the situation the United Nations faced, the solution proposed was to divide Palestine into two parts – one Arab, and one Jewish – with Jerusalem to become an

---

3 The Balfour Declaration of 1916, promising a Jewish national home in Palestine, was named for Arthur Balfour, the British Foreign Secretary. The second Balfour Declaration of 1926 confirming the independence of the British Dominions was then embodied in the Statute of Westminster of 1931.

international city. I had never been able to get myself interested in the special problem of Jerusalem, and I was for a long time unwilling indeed to become involved in the larger question of Palestine and the Jewish State. Nevertheless I found I had to take part in this great debate. Gradually I became very interested indeed in the wider question of Palestine.

Generally the United Nations proposals seemed to be the best that could be adopted in the circumstances as they existed. For there was no clean sheet on which the members could write at choice. This was an age-old problem, dating back for thousands of years, complicated by large and wide human developments, and bedevilled by misunderstandings and cross-promises. The Arabs had a case that no power, great or small, had a right to give away land that had been Arab for centuries. The Jews had a case, essentially weaker, in the Balfour Declaration, with its concept of a National Home.

The decisive new fact was the large scale Jewish immigration into Palestine, encouraged by the Great Powers, and tolerated by the Arabs for a time, until they began to fear for their own position. The Mandate itself had done nothing to solve the insoluble. In this unhappy situation, Partition provided the best solution available at the time. The Jews might, I believe, have been persuaded to accept Partition, but the Arabs remained intransigent. Both sides behaved badly as the United Nations proposed and considered all kinds of plans. Campaigns of murder and intimidation should have nerved the United Nations to put through its considered plan, by force if necessary. But recoiling from this prospect in crass fear, the Assembly allowed its decision to be flouted.

At this time, with none other than General Eisenhower preceding me, I was the principal speaker at the New York Bar Association's annual dinner. I made one of my best speeches and was then asked to the annual Law Faculty dinner at Syracuse University. There, to my discomfiture, as no one could emulate that great master, I was billed as a second Churchill. The Law Dean was a strong proponent of the movement for world government. Indeed I am too. My problem is that I realise, as they do not, that there is no chance in the world in present circumstances of achieving anything of the kind.

I had to decline another invitation, this time from the American Bar Association, but did address a distinguished group of journalists, the Overseas Writers, on the veto and its effect on the United Nations. The

President of the Overseas Writers, Bob Considine, was a devout Roman Catholic and a warm protagonist of the principle that the United Nations should open its meetings with prayer. He did not achieve this, but his wish that the United Nations should set aside a place for reflection was to be attained during Dag Hammarskjöld's Secretary-Generalship.

Early in 1948 Nellie and I had returned to New Zealand for consultations with the Government. On the way we stopped in Honolulu so that I could invest two United States officers, one an Admiral and one a General, with honorary British orders. Back in New Zealand we had a chance to meet old friends and catch up with our own country. My problem was that the visit got taken up with conferences and interviews at a time when I was feeling unwell with my duodenal ulcer. The Prime Minister as usual was kind and appreciative. At one point he asked me and C.W. Boswell, our Minister in Moscow, to meet the Cabinet – why, I could not possibly hope to explain. After I had finished, the Prime Minister, unusually, hurried after me to MacIntosh's room: 'Thank you, thank you very much.' This I might say was quite unprecedented. I made broadcasts, talked to the press, spoke at the Wellington Town Hall and met the Foreign Affairs Committee of the House.

Soon we were off again, with a speech in San Francisco, on the way back to Washington where the Government, in most flattering terms, had asked us to continue. All in all, despite the effort required, it is a good thing to bring a representative abroad back home at regular intervals. It helps him avoid being enveloped in the affairs of the land to which he is accredited. Increasingly an Ambassador tends to take on the colour of his surroundings. A home visit allows him to reorient himself and reacquire his country's point of view.

Back in Washington I found myself, a complete newcomer, elected President of the Annual Conference of the Food and Agriculture Organization. This was in one way an easy task, but in another difficult because of the condition of my voice. I found great difficulty in speaking with the force necessary to be heard by a large gathering of several hundred.

Then it was back to New York for the Trusteeship Council and the Special Meeting of the United Nations Assembly on Palestine. My voice was a liability, yet I managed to address the Assembly many times in some of my most quoted speeches. Pusillanimity, I argued, would never maintain peace and order and justice, and I urged the Special Assembly to act on the issue, quoting Benjamin Franklin: 'Resolve to perform what you ought; perform without fail what you resolve.'[4]

This was not my best speech, nor as widely acclaimed as the one I was to give at the Peace Conference on Japan in 1951. It was, however, a great success. It was printed and reprinted in many journals and placed in 'Vital Speeches of the Day'. Over one hundred thousand copies were distributed by the United Nations Association of the United States of America.

As is well known, when warfare flared in 1948, Israel, with American assistance in arms and supplies, easily defeated all the Arab states together. Never did a people get a more rapid and humiliating defeat at the hands of an apparently weaker foe. Their rout was abysmal and complete. In getting their war, the Arabs had thrown away sympathy by their recourse to arms. Worse, they made implementation of the Partition plan impracticable.

How was the United Nations to solve this unhappy quarrel? All that was possible was to reduce the hostilities to a simmering animosity. Anyone could see that the Arab states, thirsting for revenge, were bound to fracture the uneasy peace at the first opportunity. Despite the immense capacities of its people, and the abilities of leaders like Moshe Sharett, Eliyahu Elath and Abba Eban, coupled with the continuing inflow of Jews, the position of Israel was neither stable nor promising.

One proposal was for Palestine to be treated as a Trust Territory. I had no hesitation in telling the Trusteeship Council what I thought of such a body trying to fiddle with the Palestine problem. This was a task for which the Council was totally unfitted when the Assembly and Security Council were facing such difficulties in finding solutions.

It was at this point that President Truman cut the Gordian knot. Suddenly and without notice the United States recognised the state of Israel as an international entity. I shall not forget the face of an Arab friend, Awni Khalidi, as I told him of the President's announcement. I have never heard such plain speaking as the Arabs' reaction to this totally unexpected move.

---

4 General Debate Speech, Second Special General Assembly February–March 1948: Famous Statement by Sir Carl Berendsen on Palestine, 20 April 1948, widely credited in a tight vote for confirming the resolution, after the US hesitated, for Partition. See Appendix and *New Zealand Foreign Policy: Statements and Documents 1943–57* (Wellington: Government Printer, 1972).

At this time too my Government asked if I would make myself available as mediator between India and Pakistan. I replied that I could do it, provided my wife came with me, but I did not consider myself an unbiased arbitrator. Nor would India have considered me to be so, in the light of my criticism of India's attitude towards British policy. I would have been disappointed if I were not correct, for this would have meant my remonstrances against Indian policies had fallen on deaf ears. In any case I heard no more on the posting, which went to Admiral Nimitz.

This was the time of the Party Conventions prior to the US elections of 1948. These typically American productions appear somewhat infantile to the British mind. Devoid of reason and restraint, their oratory of a perfervid and caricatured style, subject to intrigue and negotiation for position, they are noisy, excited, seething affairs. They stand in contrast to the responsibilities thrust upon Americans by providence, responsibilities on which their fate, and the fate of humanity, depend.[5]

The American election of November 1948 caught us all out. I naturally reported on the prospects. Throughout I told my Government that Truman and the Democrats had no chance at all of being re-elected. This was the view of all my colleagues in the Diplomatic Corps and of every authority throughout the United States. Every columnist, every commentator, every editor, every radio and television station, accepted without question the defeat of the Democrats. So too did the Democrats. We knew of many busy selling or leasing their houses. One senior Democrat with whom I was intimate had been invited to run as Vice President. He had declined on the grounds that 'God himself couldn't win with Truman'. The only person who disagreed with this common view was the little President himself. He had all the courage in the world. He set out personally to win his election battle with Governor Dewey.

And he did, to the astonishment of all, and to the dismay of those of us who had pledged our judgement on his defeat. This was the biggest gaffe of my career. I had no excuse. Some of my colleagues had urged me to hedge. I declined to do so. How much better I would have appeared if I had taken this well meant advice. Such is life. My explanatory

5 Berendsen's acidulous comments about American Party Conventions receive some support from Damon Runyon in his story 'Delegates At Large', in *Runyon From First to Last* (London: Constable, 1954).

telegram to Wellington was indeed a lame one. I had made a mistake that I could never live down. Still I was only one of a red-faced group of repentant prophets all over America. All had been wrong. We had all had to learn that one can never foresee the result of an election.

At that time I gave the Wharton address to the University of Pennsylvania and a series of talks in Chicago, while increasingly finding we were having to spend up to eight months of the year in New York. So we took an apartment on the corner of Fifth Avenue and 69th Street, facing right onto Central Park, the better to attend to our United Nations duties. This was the time I had to face the Prime Minister himself with a series of personal problems, mainly related to my remuneration and my superannuation. There was a contrast, I pointed out, between the complimentary references to my work, so extreme at times that I blushed, and the singular refusal in my case to provide an adjustment offered to every other civil servant. Despite being so forthright with Fraser over this niggardly injustice, I had to wait for Holland to make the necessary adjustment.

In attending the inauguration of President Truman in January 1949 we were fortunate to get public seats for our son Keith, who had just finished his medical training, and his wife. The President's inaugural address was rather better than his usual speeches, which were for the most part terrible, at least in their delivery. Here he spoke well, and his enunciation of the Point Four policy struck a chord in world interest that made it of historic significance.[6] All possible credit should be given to the President for this policy.

In 1948 too our capitals agreed to raise our Legations to the status of Embassies. So instead of being a Minister I became an Ambassador. This was a wise step as the Americans wanted all Heads of Mission to be Ambassadors. I would not have relished being relegated to a lower place at public functions by many who had come to Washington long after me, but who outranked me while I remained a Minister. This might

6 President Truman announced his Point Four Program (1949–1953) for economic aid to developing countries in his 1949 inaugural address. This, the fourth of his foreign policy objectives, was linked to the European Recovery Program of 1948, which he had insisted, to ensure Congressional acceptance, be known as the Marshall Plan, after General of the Army George Marshall (1880–1959), famous wartime Chief of Staff of the United States Army 1939–45, Truman's Secretary of State 1947–49, Secretary of Defence 1950–51, and winner of the Nobel Peace Prize in 1953. See David McCullough's *Truman* (New York: Simon and Schuster, 1993), p. 564.

seem a minor matter, but it does affect the reputation of one's country. New Zealand was finding itself falling behind the smallest and meanest newcomers on the international scene. So eventually I presented my letters of credence as Ambassador to President Truman, a most pleasant and likeable person, who by this time we knew well.

After the June meeting of the Trusteeship Council, Nellie and I took a sea voyage to see something of South America, which was playing so important a part in United Nations affairs. Brazil, despite its huge size, pride and international standing, seemed a backward and somewhat sad land. Even the loveliest of its cities were spoilt by the horrifying favellas. Still there was Rio de Janeiro, whose vistas could not be exceeded in beauty and majesty, ranking in our minds with the Bay of Naples from Vesuvius, and the wonderful and insufficiently appreciated vistas in Wellington. We left Brazil greatly taken by the Latin American 'paseo', by the Brazilian sense of life, and by their conception of time as being not solely for work and worry, but also for enjoyment and contemplation.

In Uruguay we rapidly came to terms with one Latin American fetish, Association football, and the need to import professional referees from England, a highly paid and highly insured occupation encompassing both the temperament of Latinos and the honour of Englishmen. With the help of old diplomatic friends we then explored Buenos Aires, one of the greatest cities in the world, and a beautiful one, with everything a modern city has – everything but freedom. Under a dictatorship which had almost killed the flourishing industry on which its prosperity depended, Argentina had become a sad land.

Let me make clear my aversion. Here we felt the same sense of terror and brutality, uneasiness and deception that we had known in Nazi Germany. No one dared to discuss the dictator. Evita Peron was always referred to as Mrs Smith. We found no one who spoke aloud or who smiled or laughed. In this totalitarian state all had an eye cast over their backs watching for eavesdroppers. Underlying it all was the same uneasiness, the same sense of terror that we had sensed in Germany. In Argentina we saw what we call civilisation at its highest level; and liberty at its lowest.

By this time, though not normally of a nervous disposition, I was anxious to depart from this tyranny. I was much relieved when I got into the plane, and still more relieved, recalling my 'escape from Germany' before the war, when the plane took off. At our departure one of the airport clerks, noticing our New Zealand passports, mentioned a long lost brother resident in New Zealand. Later, after I had made enquiries, the brother was found, and the two were made known to each other after twenty years.

We were no sooner home than we were off again to the Fourth General Assembly of the United Nations. This time the President was Carlos Romulo of the Philippines. The main question to be decided was the future of Libya. This issue was a typical instance of the United Nations method of handling a problem. At its third meeting, despite its intense enthusiasm for independence, the 1948 General Assembly had voted by an enormous majority that Libya was not yet ready for independence. At this very next meeting in 1949 the Fourth General Assembly decided by a similar majority that Libya was ready for independence and must be granted it immediately.

What could be made of this? As I told the Assembly, both decisions could not possibly be right.[7] Progress towards self-government was a matter of time. In this situation nothing whatever in that direction had happened since the previous vote. But independence it was. Poor Libya, as history will record, was left to make the best of it. Libya and the Trust Territory of Italian Somaliland were indeed two cases in which, as a result of muddled humanitarianism and sordid bargaining, the United Nations behaved with the grossest irresponsibility.

About this time our household was enlivened by my wife's cousin Ella coming to us for an extended stay. She had grown up with Nellie in Dunedin and had then gone to Australia, where she had become a buyer for one of Sydney's largest department stores. Travelling all over the world for her firm, she had married a wealthy jute merchant from India. When he died, and a second marriage failed, she joined us, and was a happy companion, full of fun and life. During this period too, our son Ian, who had joined the Trusteeship Division of the UN Secretariat, married an American girl of the well-known Peabody family.

At this time I made two separate journeys on speaking engagements. The first was to the University of Alabama, which had one of the most

7 Statement by Sir Carl on the 'Question of the disposal of the former Italian colonies', Discussion of the report of Sub-Committee 17, Fourth Session of the United Nations General Assembly, New York, 4 November 1949.

beautiful campuses of any American university. The other was to the Annual Convention of the World Federalists of America. Although the goal was far distant, I had sympathy for the ideals and aspirations that lay behind the movement. World federation might not in historical terms be just round the corner, but the gathering was the largest 'live' audience I ever addressed.

After the eloquent Mayor of Minneapolis, later Senator Hubert Humphrey, I came on as the last and main speaker. My question was simple enough: how did the movement propose to amend the Charter to make the United Nations the basis for a world government? As it would require ratification by each of the five Great Powers, this was complete nonsense. There was no possibility in any foreseeable future of amending the Charter along these lines. World government remained an ideal when even that small measure of world government required to maintain the peace of the world was unattainable.

At another speech in Philadelphia for Rotary International I shared a platform with Mrs Vijaya Pandit, the sister of Pandit Nehru, and then Indian Ambassador to the United States. Unbeknownst to me, the fee, which as an Ambassador I had refused, was sent to Rotary New Zealand. Years later I found myself introduced at a Christchurch Rotary meeting as the donor of the Berendsen Bursary.

Among the tasks that fell on Ambassadors was to support worthy institutions like the Dupont Nemours Foundation, near Wilmington, for crippled and disabled children. This was a cause in which Peter Fraser had shown a warm interest. During one Nemours function we met Mrs Woodrow Wilson, and I also had a chance to talk to that sage guide of his generation, and adviser to Presidents, Bernard Baruch.

At the end of 1949 the Labour Government in New Zealand was defeated. In my view this was long after this Socialist Administration, so magnificent in war and foreign affairs, but so damaging to the local economy, should have been removed from power. I found no difficulty in working with the new Holland Government and its successive Ministers of External Affairs: my old friend Fred Doidge, and then Clifton Webb. All were considerate and sensible, even if they did continue to ask me to stay on at my own post year by year, for three more years.

CHAPTER 6

UNITED NATIONS TEST IN KOREA

After another long and demanding year of daily work at the Embassy, with sallies to highly regarded colleges like Mount Holyoke and Wellesley, as well as to other parts of the country, no sooner had we planned a summer vacation when out of the clear sky came the Korean War, in June of 1950.

The reaction of the United Nations to Communist aggression in Korea was the most inspiring and hopeful development of my whole life. The nations gathered in New York met the challenge admirably. All the muddle and intrigue, and all the wordy nonsense were stripped away. The free world gathered itself to meet the situation in the only way it could be met.

An enormous majority joined in a resolution to declare North Korea an aggressor. The members of the United Nations resolved to meet lawless force with lawful force. Each was called on to take their proportionate part in the military action required to respond to this unprovoked attack, not only on Korea, but also on the free world and the tenets of decency, honour and justice on which any civilisation must be based.

As leader of the New Zealand Delegation, I took my share in these deliberations and discussions. New Zealand could be proud of the policy of its Government in this delicate and desperate matter. Of course little of this would have been possible but for a chance of history. Why was it possible for the member states of the United Nations to resolve to act in the face of the veto power? And then to take immediate and forceful action against North Korea?

The answer was simple. At that time Jacob Malik, the Soviet representative, was absenting himself from meetings of the Security Council. He was protesting, as the Russians were always protesting against something or other, as a matter of policy, and in order to make propaganda Malik was absent and could not cast his negative vote – his veto!

THE NEW HUNTING GROUND

There was a point of law involved, and I found myself on the wrong side of the issue. The Charter specifically required the affirmative vote of each of the Great Powers. The Security Council did not receive the affirmative vote of the Soviet Union. Without that affirmative vote the resolution, however desirable in fact, was, in my view, invalid in terms of the Charter.

Most competent opinion did not agree. Those who supported the legality of the resolution, as opposed simply to its desirability, asserted that the Security Council had laid down that mere abstention from voting would not amount to a veto. That indeed was so. Moreover the Soviet representative had specifically agreed to that arrangement.

The point I held was that, however desirable, such an arrangement was beyond the power of the Security Council. The resolution was therefore null and void. In requiring active opposition to effect a veto, the Security Council was in effect amending the Charter. Such an amendment, to be legal, would have required resolutions of both the General Assembly and the Security Council, and then ratification by each of the Great Powers.

No doubt all that was done under this resolution could have been done by resolution of the General Assembly, for no one acted here because of obligation under the Charter, but voluntarily by the light of reason and the general principles of the Charter, and then very few acted at all. But there would have been a substantial delay, and this might well have meant the forces of aggression capturing the whole of Korea before the United Nations could have effectively intervened.

Then there is the issue of why the Soviet representative was not in his seat in the Security Council. If the North Korean attack was the deliberate design of the Communists in Moscow as well as in Peking, and if the attack was provoked, as well as supported by Moscow, why was Malik not there ready to veto this action against North Korea and the Communist world? After all he had vetoed some fifty other resolutions. The answer is simple and comforting. All the mistakes were not made on the western side of the Iron Curtain.

Let me examine the issues in the Korean War. Was the United Nations right to meet the aggression of North Korea – in other words the aggression of Moscow and Peking – by force? Of course it was right; there could have been no other course without the betrayal of all for which the United Nations banded together.

Did the United Nations do all that it could and should have done? No, indeed it did not. Many, indeed most, of its members did not. Apart from the usual wordy resolutions and airy support for which many member nations were noted, two thirds of those who had supported the condemnation of the aggressor and the call for action did exactly nothing at all. In the event only fourteen – some fourteen – members of the United Nations sent fighting forces to meet this fighting attack. The others talked. Even some of those who did contribute to the arms of the United Nations defending civilisation against armed attack did conspicuously less than they should have done. Others of the cooperating states that gathered together in the Washington committee to consider the higher strategy of the struggle were noticeable for their timidity and their indecision. They held back rather than marched forward. So they contributed largely towards the indecisive and ominous result of a divided Korea.

Was the United Nations right, after a perilous period of overwhelming Communist attack, when its forces gathered strength, to advance beyond the thirty-eighth parallel? Remember this was an artificial and temporary boundary drawn solely to allow the Russians to accept the Japanese surrender north of the line. Of course it was right, and no one argued, or even thought to the contrary, at the time.

Was the United Nations right in endeavouring then to restore the unity of Korea? Of course it was right. The unity of Korea was a matter to which every member of the United Nations was pledged in honour – and in commonsense – and indeed the country was physically reunited when MacArthur's forces reached the northern boundary on the Yalu River.

Why did the Chinese attack? Was it due to the belief, as alleged, that the United Nations intended to attack China itself? That was nonsense. No such fear could have been held in any quarter. The Chinese attacked as part of a Communist strategy to make mischief.

And why were the massive Chinese forces not seen and evaluated to prevent the United Nations forces walking right into their arms? The blame had to fall on the limitations of MacArthur's intelligence organisation, led by the egregious General Willoughby.

Was it right to agree to the armistice when the UN appeared be on the point of defeating the enormous Chinese forces? That question history must answer. But in my view we were wrong. We allowed ourselves to be tricked; to be caught in a trap; to be deceived by a simple ruse to gain time for the hard-pressed Communists. As a result the Communists were able to drag out the negotiations for years. The United Nations was left with an armistice but no peace. The Communists simply used the time they gained to strengthen their positions.

Was the United Nations right to parley with evildoers in the search for a patched up peace? As an experienced observer and opponent of appeasement, I believe we were wrong. Having set out to vindicate the right, the United Nations should have continued to do so, despite the waste and suffering in meeting force with force, to vindicate the right. Instead, millions of innocents were added to those imprisoned behind the Iron Curtain, and the standing of the United Nations fell.

Should the United Nations have refrained from bombing beyond the Yalu after the Chinese had attacked? I looked on this as a cardinal error. Nor was this the fault of MacArthur or the United States. The blame lay with the Allies, who contributed little in the way of armed forces, but much in meddling with strategy. As the New Zealand representative on the Allied Committee I can testify that, except in the early stages of the conflict, these Allies dragged on the American coat tails, pulling back as hard and as often as they possibly could. They argued if the Allies were not too 'beastly' the Communists would become good international citizens. As a result the Korean problem was left like a canker to future generations to cauterise or solve.

Here we had an armed band of aggressors, declared as such by the United Nations, and properly and inescapably so, being fought back by the forces of international order, just as armed criminals are constantly being fought by the police forces of every civilised nation in the world. In this situation I have never heard anyone suggest that we should take the criminals to our bosom in the hope that they would cease from crime. Such a course would universally be recognised as absurd and dangerous. While we may seek to rehabilitate the criminal, the first step is to defeat him so as to prevent further crime.

Yet our approach to international problems is entirely different. The UN's handling of the international criminal involves a mental and moral cowardice that in this case was influential and, in the end, decisive. In this matter I stood as a convinced supporter of MacArthur and his successor Van Fleet. The United Nations could not fight a war against barbarism with one hand tied behind its back. No war could be won that way.

Let me be clear. There was no sense or morality in compromising, in attempting to placate the implacable, in pretending one can treat with evil doers, and in dreaming of making friends of declared and active enemies. It was wrong to pretend that the mere cessation of warfare was a supreme good in itself. If this sort of peace was the ultimate good we should not have gone to war in the first place. Nor should we fight in the future for justice and order and liberty. How dishonest to pretend that South Korea, or South Vietnam for that matter, could stand against China. Lack of courage in this matter might well leave Asia to be swept up into the Communist fold.

The outbreak of the Korean War in the middle of 1950 made for a busy and anxious year. The Allied Policy Committee in Washington was meeting twice a week with high-ranking representatives of the cooperating countries as we moved into the annual United Nations meetings in the autumn. While I was attending the 1950 General Assembly I was invited to be the guest speaker on the coast-to-coast radio programme 'United – or Not?', an intelligent weekly survey instituted by the United Nations Press Club. They were a fine and knowledgeable body, and the radio programme they prepared was always thoughtful and thought provoking. Eight or nine of the best-known journalists sat around a table with an invited guest to discuss some aspect of world affairs.

On the night the debate covered a wide range of issues, including my view that a case could be made for what was so universally condemned as colonialism. An Arab interlocutor would have none of this, as I expressed heretical opinions on the limited powers of the United Nations to rectify existing and potential evils. Controversial then, before long these views became platitudinous.

Sometime later this programme was translated onto television. This was my first appearance before a television camera as a kind of star performer. One had to learn to wear a grey suit and a blue shirt to appear naturally contrasted on the screen, and avoid altering any of one's natural behaviour. One had to remain calm and serene and not even smile at the most absurd statements. There was a particular problem in listening to the questions and thinking out answers without delay under the close scrutiny of the camera. I managed quite satisfactorily in this new and public, but intimate medium.

In the new year, January 1951, I went on tour to address the Council on Foreign Relations in Chicago, the Seattle Council of Foreign Affairs, and the Foreign Affairs branch of the San Francisco Chamber of Commerce. This tour included a formal visit to San Diego where I actually received a formal nineteen-gun salute at a parade of the US Marines and met many old Marine Corps friends from Wellington and Washington days. My final speech, to the Los Angeles Forum, added to the controversy over the British recognition of Red China. That bewildered little man Clement Attlee, harried by the visionary and crack-brained extremists of his Labour party, had done so without the United States, Canada, Australia or New Zealand following suit.

By this stage Nellie and I were getting to the end of our tether. With the daily toil at the Embassy and the incessant worries and anxieties of the United Nations, we were forced to limit the number of social engagements and the effort involved. We too often found some of our visitors, politicians and high officials, something of a trial, and occasionally guilty of misconduct. Two of our visitors were persistent and notorious chasers of women. One fortunately confined his pursuit to the type of female to whom such activities were welcome. The other had a wider sphere, including his own staff. Two more were generally known for being unable to keep their hands off women.

Although these habits were known in official circles in New Zealand, these people were still sent abroad as the representatives of our Government. What indeed placed a Cabinet Minister outside and above the responsibilities of a gentleman? Particularly an honourable gentleman supposedly representing his country his country abroad?

Others openly sponged. One simply stayed on and on at the Embassy without the barest word of gratitude or appreciation. Unwilling to pay even for a cinema ticket, let alone a sundae, he was a scrub of the first order. We found others freeloading off the junior officers of delegations, rather than use their allowances. Another sent abroad in a high capacity managed, despite his high pay and allowances, to charge a fee for his speeches, and lost the respect of all who knew of this practice. One visitor, excellent though he may have been, was so crude and vulgar that one could only reflect on the stupidity of anyone exposing New

Zealand to such humiliation and embarrassment. Another visitor had been sent to represent New Zealand when he was physically and mentally incapacitated, and still another was simple and stupid, half-witted to an extent that only political considerations could have led to his appointment. At the expense of the taxpayer, we were ruining the reputation of our country.

These grim stories may balance the concept of glamour that attends thoughts of the life of an Ambassador. By 1951 the continuous pressure had made me determined to retire.

CHAPTER 7

THE ANZUS PACT AND THE JAPANESE PEACE TREATY

At the specific request of successive Governments and Ministers I had now remained at my post for six years over my pension service of forty years. I was dealing with a mass of daily work, taking responsibility for all the work of the Embassy and the New Zealand Delegation to the United Nations, travelling this vast country and making speeches to secure friends for New Zealand, reporting on developments in the United States, looking after New Zealanders and New Zealand interests, dealing with acres of correspondence, handling all our official business with the United States Government, negotiating treaty after treaty, and attending hundreds of social functions each year.

An Ambassador's life, of course was in many respects enjoyable. But over time it was harsh, and intolerably heavy and destructive. So I was relieved when I learned that our request for retirement had been approved for 1952. But the time had not yet come. Early in 1951 I was approached in New York by John Foster Dulles, an old friend and associate. Although Dulles was a Republican, Dean Acheson, one of the most enlightened and ablest Secretaries of State, had, in the spirit of bipartisanship, appointed him to assist the Democratic Administration.

During my Ambassadorship Dulles had been constantly engaged in foreign affairs. An unusual type for an American, Dulles was reserved, earnest and solemn, highly cultured and polished, and carefully educated in the law. His career and practice, especially in international affairs, had become one of the most lucrative in the country and he had been expected, if Governor Dewey had won the 1948 election, to become the Republican Secretary of State.

A man of deep religious connexions, Dulles studied each problem from the outlook of morality. I for one know of no better or more reliable guide on all matters of international, national or personal difficulty. As a result of his probity and competence Dulles was so fully in the confidence of the Administration, and particularly of Dean Acheson, that he was entrusted almost entirely with the negotiations that led to the peace treaty with Japan and consequently the ANZUS Pact.

In any case I found myself called to the Dulles home in the East Sixties. There Dulles outlined to me his idea of some form of collective security arrangement for the South Pacific. I made careful note of Dulles's suggestions and clarified his proposals as circumstances seemed to indicate. After a conversation of some hours I went back to the office and drafted a telegram to Wellington. Dulles also talked with the Australian Ambassador.

So we began work on the ANZUS Pact. All the detailed negotiations took place in the Pacific. Personally I had no part in them except for a few queries and explanations from time to time. At the request of my Government, with whose general attitude I was in entire agreement, I did give a full exposition of my own views on the matter.

Finally Dulles and the Australian and New Zealand Ministers reached full agreement on the text of the ANZUS Pact. I was called upon to initial the draft at a formal ceremony covered by radio and television and well publicised in the press. Having done this, I realised that I would be required to attend, either alone or with Prime Minister Holland or Minister Webb, the conference to negotiate and sign a peace treaty with Japan, set for the autumn of 1951.

In the event it was left to me to lead the New Zealand Delegation to the Japanese Peace Conference. Before that of course we spent months negotiating and discussing the details of a treaty of fundamental importance to Australia and New Zealand. Our destinies inevitably lay in the Pacific, adjacent to a reinstated and possibly resurgent Japan.

The questions involved for New Zealand were difficult and delicate. Many might believe that as a result of the American occupation and the inestimable privilege of MacArthur's tutelage, the Japanese people had changed overnight from a warlike and aggressive people to a smiling and friendly race, anxious only to live on terms of peace and amity with their neighbours.

Many in Australia and New Zealand, however, found it impossible to divest themselves of doubt that the Japanese had indeed changed at all. We could not shut out from contemplation the possibility that this powerful and enigmatic people might bide their time, wait for the end of the Occupation, and resume those national policies that best met Japanese interests, even at the cost of renewed war.

This was a fundamental question for the Australian and New Zealand Governments. Here we did not have a clear table. We were signing a treaty against a background of Communist aggression that had absorbed many countries and many more millions of people. If Japan were to join the Communist conspiracy, the prospects for our two countries in the Pacific were gloomy indeed.

On these grounds, as well as on grounds of fairness and equity, our Governments concluded that we must offer a generous and friendly peace to Japan.[1] This was the basis on which a treaty evolved. Much work and many long and detailed discussions were required. Finally all was ready for signature in San Francisco in the autumn of 1951. The exception of course was the Soviet Union and its satellites, who, as always, made difficulties, and looked to make more.

Australia and New Zealand were in full accord with the need for a generous peace settlement, except for one essential preliminary. If Japan were, as was planned, to be reinstated to full membership in the community of nations, and with the possibility of rearmament, what about our security? In the past Australia and New Zealand had happily, if selfishly, relied for protection on the British navy and on British arms. This shield and buckler was no longer available. Britain was no longer able to shoulder its former worldwide responsibilities. Unless some other means of defence were found, in case of renewed Japanese aggression, Australia and New Zealand could not possibly sign a treaty of peace with Japan.

This was the fundamental reason for the negotiation of the ANZUS Pact. The United States agreed with Australia and New Zealand that any attack on any of them in the Pacific would be a threat to the safety of the others. This would require them to consult together and act according to their constitutional procedures. The ANZUS Treaty was for Australia and New Zealand an essential substitute for the powerful shield of Britain. Once we had the ANZUS Pact in place, we would be

1 'Allied Policy Towards Japan', Speech by Sir Carl Berendsen, Washington, 11 December 1947. See Appendix.

able to sign the proposed Japanese Peace Treaty to be finalised in San Francisco.

So I found myself instructed to go to San Francisco in a two-fold capacity. As the New Zealand plenipotentiary I had formal powers to sign the ANZUS Pact on behalf of New Zealand. Then as the leader of the New Zealand Delegation to the Japanese Peace Conference I was to sign the Japanese Treaty.

In September 1951 my wife and I set out on the last important assignment of our official life. It was an impressive as well as a valuable end to my long service. My apprehension was that the Soviet Delegation would make a good deal of trouble, particularly in the period before the conference had adopted its rules of procedure and got off the ground.

The functions for the ANZUS Treaty focussed on the Presidio, which was the historical centre of San Francisco and the headquarters of the Spanish authorities. The Secretary of State, Dean Acheson, the Australian Ambassador, Percy Spender, and I met the various dignitaries and then went to the hall where the public was gathered.

The proceedings for signature, though simple, were dignified and indeed moving. The three of us spoke, I from the written text which my new colleague, Malcolm Templeton, who had just arrived from New Zealand, had arranged at my place so that it was easily readable. Then the Protocol Officer opened the copies of the treaty for signature.[2] Dean Acheson signed for the United States, and with him a considerable number of American politicians of both parties to provide a proper bipartisan approval to the epoch-making treaty. Spender and I alone signed for our countries.

After the signing ceremony, we attended a reception and later a three-nation celebratory dinner. I found myself in demand for radio and television broadcasts on national hookups. One of the TV programmes was with Senators Smith of New Jersey and Sparkman of Alabama. This then led onto a major session to discuss the prospects of the Japanese Peace Conference before its opening by President Truman.

The press were soon alerted to the fact that the Assistant Secretary of State, the able Dean Rusk, had asked me to gazump any Russian

2 Statement by Sir Carl Berendsen at the signing of the ANZUS Treaty, San Francisco, 1 September 1951. See Appendix and *New Zealand Foreign Policy: Statements and Documents 1943–57* (Wellington: Government Printer, 1972).

manoeuvre to stall the Japanese Peace Conference before the adoption of its rules of procedure. He wanted me to move the adoption of the rules of procedure at the very opening of business, before any Russian distraction. After some hesitation I agreed, mainly because the Americans pressed me, but partly because I could see what serious mischief the Soviet group could do in the absence of accepted rules. The Soviet spokesman, Gromyko, an unpleasant Pole named Wierblowski, and an unequally unpleasant Czech, Dr Sekaninova, all did their best to sow dissension and discord, and delay proceedings.

So it was arranged. Acheson was to start speaking, and as he would be brief, I was to stand almost immediately to indicate that I sought the floor. The problem was that I was in the middle of the row. By the time I got to the aisle I found myself brushing shoulders with Gromyko. Fortunately I brushed harder than he, and got to the platform first. He had no option but to wait while I moved my motion, which was immediately seconded.

What Gromyko wanted was to move for the admission of Red China. This Acheson ruled out of order. It was the New Zealand motion that was before the conference. No extraneous matter could be discussed until that motion had been disposed of, and the rules of procedure for the conference adopted. Gromyko protested vigorously and so did Wierblowski and Sekaninova. There was a considerable scene, with shouts and objurations. Acheson was polite but icy. Over and over again he repeated: 'The gentleman is out of order'. This demonstration carried on for half an hour or more, but got no further. The draft rules were adopted and these provided that only countries that had fought against the Japanese might be represented.

It was here at San Francisco, that I saw Dean Acheson, whom by this stage I had got to know well, develop as an American statesman. He was elected Chair of the conference, and Spender was elected Vice Chairman. I never saw Acheson, whom I admired, at better advantage than at that conference, quietly checkmating every Soviet move to disrupt the proceedings or the timetable, never raising his voice, never departing from the strictest politeness, but never giving way on the essentials of order and decorum. The Communists tried to prevent agreement but they failed.

Gromyko was a dour, stolid and unsmiling man. He had already made a reputation at the United Nations, where in the Security Council he had exercised the veto some fifty times. So frequently had he taken to leaving a meeting in disgust and contempt, whenever something was adopted of which he disapproved, that this form of protest had become known as 'doing a Gromyko'.

In one sense we were not disappointed. On the announcement at San Francisco of one more in a long series of Soviet defeats by some forty votes to the Soviet bloc three, he rose and, without a flicker on his gloomy and savage countenance, stalked solemnly from the room. All his Soviet colleagues and his bodyguard then rose and followed him, each putting on their own personal exhibition of outraged insult. Each marched majestically down the long corridor to the entrance and disappeared. The Pole then woke to what he thought was afoot. He rose and beckoned to his staff, and the Polish contingent followed its masters. The Czech representative also gathered her papers and colleagues, and tripped out with a face like a thunderous martyr.

What a sensation: for the delegates, the spectators, and above all the press. Reporters crowded in on Gromyko and his guards. Flash bulbs went off like a battery of guns. There was a stirring and a humming like a hive of bees. Gromyko had not, however, left the meeting to state an objection. He had left for personal reasons. Within the minutes that required, he had swept back into the hall, to the discomfiture of Sekaninova, whose assistance was not what he had required.

All this was important, because for the first time it had been possible to arrange for all of the transactions of the conference to be broadcast on television throughout the United States. The new medium brought all sorts of new problems to international conferences. It was a matter of real moment to make one's appearance, and one's remarks, as effective as possible, for one was always, on the rostrum, and possibly at other times, in a pitiless spotlight.

This necessity disturbed some, and exhilarated others. I confess that I was one of the latter. When I spoke from the rostrum I chose my time knowing that Eastern time was three hours ahead of San Francisco. My audience, officially, was some fifty million, of whom twenty million were actually looking at a television screen, and the other thirty million listening on radio. The potentiality of this new medium, and its impact for good and ill on orderly government, gave pause for thought.

Delegates at the Peace Conference for the first time had to confront a portable transmitter, which enabled the reporter to catch his victim wherever he chose.

One morning Foster Dulles came up to talk to me and I heard Mr Winters behind me: 'Good morning Mr Dulles; good morning Sir Carl – you're on television throughout the United States.' 'Dear me!' ejaculated Mr Dulles. 'The hell I am!' I exploded. Such are the pitfalls of the march of science.

My service at this conference was the most widely publicised in all my forty-six-year career. Everywhere I went people stopped me and told of their recognition and appreciation, even to the extent of my being embraced once in public by a young woman. Nellie was not amused.

My main speech at the San Francisco Peace Conference was certainly the most widely publicised and approved of all the hundreds I have made.[3] I had discussed it with my colleagues in Washington, particularly with Frank Corner, and had included many of his suggestions.

I did speak firmly and with conviction, and with complete honesty. I believe it is this latter quality that gained me public appreciation and public confidence. I told the Russians what I thought of their conduct. I then told the Japanese what I thought of theirs. But I also told them what I hoped from Japan in the future – with trust, I stressed, rather than complete confidence.

Of course it was no new thing to address great gatherings, with millions more listening in. I had learned some of the tricks of a trade of what is at bottom a meretricious art. But one never knew. Long years of experience could not predict what would hit the public's fancy. My very best speech, in my opinion, in the full glare of the United Nations spotlights, radio, television and the press, met with no public comment or approbation. But at the Japanese Peace Conference I rang a very loud bell, which resounded throughout the radio and television and press and all over the United States.

In the usual way we had prepared a small number of copies of the address to the Peace Conference. But it became incredibly popular, and we had to bring out edition after edition to satisfy the demand. I received

3 'Japanese Peace Treaty', Statement by Sir Carl Berendsen at the San Francisco Conference, 6 September 1951. See Appendix and *New Zealand Foreign Policy: Statements and Documents 1943–57* (Wellington: Government Printer, 1972).

complimentary comments from Europe, Africa, Asia and America. In my own country the response was friendly and appreciative. But in San Francisco the editorials about this 'colourful, brilliant statesman' made me blush.

So the conference talked itself successfully to its close. The large Japanese Delegation led by Prime Minister Yoshida, even if uncomfortable and out of their element, had sat listening silently but keenly to the proceedings. They were so calm, restrained and enigmatic, I found it difficult to calculate their reactions or assess what they might do. In the event, however, the draft Treaty was acceptable to the Japanese. Nor were the prospects ruined, as they might have hoped, by the absence in the latter stages of the Soviet group. The Indians too were absent. They had decided to make their own peace.

The Treaty was signed in a formal and glittering ceremony. For me it meant a startling degree of recognition and appreciation when I came alone, as I alone had full powers, to sign. On my long walk to the front of the hall and up the steps to the dais – and indeed until long after I had finished signing and returned to my seat – I received the greatest ovation I have ever experienced in my life: indeed it was something that does not usually occur in a lifetime.

I claim no personal credit for this. It was a mark of the esteem in San Francisco, and in the United States, for the part played by New Zealand. My satisfaction, and it was deep but modest, was that I had worthily and adequately represented the views and policies of my country so that no one could misunderstand them.

The Japanese Peace Conference and the signing of the Peace Treaty was in fact the last important act of my official life. There could have been no more gratifying conclusion.

ENVOI

So Nellie and I returned to Washington and the end of our long Ambassadorial road. In the capital we fell into a ceaseless round of work. Its burdens were broken by the charm, for Commonwealth representatives, of the visit of Princess Elizabeth and the Duke of Edinburgh.

The visit too of Winston Churchill stood out both for his presence and his oratory. The speech of this, for me, the greatest of orators, to the United States Congress was impressive enough, but at the National Press Club, where he had more freedom for those brilliant asides and *obiter dicta* for which he was famous, he excelled himself. His handling of the Irish issue had a humour that had even his bitter Irish questioners laughing with the crowd. 'My advice to the well wishers of Ireland is that they should woo Ulster, and not rape Ulster.'

The high mark of Churchill's oratory on this visit was at a most moving ceremony where he was inducted into the Order of the Cincinnati, a select organisation of the eldest sons of families whose ancestors had fought as officers against Britain in the War of Independence. Churchill qualified through his mother Jenny Jerome. On this stage Churchill did not fail to expound the lessons he had learned on the mutability of human affairs. So too he emphasised the true association and friendship, despite the quarrels and wars of the past, that had grown up between the British and American peoples.

In sonority, in spontaneity, and in imagery, Churchill's was a masterly and majestic effort, rich and impressive in tone, and impeccable and unerring in the choice of words. Never again may we hear language equal to Churchill's. In our time, and perhaps for all time, he was incomparable: an heroic war leader, a wise and judicious statesman, an historian of world reputation, a painter of repute and even a builder . . . with his brick laying. No man in history can have done more for liberty and decency in human affairs. Certainly no one has done more to strengthen the ties of understanding and collaboration that join the English-speaking peoples together.

Churchill stood in marked contrast to my experience of Clement

Attlee. No doubt well meaning, Attlee had no idea how to deal with the American people, and worse, the American press. His attitude was close to condescension. He would take the trouble to tell the Americans where their policies – that others saw as justified by the event and the situation – were wrong. So the Americans smiled at Attlee while they listened in admiration to the large-minded Churchill, firm as granite.

So we made our final formal calls, the first on my old friend and colleague, Secretary of State Dean Acheson. The other was of course on President Truman. He moved us greatly by asking Mrs Truman to share in our 'family' ceremony in the Presidential office, where the President made little gifts of remembrance to the two of us.

Once we left the Embassy, Nellie and I never looked back. We had had a wonderful, exhilarating and amazing official life. From simplicity and poverty we had come to mix with kings and queens and presidents, with lords and ladies, and of course ambassadors.

Knighted at home, and recognised abroad, we had in the work of a lifetime done some service to our magnificent country. The comment on that service that I treasure most was that of the *Washington Post* on my retirement:

> With seventy-four chiefs of foreign Missions established in Washington, their comings and goings for the most part pass unnoticed, but the approaching retirement of New Zealand's Ambassador, Sir Carl Berendsen, deserves attention.
>
> Sir Carl has been here for more than seven years. In that time he and Lady Berendsen, a good wife and a perfect partner, have made a host of friends for themselves and for New Zealand.
>
> Sir Carl has the convictions which square with the ideals of our own society, and he expresses them in private and in public with a saltiness and sincerity, which arrest and persuade.
>
> He had a personal success at the San Francisco Conference on the Treaty with Japan. There was a Lincolnesque directness and simplicity about his speech which made the Opera House a ringing Hall of Liberty.
>
> Sir Carl Berendsen will be missed both here and in the Assembly of the United Nations, but he will have the satisfaction of knowing that in the opinion of his American friends, he has fought the good fight.

Berendsen was often approached at the United Nations by people who knew, or professed to know, him and he developed a series of responses enabling him to cope with either possibility.

'Oh! Oh! How nice to see you!'

'And, and how's your husband?'

'And those lovely children?'

'Well goodbye now. Come and see me anytime.'

And (to his staff, in the appropriate circumstance):

'Who the bloody hell was that?'

He was once approached in the UN dining room by an earnest New Zealander bursting with enthusiasm over a meeting of UNESCO and eager to tell him all about it.

Berendsen cut him short before he could get far.

'I've got three things to say to you,' he said. 'First, I'm having my lunch! Second, UNESCO and all those other alphabetical conglomerations are not worth a tin of fish! And, third, you ought to be in a lunatic asylum!'

Charles Craw

LIST OF CHARACTERS

DNZB = *Dictionary of New Zealand Biography* (Auckland: Auckland University Press) Volume One, 1769–1869 (1990); Volume Two, 1870–1900 (1993); Volume Three, 1901–1920 (1996); Volume Four, 1921–1940 (1998); Volume Five, 1941–1960 (2000)

Dean Acheson 1893–1971
Distinguished and eloquent American lawyer and statesman; Secretary of State 1949–53 in President Truman's elected second term. Author of *Present at The Creation: My Years at the State Department* (New York: W.W. Norton Inc., 1969).

Rashid Ali al-Gaylani 1892–1965
Descendant of a Muslim saint and one-time Prime Minister of Iraq. With the break up of the Turkish Empire, Iraq had become a British mandate 1919–32. Unrest, intrigue and violence remained endemic until World War II. Prime Minister Nuri al-Said then sided with Britain. In the spring of 1941 Rashid Ali led an army coup d'etat sympathetic to Germany. Britain sent forces from Syria to Bagdad, and also to Basra, to protect its position and the vital oil fields.

Colonel Stephen Allen 1882–1964
Born in England. Cambridge graduate in Arts and Law. Came to New Zealand in 1892, distinguished war record in World War I and World War II. Known to Coates in both military and political spheres. Coates asked him to succeed Richardson in Samoa. (*DNZB* Vol. 4, p.9)

Leo S. Amery 1873–1955
Influential British MP 1911–45. Assistant Secretary of War Cabinet 1917, Under Secretary 1919–22, First Lord Admiralty 1922–24, Secretary of State for the Colonies and Dominions 1924–29 (when he visited New Zealand), and for India and Burma 1940–45. Author of *Thoughts on the Constitution* (London & New York: Oxford University Press, 1948), and *My Political Life* (London: Hutchinson & Co Ltd, 1955).

Marian Anderson 1902–1993
Famous American contralto who, with Eleanor Roosevelt's help, broke a long tradition of racial discrimination in the arts; delegate to the United Nations in 1958. Author of *My Lord, What a Morning* (New York: Viking Press, 1956).

Oswaldo Aranha 1894–1960
Brazilian Foreign Minister during World War II. President of First Special Session of United Nations General Assembly (Question of Palestine) April 1947; President of Second Regular United Nations General Assembly 1947.

Admiral Georges d'Argenlieu (Louis de la Trinité) 1889–1964
One of the leading Free French figures. A naval officer, of a family of Breton naval officers, he served in World War I, and post-war joined the Carmelite Order, rising to be Superior of Paris. Mobilised into the Navy in 1939, he was captured defending Cherbourg. He escaped to join de Gaulle, was given dispensation due to the shortage of naval officers, and made chief of staff in July. He served at the battle of Dakar and in Gabon; was sent as de Gaulle's troubleshooter to the Pacific; and in 1943 became commander of the naval forces in Britain, ferrying de Gaulle to France on 14 June 1945 and entering Paris with him. After the defeat of Japan he served in Indochina until 1947, then as Inspector General of Naval Forces, before retiring to a convent.

Dr Val Armstrong 1913–1994
Notable chemical engineer. Served 1942–45 as Manager of New Zealand Munitions Factory. Post-war he served as Head of the New Zealand Scientific Liaison Office at NZ House, London. His son Wade Armstrong is a senior serving New Zealand Foreign Service officer.

Morris Asher 1818–1909
Father of Philip Asher and Grandfather of Oswald Asher and Carl Berendsen, Morris Asher was born in London, emigrated to Sydney 1839 and then to Wellington, where he opened a store, fitting up whaling stations in Cook Strait, and importing sheep and merchandise from New South Wales. In 1846 he returned to New South Wales, building hotels, a store, a flour mill and a rendering works. He served briefly in the New South Wales Legislative Assembly as Member for Hume, June 1859–November 1860.

H.H. Asquith 1852–1928
Distinguished British lawyer, Liberal MP and Home Secretary 1892, Chancellor of the Exchequer 1905–08. Long serving and significant Liberal Prime Minister 1909–16. Author of *Memories and Reflections 1852–1927* (Boston: Little, Brown & Co., 1928).

Nancy Astor 1879–1964
Anglo-American wife of Waldorf Astor. When he became Lord Astor of

Cliveden, she took his seat, becoming the first woman in the House of Commons (1919–45). Champion of women's rights and social reform, and influential hostess of 'the Cliveden set'. Author of *My Two Countries* (London: William Heineman, 1923). William Waldorf (1907–66), her son, was Principal Private Secretary to Samuel Hoare 1936–37. John Jacob Astor, Waldorf's brother, was influential Chairman of *The Times* during the long 'appeasement' editorship 1923–41 of Geoffrey Dawson (1874–1944).

Clement Attlee 1883–1967
Eminent British Labour MP and Minister, Leader of the Opposition 1935; Member of the War Cabinet; Minister of Dominion Affairs and Deputy Prime Minister 1942–45; Prime Minister 1945–51.

Stanley Baldwin 1867–1947
Notable British Conservative Prime Minister 1922–24, 1924–30, and 1935–37. As Lord President of the Council, led the British delegation to the Imperial Economic Conference in Ottawa 1932. A great career ending in the failures of the Hoare–Laval Pact, the Abdication, and delays in rearmament.

Arthur Balfour 1848–1930
Long-serving British Conservative politician, present at the Congress of Berlin with Disraeli and the 3rd Marquess of Salisbury. Succeeded Salisbury (his uncle) as Conservative Prime Minister 1902–05. In 1915 he became First Lord of the Admiralty in the first British wartime Coalition Cabinet. In 1916 he became Foreign Secretary, and was responsible for the Balfour Declaration, which promised a Jewish national home in Palestine. One of four members of Prime Minister Lloyd George's War Cabinet and his second-in-command at the Versailles Peace Conference. As Lord President of the Council he was responsible for the Second Balfour Declaration confirming the independence of the members of the British Commonwealth.

General Sir Harold Barrowclough 1894–1972
One of New Zealand's outstanding citizen soldiers, he served in the Rifle Brigade and led the storming of Le Quesnoy in World War I. After the war he served in the Territorial Army. He was a World War II senior officer in Greece and the Western Desert, and Commander of the Pacific section of the Second New Zealand Expeditionary Force. He was Chief Justice 1953–66, when New Zealand established its Court of Appeal. (*DNZB* Vol. 5, p. 37)

Bernard Baruch 1870–1965
United States financier and statesman, famous as adviser to presidents, and to Winston Churchill.

Francis Henry Dillon Bell 1851–1936
Lawyer and leader of the Legislative Council 1912; Attorney General responsible for the Western Samoa Mandate legislation 1919; briefly Prime Minister 1925; Attorney General and Minister of External Affairs 1925–28. (*DNZB* Vol. 2)

Ian Berendsen 1919–
Elder son of Carl and Nellie. Rhodes Scholar 1939; Captain in the Second New Zealand Expeditionary Force in the South Pacific and Italy; was part of the United Nations Secretariat as Political Affairs Officer in the Trusteeship Division; Chief Ed Control 1969–79.

Keith Berendsen 1921–1997
Younger son of Carl and Nellie. Influenced by his infantile poliomyelitis, Keith became a doctor and medical administrator. As Medical Superintendent-in-Chief of the notable teaching hospital of the Otago Medical School, Keith oversaw a model redevelopment of the Dunedin Hospital Ward Block, the Geriatric Assessment Unit, Psycho-Geriatric Services, a Paediatric Hospital, and a Hospital Ethics Committee. The career of this 'principled, kind and gentle man' in face of challenging and rapid changes in public health was, his hospital board chairperson, Dame Dorothy Fraser reflected in her valedictory speech, one of 'wise and unstinting service'.

James Bertram 1910–1993
Distinguished New Zealand Rhodes Scholar 1932–35. Newspaper correspondent and relief worker in China 1937–40; employee of British Ministry of Information (Far East) 1940–41; soldier in Hong Kong Defence Force and prisoner-of-war in Japan 1941–45; part of New Zealand delegation to Far Eastern Commission 1946; Department of English Professor at Victoria University of Wellington 1947–76; Emeritus Professor; Visiting Fellow at Balliol College 1968. Author of *Crisis in China* (London: Macmillan, 1937), *North China Front* (London: Macmillan, 1939), *The Shadow of a War* (Australia: Whitcombe & Tombs, 1947), *Rip Tide in the Pacific* (Auckland University Labour Club, 1948), *Return to China* (London: Heinemann, 1957), *Occasional Verses* (Wellington: Wai-te-Ata Press, 1971), *The Letters of Thomas Arnold the Younger (1850–1900)* (Auckland: Auckland University

Press & Oxford University Press, 1980), *Charles Brasch* (Wellington: Oxford University Press, 1976), and a brilliant autobiography, *Capes of China Slide Away* (Auckland: Auckland University Press, 1993).

William Watson Bird

Born Hants, England. Otago University Honours graduate 1893. Senior Inspector for Schools, licensed interpreter, and headmaster. Adviser on education for Cook Islands from 1913 and then Samoa from 1921.

Lord Birkenhead (F.E. Smith) 1872–1930

Notable Conservative politician: Attorney General 1915–18, Lord Chancellor 1919–22, Secretary for India 1924–28. A brilliant barrister and orator, reckoned the finest after-dinner speaker known. Prolific author, viz *Toryism until 1832; Speeches 1906–09* (1910), *Famous Trials of History* (1927), *Fifty Famous Fights in Fact and Fiction* (London: Cassell & Co., 1938), *Law, Life and Letters* (Hodder & Stoughton, 1927), *Turning Points in History* (Ayer Publishing, 1930). See *Who Was Who: Volume III, 1929–40* (London: A&C Black, 1967).

Charles Boswell 1886–1956

Schoolteacher and Labour MP. Minister to Moscow 1943–49. See M.J.C. Templeton, *Top Hats Are Not Being Taken* (Wellington: New Zealand Institute of International Affairs, 1989).

Stanley Melbourne Bruce 1883–1967

Decorated Anzac in World War I. Federal MP 1918, and Treasurer in Hughes's National Government in 1919. Attended League of Nations and Imperial Conference as Coalition Prime Minister and Australian Minister of External Affairs 1923–29. Defeated by J.H. Scullin who then served as Prime Minister 1929–32. Bruce was appointed High Commissioner in London by the Lyons Government 1933–45. First Chancellor of the Australian National University 1951–56.

James Byrnes 1879–1972

Lawyer, member of the House of Representatives 1911–25, Senator for South Carolina 1931–41, Associate United States Supreme Court 1941–42, Director for Economic Stabilisation 1942–43 and Mobilisation 1943–45, Secretary of State 1945–47, and Governor of South Carolina 1951–55.

Dr R.M. Campbell 1897–1974
A Waipu Scot and distinguished civil servant with a doctorate in economics. From 1926 he became a principal adviser to Coates and successive governments. Served in Wellington and London (twice) and at international conferences, retiring as Acting High Commissioner in London 1958. (*DNZB* Vol. 5, p. 91)

R.G. Casey 1890–1976
Son of a wealthy mining magnate. World War I soldier. Casey served Australia in London in the 1920s, in federal politics as Treasurer in the Lyons Government 1935–39, as Australian Ambassador to Washington 1940–42, as member of the British War Cabinet and Churchill's Minister of State in the Middle East 1942–43, as Governor of Bengal 1943–46, as Minister for Supply 1950 and as Minister of External Affairs 1951–60. The first Australian-born Governor General 1965–69.

The Cecils
Aristocratic British family descended from Lord Burghley, chief adviser to the great Queen Elizabeth I, and his son Robert Cecil, the Earl of Salisbury (1563–1612) chief adviser to James I. Robert Cecil, third Marquis of Salisbury (1830–1903) was Foreign Minister under Disraeli and then Conservative Prime Minister 1886–93 and 1895–1902. His son, James Edward Hubert Cecil, fourth Marquess of Salisbury (1861–1947) was President of the Board of Trade 1902, Lord President of the Council 1922–24 and Leader of the House of Lords 1925–29. His younger son Edward Algernon Robert Cecil, Viscount Cecil of Chelwood, was Lord Privy Seal 1923–34; Chancellor of the Duchy of Lancaster 1924–27; and importantly, as President of the League of Nations Association 1923–45 and Life President of the UNA, winner of the Nobel Peace Prize. His grandson Lord Cranborne, to whom Berendsen refers, was a Conservative Minister, Secretary of State for the Dominions 1940–42 and 1943–45, and later the fifth Marquess of Salisbury, and author of *The Way of Peace* (London: Philip Allan, 1928).

Austen Chamberlain 1863–1937
Son of Joseph Chamberlain, of the great Liberal Unionist Birmingham political dynasty, and half brother of Neville Chamberlain. Unionist MP. Chancellor of the Exchequer 1903–06 and 1919–21; Foreign Secretary 1923–29, at the time of the Locarno Pact and Statute of Westminster. Won the Nobel Peace Prize in 1926. Author of *Peace In Our Time: Addresses on Europe and the Empire* (London: Allan, 1928). See *Who Was Who: Volume III* (London: A&C Black, 1967).

Neville Chamberlain 1869–1940
Half brother of Austen Chamberlain. Long-serving British Conservative MP and Minister. His career as Prime Minister 1937–40 failed at time of appeasement, the Munich Agreement and the countdown to World War II. See *Who Was Who: Volume III* (London: A&C Black, 1967).

The Clarendons
Another aristocratic British family with long service to the State. Descended from Edward Hyde, First Earl of Clarendon (1609–1674), Chancellor of the Exchequer to Charles I and principal adviser of Charles II in exile, and Lord Chancellor 1658–1667. Berendsen's reference is to George Herbert Hyde Villiers, Sixth Earl of Clarendon (1877–1955), Under-Secretary for Dominion Affairs 1922–25, Chairman of the British Broadcasting Corporation 1927–31 and Governor General of South Africa 1931–37.

Joseph Gordon Coates 1878–1943
Farmer and soldier; MP for Kaipara 1911–43; inter alia Minister of Justice, Public Works and Native Affairs 1919–25; Prime Minister 1925–28, 1931; Minister of Public Works and Transport 1931–35; Minister of Finance 1933–35; Minister in the War Cabinet 1940–43. See Michael Bassett, *Coates of Kaipara* (Auckland: Auckland University Press, 1995). (*DNZB* Vol. 3, p. 104)

G.D.H. Cole 1889–1958
Economist and historian of Fabian Society and British working classes. He often worked with his wife Margaret Postgate and her brother Raymond Postgate, though it was he who signed the article in the *New Statesman* detailing 'American plans for world conquest that began with the "invasion" of North Korea'. Later became Chichele Professor of Social and Economic Theory at Oxford. Author of *The Life of William Cobbett* (New York: Harcourt, 1924), and *Life of Robert Owen* (London: Ernest Benn Ltd, 1925).

Senator Tom Connally 1877–1963
Democratic Representative 1917–29 and Senator 1928–52 who, as Chair of Senate Foreign Relations Committee, was involved at San Francisco in the formation of the United Nations and its first two Assemblies in London and New York.

Frank Henry Corner 1920–
Formidable and highly regarded founding New Zealand Foreign Service officer 1943–80; Counsellor, London 1954–57; Deputy Secretary of Foreign

Affairs 1957–62; Permanent Representative to the United Nations 1962–67; Ambassador to the United States 1967–72; Secretary of Foreign Affairs 1973–80. Author of 'New Zealand and the South Pacific' in T.C. Larkin (ed.) *New Zealand's External Relations* (London: New Zealand Institute of Public Administration, Oxford University Press, 1963), and 'The Trusteeship Council' in Prof. Peter Munz (ed.) *The Feel of Truth* (Wellington: A.W. & A.H. Reed, 1969). See M.J.C. Templeton (ed.) *An Eye, an Ear, and a Voice: Fifty Years in New Zealand's External Relations 1943–1993* (Wellington: Ministry of Foreign Affairs and Trade, 1993).

H.H. Cornish 1887–1952
Eminent New Zealand jurist and judge; Professor of Law at Victoria University of Wellington 1930–34; Solicitor General 1934–45. Cornish drafted Savage's iconic broadcast declaration of war against Germany on 3 September 1939: 'Where Britain goes, we go'.

Dr George Craig 1873–1947
Civil servant who, like Berendsen, took an LLM, and rose through the ranks to the prestigious post of Comptroller of Customs in 1928.

Lord Cranborne, Fifth Marquess of Salisbury 1893–1972
The elder son of the Fourth Marquess of Salisbury, Robert Arthur James Gascoigne-Cecil. Conservative Under Secretary of State for Foreign Affairs 1935–40; Secretary of State for the Dominions 1940–42 and 1943–45; Leader of Lords 1942–45 and 1951–57; Secretary of Commonwealth Relations 1952; and Lord President of the Council 1952–57. His younger brother Lord David Cecil was a notable Professor of English and author of many books, including *The Young Melbourne* (Constable & Co., 1939) and *The Cecils of Hatfield House* (Constable & Co., 1973).

Charles Craw 1918–1994
Entered External Affairs in 1946 after war service – often in situations of great risk which he would never discuss – with the Fleet Air Arm. A most talented man, he trained as an historian at Otago University. He was equipped with a vast store of reading, experience, reminiscence and incident, with a sharp eye for telling debate, and with an ear that was always sensitive to the nuances, and especially the oddities of what was being said around him. He worked for a long time at the United Nations under Berendsen, particularly in Trusteeship and related issues. Those years called for special qualities – competence, a cool head, courage and commonsense – all of which he had in large measure. He had

an abiding distaste for the pompous and overstuffed, and for all the eminence that he attained – Charge d'Affairs in Thailand, Deputy High Commissioner in London, Ambassador to France and to the United Nations – he remained unpretentious in what he said. Regrettably there is little on public record to show his abilities. But for those who knew him, he is clearly remembered for his dark, glossy good looks, his easy talk, and his bright mind. (Tom Larkin)

Admiral Andrew Cunningham 1883–1963
Vice Admiral of the battlecruiser squadron 1937–38; Commander in Chief Mediterranean 1939–42. Led battles in Taranto and the Ionian Sea. Commander in Chief North Africa 1942; Allied Commander in Chief for Operation Overlord; First Sea Lord and Chief of Naval Staff 1943–46. His brother, General Alan Cunningham, commanded British forces that defeated Italian forces in Ethiopia and Libya 1941.

Rex (R.R.) Cunninghame 1918–2004
Distinguished first generation officer in New Zealand Department of External Affairs. Attended Wellington College with Ian Berendsen; the two sailed in 1939 to Britain, Berendsen as a Rhodes Scholar, Cunninghame as a Post Graduate scholar to Merton. There, joining the navy as a rating, he was asked to train as a Japanese language specialist. He served as a lieutenant in the Pacific, the second New Zealander into Japan after the surrender. Meeting him in Japan, Sir Carl suggested he join External Affairs. He served in Tokyo 1955–59, as Deputy High Commissioner in Ottawa 1961–65, and Minister to The Hague 1965–67.

John Curtin 1885–1945
Leader of the Labour Party and fourteenth Prime Minister of Australia during the darkest days of World War II.

Sir Cecil Day 1884–1963
English born, came to New Zealand as secretary to Governor General Islington 1910–12, stayed on as Official Secretary at Government House, Wellington, 1912–36, and then as Official Secretary at NZ House, London, responsible for liaison with the Foreign Office.

Governor Thomas Dewey 1902–1971
Republican Presidential candidate 1944 and 1948, a United States lawyer who had made his name as special prosecutor and attorney in New York 1935–38 and Governor of New York 1942–54. As Berendsen notes, he was almost

unanimously expected to win the 1948 election. One lifelong Republican was to explain: 'In the polling booth, I just couldn't vote for the little man on the wedding cake.'

Frederick Doidge 1884–1954

Australian-born, talented New Zealand journalist who made his career in Britain with Lord Beaverbrook, the famous Canadian-born press lord of the *Daily Express*. Doidge was responsible for recruiting David Low and Arnold Bennett, organising the Empire Free Trade Crusade, and earning status as 'the man who got the million readers'. Returning home in 1935 he became an MP 1938–51, and Minister of External Affairs 1949–51 during the signing of the Japanese and ANZUS Treaties, the Korean War and the Colombo Plan. High Commissioner in London 1951–54. (*DNZB* Vol. 5, p. 148)

Eric Drummond, Lord Perth 1876–1951

Entered the Foreign Office in 1900, serving as Private Secretary to Asquith 1912–15 and Balfour 1915–19. First Secretary General of the League of Nations 1919–33. France supplied the Deputy Secretary General, M. Avenol.

John Foster Dulles 1888–1959

President Eisenhower's powerful United States Secretary of State from 1953 to 1959, at the height of the Cold War. As a young man he had attended The Hague and Versailles Conferences. A powerful advocate of a World Organisation, he participated in founding the United Nations and in default of an effective organisation, he became a notable proponent of regional pacts like SEATO and CENTO. Author of *War or Peace* (New York: Macmillan, 1950). See Richard Goold-Adams, *John Foster Dulles: A Reappraisal* (New York: Appleton-Century-Crofts, 1962).

Abba Eban 1915–2002

Notable and eloquent South African-born Israeli diplomat and politician; first Permanent Representative of Israel to the United Nations 1948; Ambassador in Washington 1950–59; Foreign Minister 1966–74. Author of *Personal Witness: Israel Through My Eyes* (New York: Putnam, 1992).

Anthony Eden 1897–1977

Served in World War I. Became a Conservative MP in 1923, and, in 1931, Under Secretary of Foreign Affairs. In 1935 he became Minister for the League of Nations; 1936–38 Foreign Secretary; 1939 Minister of Dominion Affairs; 1940–45 and 1951–55 Foreign Secretary; and 1955–57 Prime Minister. His distinguished career ended in the failure of Suez. Author of *Foreign Affairs* (London: Faber & Faber, 1939), and *Freedom and Order* (London: Faber & Faber, 1947).

General Dwight Eisenhower 1890–1969
Famous American Commander of Allied Forces in World War II, and 34th United States President at the height of the Cold War.

Eliyahu Elath 1903–1990
Zionist Representative in United States and first Israeli Ambassador to United States 1948–49. Ambassador to the United Kingdom 1955. President of the Hebrew University.

Dr Herbert Evatt 1894–1965
Distinguished Australian Attorney General, Minister of Foreign Affairs 1941–49 and Deputy Prime Minister 1946–49. Third President of the United Nations General Assembly 1947.

General James Van Fleet 1892–1992
Graduated from West Point in 1915 with Eisenhower, Bradley and Clark. His career suffered through a mistake in identity but took off late in Normandy when he became one of the top United States fighting commanders. He spent 1947–49 training and advising the Greek army in the bitter Greek Civil War. In 1951 he followed General Ridgeway, General McArthur's successor in Korea, as commander of United Nations forces in important battles in April and May 1951 that stabilised the front and led to the ceasefire. See Billy Mossman, *Ebb and Flow: November 1950–July 1951* (Washington DC: Center of Military History, US Army, 1990).

George Forbes 1869–1947
Liberal politician 1908–43 who followed Ward as Prime Minister 1930–35 during the Great Depression. Dubbed 'His Master's Voice' because of his reliance on Robert Masters MLC. (*DNZB* Vol. 3, p. 161)

Peter Fraser 1884–1950
Born Cromarty Scotland. Long-serving Labour MP from 1918, Deputy Prime Minister 1935–40 and Wartime Prime Minister 1940–50. Statesman of the United Nations Charter. See Michael Bassett, *Tomorrow Comes the Song: A Life of Peter Fraser* (Auckland: Penguin, 2001), and Margaret Clark (ed.), *Peter Fraser: Master Politician* (Palmerston North: Dunmore, 1998). For a

contemporary account, see James Thorn, *Peter Fraser* (London, 1952). (*DNZB* Vol. 4, p. 102)

Bernard Freyberg 1889–1963
New Zealand's greatest soldier. Commander of the Second New Zealand Expeditionary Force, and Governor General 1946–52. See Paul Freyberg, *Bernard Freyberg, V.C.: Soldier of Two Nations* (London: Hodder & Stoughton, 1991); W.G. Stevens, *Freyberg V.C.: The Man 1939–45* (Wellington: A.H. & A.W. Reed, 1965); and Laurie Barber & John Tonkin-Covell, *Freyberg: Churchill's Salamander* (London: Hutchinson, 1990). (*DNZB* Vol. 5, p. 177)

Senator J. William Fulbright 1905–1995
Rhodes Scholar, Representative 1942–44 and famous liberal Senator for Arkansas 1944–74. Made his name advocating creation of United Nations, in creating Fulbright Scholarships in 1946, and in opposing Senator McCarthy, and later the Vietnam War. Author of *The Arrogance of Power* (New York: Random House, 1966), and (with Donald R. Kelley and Hoyt Purvis) *Old Myths and New Realities in United States–Soviet Relations* (New York: Praeger, 1990). See Eugene Brown, *J. William Fulbright: Advice and Dissent* (Iowa City: University of Iowa Press, 1985).

General Charles de Gaulle 1890–1970
The charismatic, iron-willed, clear-minded, eloquent leader who after the Fall of France in 1940 set up a Government in exile in London. 'The flame of French resistance must not die.' Despite 'une nation prostree et stupefaite, sans foi and sans espoir' he led the Free French in the fight back against Nazi Germany to march in August 1944 into Paris with a French Army and form a Provisional Government and the Fourth Republic. He served subsequently as President and Constitution maker at various times until his death. One of the great men of history, as a latter day Jeanne d'Arc, de Gaulle claimed the leadership not in the name of France, but as France, as the embodiment of France: 'c'etait a moi d'assumer la France!'

Admiral Robert Lee Ghormley 1883–1958
Commander South Pacific Area and Force June–October 1942 during the critical early stages of the Guadalcanal campaign.

Air Marshall Sir Victor Goddard 1897–1987
British airman. Royal New Zealand Air Force Chief of Air Staff and

Commander South Pacific 1941–43. Author of *Skies to Dunkirk: A Personal Memoir* (London: William Kimber, 1982).

Edward Grey 1863–1933
British Foreign Secretary 1905–16 in the Liberal Government of Prime Minister Herbert Asquith at the outbreak of World War I, who in 1914, having failed to hinder the outbreak of the Great War, presciently intoned 'The lights are going out all over Europe.' See G.M. Trevelyan Grey of Falloden, *Twenty Five Years 1892–1916* (New York: Frederick A. Stokes Co., 1925).

Andrei Gromyko 1909–1989
Dour Cold War warrior; Soviet Ambassador to Washington 1943; Permanent Representative at the United Nations; Foreign Minister 1957–85, until the era of Gorbachev and Perestroika.

Fiorello La Guardia 1882–1947
Lawyer who served in the United States House of Representatives 1917–21 and 1923–33. He became so famous as the dynamic Mayor of New York 1934–45 as to inspire a musical, *Fiorello!*. Chief of United States Office of Civilian Defence 1941–42.

Fleet Admiral William Halsey 1882–1959
Admiral in command of the United States Third Fleet during much of the Pacific War. With much experience in naval aviation and aircraft carriers, he was at sea in the USS *Enterprise* during the attack on Pearl Harbour. He replaced Ghormley mid-October 1942 in the critical stages of the Guadalcanal campaign. He then led the Third Fleet for the rest of the war, taking the Japanese surrender on its flagship, USS *Missouri*, on 2 September 1945.

Adam Hamilton 1880–1952
Southland farmer and businessman. MP for Wallace 1919–22 and 1925–46. Minister of Internal Affairs, Postmaster General 1931–35; Leader of National Opposition 1936–40 and Opposition member of various War Cabinets 1940–45, with Gordon Coates until 1943. (*DNZB* Vol. 4, p. 218)

Dag Hammarskjöld 1905–1961
Brilliant Swedish civil servant, chairman of the Bank of Sweden, and Foreign Minister 1951–53. Second Secretary General of the United Nations 1952–61. 'A secular Pope' – one of the great thinkers and men of action of the twentieth century.' See Dag Hammarskjöld (translated by Leif Sjoberg and W.H.

Auden), *Markings* (London: Faber & Faber, 1964); Wilder Foote (ed.), *Dag Hammarskjöld: Servant of Peace: A Selection of Speeches and Statements* (New York: Harper & Row, 1963); and Joseph Lash, *Dag Hammarskjöld: Custodian of the Brushfire Peace* (New York: Doubleday, 1961).

General Herbert Hart 1882–1968
A lawyer, and another of the distinguished First New Zealand Expeditionary Force citizen soldiers who at brigade level helped make the name of the New Zealand Division in Gallipoli and France. From 1931 to 1935 he served as Administrator of Western Samoa and 1936 to 1943 as Deputy Controller of the Imperial War Graves Commission. (*DNZB* Vol. 3, p. 201)

J.B.M. Hertzog 1866–1942
Afrikaner General and Prime Minister of South Africa 1924–39. His sympathies for Germany allowed the Imperial icon Field Marshall Smuts to take over and lead South Africa into World War II.

Sidney Hillman: 'Sidney the Kingmaker' (1887–1946)
Franklin D. Roosevelt laid down the rules on the momentous 1944 selection for Vice President among the Democratic contenders Wallace, Byrnes and (not by his wish) Truman: the Democrat bosses were to 'clear it with Sidney', a Lithuanian-born American who had founded the Amalgamated Clothing Workers Union of America. Wallace was unacceptable to FDR, but so was Byrnes to organised Labour. So Truman came through the middle. See David McCullough's great biography *Truman* (New York: Simon & Schuster, 1992).

Alger Hiss 1904–1966
United States State Department officer; adviser at Dumbarton Oaks and Yalta Conferences; and President of the Carnegie Endowment for Peace 1946–49. Was tried and convicted in controversial trials for allegedly passing secret documents to Whittaker Chambers, an agent for an international communist spy ring. See Whittaker Chambers, *Witness* (New York: Random House, 1952).

Colonel William Hodgson 1892–1958
Secretary of Australian Department of External Affairs 1939–45; High Commissioner to Canada 1945–48; Ambassador to France 1949–50; Australian Mission to Japan 1949–52; High Commissioner to South Africa 1952–57.

H.E. 'Harry' Holland 1868–1933
Socialist journalist, orator and author who came to New Zealand from Australia in 1913 at the time of the Waihi Strike. Labour MP from 1918 and leader of the New Zealand Labour Party 1919–33. See P.J. O'Farrell, *Harry Holland, militant socialist* (Canberra: Australian National University, 1964). (*DNZB* Vol. 3, p. 227)

Sidney George Holland 1893–1961
Became an MP in 1935 and Leader of the National Opposition in 1940. Fourth New Zealand-born Prime Minister 1949–57, at the time of the signing of the ANZUS Treaty 1951. (*DNZB* Vol. 5, p. 229)

William 'Billy' Hughes 1864–1952
Founder Federal MP 1901; Minister 1904, 1908–09, and 1911–13; Prime Minister of Australia 1915–1923. Variously Minister of the Crown 1934–35, 1937–38, External Affairs 1939–40, Attorney General 1940–41, Navy 1941–44. See F.C. Browne, *They Called Him Billy* (Sydney: Peter Huston, 1946).

Cordell Hull 1871–1955
Senator and Roosevelt's long serving American Secretary of State in the lead-up to and during World War II 1933–44; won the Nobel Peace Prize in 1946.

Senator Hubert Humphrey 1911–78
Mayor of Minneapolis 1945. Liberal and eloquent United States Democratic Senator for Minnesota 1948–64. Vice President to Lyndon Johnson 1964–68. Democratic Presidential nominee in 1968, defeated by President Nixon.

Thomas A. Hunter 1863–1958
Born in England and trained at University of Otago (First in Philosophy). Rugby player, inspirational teacher and administrator. First Vice Chancellor of the University of New Zealand 1929–47; Principal of Victoria University College 1938–51. Had close links with H.E. Holland and Peter Fraser. (*DNZB* Vol. 3, p. 243)

Ambassador Patrick Jay Hurley 1883–1963
United States Secretary of War 1929–33; United States Minister to New Zealand February 1942–March 1943; United States Ambassador to China 1944–45.

Thomas Inskip (later Lord Caldecote) 1876–1947
Conservative politician and law minister, notably as British Attorney General. Baldwin gave him a place in history by his remarkable appointment – 'one of the most extraordinary since Caligula appointed his horse as Consul' – as Minister for Coordination of Defence 1936–39, to sidestep Winston Churchill. Neville Chamberlain had him serve briefly as Dominions Secretary before Churchill moved him upstairs as Lord Chief Justice 1940–46.

Edmund Ironside 1880–1959
British General who served in the Boer War and World War I in Archangel, Turkey and Persia. Served as Commander in Chief of India 1926, and Commander in Chief of the Middle East in 1936. Chief of the Imperial General Staff 1939–40.

Cecil Jeffrey 1888–1970
Civil servant. Clerk in Postal and Telegraphic Services Department 1903. Member of First New Zealand Expeditionary Force. Private Secretary to Massey, Bell, and Coates 1920–45, and Chief Private Secretary to Coates, Ward, Forbes, Savage and Fraser. Clerk of Executive Council and Secretary to Cabinet 1936. Head of Prime Minister's Department 1943–46.

Fred Jones 1885–1966
Footwear worker and trade unionist. Labour MP for Dunedin South and St Kilda 1931–51. Minister for Defence 1935–49 and Government member of War Cabinet.

Thomas Jordan 1880–1945
Graduated with an MA in 1902. Member of First New Zealand Expeditionary Force 1914–18. Lawyer and long-serving Mayor of Masterton 1925–41.

W.J. Jordan 1879–1959
Born in Kent, England. First Honorary Secretary of the New Zealand Labour Party 1907. Member of First New Zealand Expeditionary Force, wounded in France. Labour MP 1922–35. Methodist trustee and lay preacher. Long-serving New Zealand High Commissioner in London 1935–51. New Zealand Delegate to the League of Nations 1936–39. (*DNZB* Vol. 4, p. 260)

Rudyard Kipling 1865–1936
Immensely influential writer and poet of the British Empire, whose works include *Life's Handicap* (London: Macmillan & Co., 1891), *Barrack Room*

Ballads (London: Methuen & Co., 1892), *The Jungle Books* (1894–95) *Kim* (1901), and *The Light That Failed* (London: Macmillan & Co., 1891). See Charles Carrington, *Rudyard Kipling His Life and Works* (London: Macmillan, 1955), and Harry Ricketts, *The Unforgiving Minute: A Life of Rudyard Kipling* (London: Chatto & Windus, 1999).

Fritz Kreisler 1875–1962
Famous Austrian virtuoso violinist and composer of the operetta 'Apple Blossoms' with Victor Jacobi.

Miles Lampson 1880–1964
Proconsular British High Commissioner to Egypt and Sudan 1933–36 and Ambassador 1936–45; later Lord Killearn. See Trefor Evans, *Mission to Egypt 1934–1946* (Cardiff: University of Wales Press, 1971).

Frank Langstone 1881–1969
Important Labour politician, orator, and polemicist. Minister of Lands and Forests, and Maori Affairs, and later High Commissioner in Canada. (*DNZB* Vol. 4, p. 279)

Tom Larkin 1918–
Educated New Plymouth Boys High School 1930–35, was Taranaki cricket representative at fifteen. Victoria University 1936–40, MA Naval service in destroyers and motor launches in Mediterranean. Boarded out (for deafness) in 1945. Joined External Affairs 1946 and became an influential senior officer in Wellington. Official Secretary Canberra 1953. Ambassador to Japan 1972–76. Spent twelve years as Chairman of the New Zealand Press Council. Author of *New Zealand and Japan in the post war world* (Wellington: New Zealand Institute of International Affairs, 1969), and editor of *New Zealand's External Relations* (Wellington/London: New Zealand Institute of Public Administration/Oxford University Press, 1962), and *Tourism from Japan*. Wrote review articles in *NZ Listener* and *NZ Review of Books*, and articles on New Zealand in international affairs, New Zealand and Japan, cricket, personalities in New Zealand sport, and the press. Married to Sarah Marianne Williams; they have three children: Tom, Adam and Daisy. After representing Taranaki pre-war, played senior cricket for Varsity in Wellington till nearly forty, his innings of 205 not out in 1947 still the highest score by a Varsity player in Wellington cricket. Member of the senior champion Varsity cricket and rugby teams of 1946. (M.J.C. Templeton)

John A. Lee 1890–1982
Decorated soldier with a Distinguished Conduct Medal, charismatic Labour MP and orator 1922–28 and 1931–40, polemicist and writer of *Children of the Poor* (London: T. Werner Laurie, 1934), *Civilian into Soldier* (London: T. Werner Laurie, 1937), *Socialism in New Zealand* (London: T. Werner Laurie, 1938), *Simple on a Soap Box* (Auckland: Collins, 1963), and more. See Erik Olssen, *John A. Lee* (Dunedin: University of Otago Press, 1977), *DNZB* Vol. 4, p. 284.

Herbert Lehman 1878–1963
American banker and Democratic politician; Lieutenant Governor of New York under Roosevelt; Governor of New York 1932–42; Director, Foreign Relief and Rehabilitation 1942–46.

Trygve Lie 1896–1968
Norwegian Minister from 1935; Foreign Minister in exile in London 1941–46; First Secretary General of the United Nations 1946–52, whom Dag Hammarskjöld succeeded.

Senator Huey Long 1893–1935
Demagogic political boss, Governor of Louisiana 1928–31 and Senator 1931–35. He was assassinated in 1935. See Robert Penn Warren's superb *All the King's Men* (New York & London: Harcourt, Brace & Co., 1946).

Lord Lugard 1858–1945
British soldier and Colonial administrator who secured Uganda for the British Empire and introduced the concept of Indirect Rule in Nigeria. Member of the Permanent Mandates Commission 1922–36. Author of *The Dual Mandate in British Tropical Africa* (London: Blackwood, 1922). See Margery Perham, *Lugard. Volume 2: The Years of Authority, 1898–1945* (London: Collins, 1960).

J.A. Lyons 1879–1958
Premier of Tasmania, Labour MP from 1929, and Minister. He resigned in 1931; that year he became leader of a Coalition Government with the Country Party, and went on to win the 1934 and 1937 federal elections.

General Douglas MacArthur 1880–1964
Commander of the Rainbow Division, France 1917–18; General and Chief of Staff 1930; Head of the United States Military Mission in the Philippines

1935; Commander of the United States Forces in the Far East 1941; Supreme Commander of the South West Pacific Area 1942; Supreme Commander of the Allied Powers and Pro Consular Ruler of Japan 1945; Commander in Chief of the United Nations Forces in South Korea from 1950 until relieved by President Truman in 1951.

Ramsay MacDonald 1866–1937
Leader of the British Labour Party 1911. First Labour Prime Minister briefly in 1924 and then 1929–31. Prime Minister of National Government 1931–35.

Alister McIntosh 1906–1978
'The man who shaped our foreign service.' History graduate, librarian, collector. Proposer of a National Library. Founding Secretary/Treasurer of the Institute of International Relations. Berendsen's Deputy in the Prime Minister's Department from 1935 to 1943, when he succeeded Berendsen as Secretary of the War Cabinet. Founding Secretary 1943–66 of the new Department of External Affairs. Famed for his political intuition and realism and honoured for his sensitivity and humanity. Recruited the present writer at Oxford to the Department, and advised me briefly as Chairman of the Broadcasting Council 1973–76 in my Broadcasting portfolio. See *Undiplomatic Dialogue: Letters between Carl Berendsen and Alister McIntosh 1943–1952* (Auckland: Auckland University Press, 1994) by Ian MacGibbon, *DNZB* Vol. 5, p. 313.

Jane 'Jean' McKenzie 1901–1964
Born in Southland. Began work as a secretary in the Public Works Department. Moved to the Imperial Affairs Section in 1926 as Secretary to Carl Berendsen, then worked with High Commissioner Bill Jordan in London. Delegate to the First General Assembly of the United Nations and then First Charge d'Affairs and Minister at the new New Zealand Legation in Paris 1949–56. (*DNZB* Vol. 4, p. 315)

W.L. Mackenzie King 1874–1950
Grandson of the political rebel and reformer William Lyon Mackenzie. MP 1908–11 and 1919–48, and from 1921 three times Prime Minister of Canada. One of the world's longest serving leaders, he developed concepts of Canadian nationhood and imperial and international cooperation.

Jacob Malik 1906–1980
A favourite junior of Stalin, Ambassador to Japan 1942–45, Deputy Foreign Minister, Soviet Representative at the United Nations 1948, Ambassador to

Britain 1953–60, Deputy Foreign Minister 1960, and Ambassador to the United Nations 1968–76. 'The last of the Stalinists, a man with a deeply cultivated propensity for lying.'

William Ferguson Massey 1856–1925
Born in Northern Ireland; arrived in New Zealand in 1870. Farmer and advocate of freehold tenure. Conservative MP from 1894 and Opposition party leader from 1903; founder of Reform Party in 1909; Prime Minister 1912–15 and 1919–25; Prime Minister in coalition with J.G. Ward 1915–19. James Allen, Francis Dillon Bell, J.G. Coates, and Downie Stewart were among his major lieutenants. Signed the Treaty of Versailles for New Zealand in 1919. (*DNZB* Vol. 2, p. 316)

Captain John Mawson 1875–1954
Long serving Master Mariner of the Union Steam Ship Company, founded in Dunedin and famed for its coastal, inter-colonial and Pacific services. Mawson was in charge of the USS *Talune*, which through administrative failure let loose the black flu in Western Samoa late in 1918. Some twenty per cent of the Western Samoan population died in the epidemic, which American Samoa avoided by quarantine. O.F. Nelson, who lost his mother, sister, only brother, and sister-in-law in six days, cannot have been impressed by a New Zealand failure which still rankles. See Michael Field, *Mau: Samoa's Struggle Against New Zealand Oppression* (Wellington: A.H. & A.W. Reed, 1984). Mawson served as a lieutenant commander in World War II. His son, Brigadier John Mawson, was a noted senior New Zealand army officer.

Krishna Menon 1896–1974
Secretary of the Indian League, High Commissioner of India in London 1947–52, Permanent Representative to the United Nations 1952–57, and Minister of Defence 1957–62.

Senator Wayne Morse of Oregon 1900–1974
Out of Wisconsin farm country, he became Professor of Law at the University of Oregon, an expert on legal procedures and a notable labour arbitrator. He had a long political career, beginning in 1944 as an independent, liberal, feisty, Oregon senator, then as a Republican 1944–52, an Independent 1952–56, and a Democrat 1956–1968. He was one of two senators that voted against the Gulf of Tonkin Resolution and the Vietnam War. After losing his seat in 1968, he died during a campaign for re-election in 1974. See A. Robert Smith, *The Tiger in The Senate: The Biography of Wayne Morse* (New York: Doubleday, 1962),

and Lee Wilkins, *Wayne Morse: A Bio-Bibliography* (Westport, Connecticut: Greenwood Press, 1985).

Michael Myers 1873–1950
Eminent lawyer; the first New Zealand-born Chief Justice 1929–44 and Privy Councillor 1936; New Zealand delegate to Post War Conferences. (*DNZB* Vol. 4, p. 369)

Walter Nash 1882–1968
Born in Kidderminster, England. Long-serving Labour Party Secretary, Minister of Finance 1935–49 and Prime Minister 1957–60. See Keith Sinclair, *Walter Nash* (Auckland: Auckland University Press, 1976). (*DNZB* Vol. 4, p. 370)

Pandit Jawaharlal Nehru 1889–1964
Secretary of the Indian National Congress 1929–39, and thrice Indian National Congress President. Elegant and eloquent first Prime Minister of India 1950–66. Brother of Madame Pandit, and father of Prime Minister Indira Gandhi. Author of *The Unity of India* (London: Lindsay Drummond, 1941). See Judith M. Brown, *Nehru A Political Life* (New Haven & London: Yale University Press, 2003).

O.F. Nelson 1883–1944
Leading Samoan businessman who stimulated opposition to General Richardson's administration and organised and led the Mau. An able politician and publicist who continued, in exile in New Zealand and on his return after the Labour Government came to power in 1935, to influence events as a member of the Samoan Legislative Council. His grandson Tupuloa Taisi Efi was educated in New Zealand and became the third Prime Minister of an independent Samoa and later member of the Council of Deputies. (*DNZB* Vol. 4, p. 376)

Fleet Admiral Chester W. Nimitz 1885–1966
Commander of the United States Pacific Fleet after Pearl Harbour and during World War II, director of the United States victories of Midway, Iwo Jima and Okinawa. Co-author with E.B. Potter of *Sea Power: A Naval History* (New Jersey: Prentice-Hall Inc., 1960).

Kevin O'Higgins 1892–1927
A member of Sinn Féin and participant in the Easter Rising 1916, he was elected as an MP while in prison and became Minister for Justice in the Cosgrove Government in 1922. He established the Civil Guard, putting down

disorder firmly. In June 1927 he became Minister for External Affairs. The ablest figure in Irish public life, he was assassinated in July 1927. Author of *History of Ireland*. See Terence de Vere White, *Life of Kevin O Higgins* (London: Methuen & Co., 1948).

Madame Vijaya Lakshimi Pandit 1900–1990
Younger sister of Jawaharlal Nehru. Originally known as Sarup Kumari Nehru, she was renamed Vijaya Lakshimi by Mahatma Gandhi. She married Ranjit Pandit, a Brahmin aristocrat, in 1921. She was Minister of Local Self Government and Public Health of the Indian state Uttar Pradesh from 1937. After India's independence she served as Ambassador to the USSR (1947–49), the USA and Mexico (1949–51), and Spain (1958–61), and High Commissioner to the UK and Ireland (1955–61), and was Head of the Indian Delegation to the United Nations, 1946–68. She became the first woman president of the United Nations General Assembly in 1953. She later became a Member of the Rayja Sabha, or Upper House.

C.J. Parr 1869–1941
Leading lawyer, Mayor of Auckland and MP 1899–1936. Reform MP for Eden 1914–26; from 1920 inter alia Minister of Health, Education (during which he established the Correspondence School and Education Gazette), Justice, and Post and Telegraph. Leader of the Legislative Council 1930–33. High Commissioner to London and Representative to the League of Nations 1926–29 and 1933–36. (*DNZB* Vol. 3, p. 384)

Lester Pearson 1897–1972
Canadian diplomat. Ambassador in Washington 1945–46, involved in formation of United Nations. Secretary of State for External Affairs 1948–57, President of General Assembly 1952–53, Leader of the Opposition 1958. Prime Minister 1963–68, when Canada adopted the maple leaf flag.

General Arthur Percival 1887–1966
British General who served in the Great War, at Murmansk, Ireland, Malaya, and the British Expeditionary Force in World War II, and was General Officer Commanding at the fall of Singapore in 1941. Author of *The War in Malaya* (London: Eyre & Spottiswoode, 1949).

Evita Peron 1919–1952
Politically powerful and charismatic second wife of Fascist President of Argentina, General Juan Peron.

General Juan Peron 1894–1974
President ('El Lider') of Argentina 1946–55; and after exile, briefly again 1972–73.

Marshall Henry Petain 1856–1951
The soldier hero of Verdun who restored the morale of the French army in 1917, in the inter-war years built the Maginot Line, and after the defeat in the Battle of France in June 1940 formed the Vichy Government that negotiated peace and until 1944 'collaborated' with Nazi Germany. Safe in Switzerland in 1945, where de Gaulle hoped he would stay, the old Marshall returned to France. After a perfunctory trial he was found guilty of treason. His defence: 'Every day with a knife at my throat I struggled against the enemy demands.'

Sir Guy Powles 1905–1994
Distinguished New Zealand lawyer, citizen soldier, and diplomat who made his name as High Commissioner for Western Samoa 1949–60, preparing the way for self government, and then, after serving briefly as High Commissioner to India, in inaugurating the Office of the Ombudsman, the first in the English-speaking world. Later became New Zealand's first Race Relations Conciliator. (*DNZB* Vol. 5, p. 421)

General Sir Edward Puttick 1890–1976
Territorial soldier. Battalion Commander, First New Zealand Expeditionary Force. Joined post-war Army and rose to Quarter Master General. Brigadier in Egypt, Greece and Crete, 1939–42. Highly capable Chief of General Staff and head of New Zealand Army 1942–45. Author of *25 Battalion* (Wellington: Department of Internal Affairs, 1960). (*DNZB* Vol. 5, p. 425)

William Pember Reeves 1857–1932
As a young man he was a brilliant scholar and good cricketer. He began in journalism and turned early to politics, where he shone as a speaker and orator. While Seddon led and Ward provided the legislative framework, Reeves was the principal intellectual and ideologist of the Liberal Party that dominated the politics of New Zealand in the 1890s and 1900s. As Minister of Justice and Education and as the first Minister of Labour, he pioneered compulsory arbitration in industrial disputes, and a range of legislation governing the workplace under a Department of Labour. In conflict with Seddon he accepted the Agent Generalship in London, where he was a great success, not only as a speaker, but also in raising loans. He became a great friend of the Fabians, notably the Webbs and G.B. Shaw, through whom he became Director of the

London School of Economics. Though not an academic or administrative success there, he did put the finances of the school on a sound footing. Author of *The Long White Cloud* (London: Horace Marshall & Son, 1898), and *State Experiments in Australia and New Zealand* (London: Grant Richards, 1902). See Keith Sinclair, *William Pember Reeves: New Zealand Fabian* (New York: Oxford University Press, 1965).

Major General George Richardson 1868–1938
English-born soldier who rose from the ranks to command all New Zealand troops in the UK during the Great War. Served as Administrator of Western Samoa 1923–28. (*DNZB* Vol. 3, p. 429)

James Rolph II ('Sunny Jim') 1869–1934
Banker, shipbuilder, Mayor of San Francisco 1912–31, and Governor of California 1930–34. Despite his ebullient nature, his political career ended in failure after his support for a mob lynching.

General Carlos Romulo of the Philippines 1899–1985
World War II General who returned with General MacArthur to the Philippines. He later served as an influential Philippine Representative at the United Nations, and Fourth President of the General Assembly 1949.

Eleanor Roosevelt 1884–1962
First Lady 'extrordinaire' 1932–45. Author of, inter alia, *This is My Story* (New York: Simon & Schuster, 1956), *The Moral Basis of Democracy* (New York: Howell, Soskin & Co., 1940).

Franklin Delano Roosevelt ('FDR') 1882–1945
Thirty-second President of the United States 1932–45. Assistant Secretary of the Navy under President Wilson 1913–20; Governor of New York 1929–33; Great populist New Deal President: 'We have nothing to fear but fear itself'. The only third and fourth term American President 1933–45. Famous internationally for the Atlantic Charter and Lend Lease, and, as War President after 'the Day of Infamy', for the policies of unconditional surrender, the invasion of Europe in 1944, the island-hopping Pacific campaign, the development of the atomic bomb, the formation of the United Nations, and the selection of Harry Truman as his successor.

Franklin Roosevelt Jr 1914–1988
Third son of the great President, three-term US Congressman 1948–54. After

failing to secure the Democratic nomination for the New York Governorship, he retired from politics.

James Roosevelt 1907–1991
Eldest son of FDR and Eleanor. Had a varied life in business, films, WII combat, and politics. Was in Congress for six terms, Ambassador to United Nations Economic and Social Council 1966, and worked on the Nixon, Carter and Reagan Presidential campaigns. Co-author, with Sidney Shalett, of *Affectionately FDR: A Son's Story of a Lonely Man* (New York: Harcourt, Brace & Co., 1959), and, with Bill Libby, of *My Parents: A Differing View* (Chicago: Playboy Press, 1976).

Dean Rusk 1909–1994
American Rhodes Scholar, soldier, and professor. Worked for the US Department of State as President Truman's Assistant Secretary of State 1947–51, during the Korean War. Was distinguished Secretary of State 1961–69, during the Vietnam War, under Presidents Kennedy and Johnson.

John Sankey 1866–1948
Judge who, after the Great War, recommended nationalisation of coal mines. This won the interest of British Labour Party, who made him Labour Lord Chancellor 1929–31. He remained Lord Chancellor in the National Government 1931–35. Later he was Judge of the Permanent Court of Arbitration at The Hague.

Michael Joseph Savage 1872–1940
First New Zealand Labour Prime Minister. Australian-born, he followed his friend Paddy Webb to New Zealand in 1907. He became involved in unionism and formation of the New Zealand Labour Party in 1916, and entered Parliament in 1919, building up the Labour Party during the 1920s. He became party leader on the death of H.E. Holland in 1933, and won the 1935 election. Oversaw the founding of the Social Security State and steps towards an independent foreign policy in support of Collective Security and the League of Nations. In 1939, though a pacifist, he broadcast New Zealand's Declaration of War on Germany: 'Where Britain goes, we go'. See Barry Gustafson, *From the Cradle to the Grave* (Auckland: Reed Methuen, 1986). (*DNZB* Vol. 4, p. 455)

James Henry Scullin 1876–1953
Leader of Australian Federal Labour Party 1928–35. Prime Minister 1929–31,

responsible for appointing first Australian-born Governor General, Sir Isaac Isaacs.

Richard John Seddon ('King Dick') 1845–1906
Born in Eccleston, near St Helens in England, of Lancastrian father and Scots mother; his family were tenants of the great Earls of Derby. Saw Scots Greys march past to Liverpool to embark for the Crimea. Immigrated to Australia in 1859 and then to West Coast goldfields, New Zealand, in 1866. Vigorous leader in local politics; MP in 1879 as 'greyhound' of silver-tongued Liberal Premier Grey; Minister in Balance Liberal Government 1891. Dynamic, ebullient, populist Premier and Prime Minister 1893–1906. See P.S. O'Connor, *New Zealand Profiles: Seddon* (Wellington: Reed, 1968). For a contemporary account see James Drummond, *The Life and Work of Richard John Seddon* (Whitcombe & Tombs Ltd, 1907). (*DNZB* Vol. 2, p. 447)

Haile Selassie 1891–1975
Reforming Emperor of Ethiopia 1930–35. In exile after failure of the League of Nations to deter Italy, he never forgot New Zealand's support for Ethiopia in Geneva. In 1941 he re-entered Ethiopia with British forces. Architect of the Organisation of African Unity. Deposed in a military coup 1974.

Moshe Sharett 1894–1965
First Foreign Minister of Israel, 1948–56 and Prime Minister, 1954–55. Ukrainian-born, he immigrated to Palestine with his family in 1906; they were one of the founding families of Tel Aviv. Journalist. Deputy to David Ben Gurion in Jewish Agency and chief negotiator with the British Mandate authorities. Important architect of Zionist policy on the Jewish Brigade, 'illegal' immigration, the November 1947 Partition Plan, and admission to the United Nations.

George Bernard Shaw 1856–1950
Great Irish dramatist and Fabian polemicist. Won the Nobel Prize for Literature 1925. See Michael Holroyd, *G.B. Shaw* (New York: Random House, 1988).

Sir Frederick Shedden 1893–1971
Secretary of the Australian Defence Committee; Australian Representative to the League of Nations; key Australian defence adviser in the countdown to World War II; Secretary of Defence 1937–56; 1939–45 Secretary of War Cabinet and Principal Adviser to Prime Minister Curtin. (*Australian Dictionary of Biography* Vol. 16, p. 224)

T.J. Sherrard 1896–1992
Civil Servant, Post Office; First New Zealand Expeditionary Force; Public Service Commission 1923; Legislative Council; Prime Minister's Office. Clerk of the Executive Council 1948–67.

T.K. Sidey 1863–1933
Dunedin MP 1901–28, Member of the Legislative Council 1927. Was Attorney General and Minister of Justice in Ward Administration from 1928 until Coalition Government 1931. Famous as Father of Daylight Saving. (*DNZB* Vol. 3, p. 471)

Senator Howard Smith 1880–1966
Lawyer and University teacher. Republican Senator and member of the Foreign Relations Committee 1944–59.

Governor Wilhelm Solf 1862–1936
Imperial German Colonial Service; Governor of Western Samoa 1900–11; Imperial Colonial Secretary 1911–17. Last Foreign Minister of Imperial Germany 1918; first of Weimar Republic; German Ambassador to Tokyo 1920–28; important supporter of Liberal German tradition and opponent of Hitler and Nazis (Goethe Institute: Wellington).

Paul Henri Spaak 1899–1972
Socialist Premier Belgium 1938; Foreign Minister in exile; First President of General Assembly 1946; Premier 1946 and 1947–9; Foreign Minister 1954–57. One of the wise men Founders of the EEC; Secretary General of NATO 1957–61; Foreign Minister 1961–66.

Senator John Sparkman 1899–1985
Democratic Representative to House 1937–46, Senator from Alabama 1946–1979, US representative to the Fifth General Assembly. Unsuccessful Democratic nominee for the Vice Presidency 1952.

Sir Percy Spender 1897–1985
Australian lawyer and MP. Cabinet Minister 1939–40; Minister of External Affairs 1949–51, during development of Colombo Plan and ANZUS; Ambassador to the United States 1951–58. Judge, International Court of Justice, 1958–64, and President, International Court of Justice, 1964–67. Author of *Exercises in Diplomacy* (Sydney: Sydney University Press, 1969) and *Politics and a Man* (Sydney: Collins, 1972).

Edward Stettinius 1900–1949
Major US industrialist who chaired the War Resources Board 1939–40 and administered Lend Lease 1941–43; Under Secretary of State 1943–44; succeeded Cordell Hull as Secretary of State December 1944–June 1945, chairing the US delegation to the San Francisco Conference.

Colonel W.G. Stevens 1893–1975
London-born but with a Southland grandfather. A Duntroon-trained professional soldier. Secretary to the Council of Defence and the New Zealand Chiefs of Staff. Worked closely with Berendsen on the Organisation for National Security and the War Book. Chief of Staff to General Freyberg and Officer in Charge of the Second New Zealand Expeditionary Force Headquarters; Official Secretary, London 1946–53. Author of *Problems of 2NZEF* (Wellington: Department of Internal Affairs, 1958), and *Bardia to Enfidaville* (Wellington: Department of Internal Affairs, 1962). (*DNZB* Vol. 4, p. 494)

Robert Louis Stevenson ('Tusitala') 1850–1894
Famous Scots author. Suffering from tuberculosis, he travelled much in the South Pacific, buying land in Samoa from Harry Moors to build 'Vailima', with one of the great views of the world, over Apia Bay. As a Scot, Stevenson's particular sympathy for the Samoans can be seen in his *A Footnote to History: Eight Years of Trouble in Samoa* (London: Cassell & Co. Ltd, 1892), an extraordinarily pungent account of Samoan affairs, the gunboat diplomacy of the colonial powers, and the great hurricane of 1889 that sank the American and German vessels. The Samoans built the Road of Loving Hearts to Tusitala's memory on Mount Vaea, where he is buried. Vailima, because of its prestige, was allocated at Independence to the Heads of State, and is now a museum.

William Downie Stewart 1878–1949
Lawyer, scholar, soldier. Became an MP in 1914, and a Minister from 1921, notably a powerful Minister of Finance: he had a leading role as one of the 'academic imperialists' at the 1932 Ottawa Conference that guaranteed New Zealand its market in Britain, and in drafting the Reserve Bank of New Zealand Bill 1932. Famous for his integrity, interest in international affairs, sympathy for and friendship with John A. Lee, and resignation over 'devaluation' in January 1933. Author of, inter alia, *Journal of George Hepburn* (Dunedin: C.S.W./ Reed, 1934), *Mr Justice Richmond and the Taranaki War of 1860* (Wellington: Reed, 1947), and the unpublished autobiography 'Three Generations in New Zealand Politics'.(*DNZB* Vol. 3, p. 489)

Henry Stimson 1867–1950
Republican Secretary of War 1911–13, in Taft Cabinet; Colonel, Air Expeditionary Force, 1917–18; Governor General of the Philippines 1927–29; Secretary of State under President Hoover 1929–33; FDR's Secretary of War 1940–45.

Chief Justice Harlan Stone 1872–1946
Appointed twelfth Chief Justice by FDR: given FDR's controversy with the Supreme Court, he was one of the shorter serving Chief Justices compared with most of the sixteen between 1789 and 2005. In 1946 President Truman appointed Fred M. Vinson, the Secretary for the Treasury 1945–46, as Chief Justice 1946–53 during his Presidency. President Eisenhower then appointed – *my greatest political mistake* – the Republican, Governor Earl Warren of California as Chief Justice 1953–69.

William Strang 1893–1978
Influential British Foreign Office official 1919–53. Adviser during the Vickers trial in Moscow in the 1930s, to Anthony Eden and Neville Chamberlain during their mission to Moscow in August 1939, and to Ernest Bevin during the period of post-war settlement in Europe. Author of *The Foreign Office* (London: Allen & Unwin, 1955), *Britain in World Affairs Henry VIII to Elizabeth II* (London: Faber & Faber, 1961), and *Home and Abroad* (London: Deutsch, 1954).

Daniel G. Sullivan 1882–1947
Labour trade unionist, journalist, mayor, MP 1919–47, Senior Labour Minister 1935–47 (principally Industries and Commerce, Supply and Munitions, but also Rail and DSIR). Minister to International Civil Aviation Organization Conference, Chicago, 1944. (*DNZB* Vol. 4, p. 503)

Arthur Hays Sulzberger 1891–1968
President and Director of the *New York Times* 1935–57, publisher 1935–61.

Madame Sun Yat Sen
One of the three famous Soong sisters, Soong Ching Ling. Born to Christian parents in Shanghai. Trained at Wesley College. Married at 22 to Sun Yat Sen, Founder President of modern China. Revered as first 'active' First Lady and for her campaigning for status of women in China.

Commodore T.G.B. Swabey RN
Captain, 1918. In 1926 he became Commodore of the New Zealand Station and First Naval Member of the Navy Board.

Lord Swinton 1884–1972
Prominent Conservative politician 1920–55; served in Coalition Cabinet 1931–35; Air Secretary 1935–38; Minister for Civil Aviation 1940–45 and so attended Chicago Conference in 1944; Secretary of State for Commonwealth Relations 1952–55.

Tupua Tamasese Lealofi III
One of four 'tama aiga' or paramount chiefs. After the exile of O.F. Nelson to New Zealand, he was induced to lead the Mau and died in the Black Sunday shootings of 28 December 1929. His eldest son, Tupua Tamasese Me'ole, was to become the first co–Head of State in 1962 and his grandson, Tupua Tamasese Tupuola Tufuga Efi, the third Prime Minister. Another of his sons, Tamasese Lealofi IV, became the second Prime Minister of Samoa, after Fiame Mata'afa Faumuina Mulinu'u II.

Tupua Tamasese Me'ole 1905–1963
A wise and intelligent political leader, the eldest son of the martyred Tamasese Lealofi III. He married O.F. Nelson's daughter, Irene, and their son, Tupua Tamasese Tupuola Tufuga Efi (1938–), the grandson of O.F. Nelson, became Samoa's third Prime Minister. Tupua Tamasese Me'ole played a significant role in the move to independence, and became the first co-Head of State, with Malietoa Tanumafili II, at Independence in 1962.

Malietoa Tanumafili I 1879–1939
Important holder of the paramount Samoan title among the four 'tama aiga', or senior chiefs of Samoa. His son, Malietoa Tanumafili II (1913–2007), was to become the initial co-Head of State in 1962 with Tupua Tamasese Me'ole.

Malcolm 'M.J.C.' Templeton 1924–
Briefly attended Gore High, Berendsen's old school, then King's High School, Dunedin. Attained Double First from University of Otago, 1944. Worked for Department of External Affairs 1946–1984, serving in Washington, then New York, during New Zealand's first term on the Security Council; Minister in London; Permanent Representative to the United Nations 1973–78, representing New Zealand at Law of the Sea Conferences 1973–82. Deputy Secretary of Foreign Affairs 1978–84. Founding Director, Institute of Policy

Studies, Victoria University of Wellington 1984–86. Author of *Defence and Security: What New Zealand Needs* (Wellington: Victoria University Press, 1986), *Top Hats Are Not Being Taken* (Wellington: New Zealand Institute of International Affairs, 1989), *Ties of Blood and Empire: New Zealand's Involvement in Middle East Defence and the Suez Crisis 1947–57* (Auckland: Auckland University Press and New Zealand Institute of International Affairs, 1994), *A Wise Adventure: New Zealand in Antarctica, 1920–60* (Wellington: Victoria University Press and New Zealand Institute of International Affairs, 2000), and *Standing Upright Here: New Zealand in the Nuclear Age 1945–90* (Wellington: Victoria University Press, 2006).

Norman Thomas 1884–1968
Eloquent American Socialist leader, one-time Presbyterian minister and editor of *The Nation* 1922. Socialist candidate for the US Presidency for six consecutive elections, 1928–48. Author of *America's Way Out* (New York: Macmillan, 1931) and *The Prerequisites for Peace* (New York: W.W. Norton, 1959).

Frank D. Thomson
Significant New Zealand civil servant for thirty years. Private Secretary to successive Prime Ministers: Seddon, Massey, Coates and Forbes. Secretary to the New Zealand Delegations to Imperial Conferences 1917, 1918, 1919, 1921, 1923, 1926 and 1930. Member of the British Secretariat to the Peace Conference. Permanent Head of the Prime Minister's Department, Clerk of the Executive Council, and Secretary to the Cabinet.

Harry S. Truman 1884–1972
Thirty-third President of the United States 1945–53. Served in AIF. Senator for Missouri 1934–44. Democratic Vice President to FDR 1944. From April 1945–53 his Presidency covered the German surrender, Potsdam, the atomic bomb and Japan's surrender, the Marshall Plan and Point 4, the Truman Doctrine of Containment, the Berlin airlift of 1948, the creation of NATO 1949, the Korean War 1950, and the establishment of the CIA. See Harry S. Truman, *Memoirs*, 2 Vols. (Garden City, New York: Doubleday, 1955–56).

Alfred Turnbull 1881–1962
Civil service cadet (1899) who began in Lands and Survey and rose to be Chief Accountant 1912 and Inspector 1915 before serving in the First New Zealand Expeditionary Force. Secretary Public Service Commission 1919. Secretary to the Government of Western Samoa 1930–35 and then Administrator 1935–46.

Eamon de Valera 1882–1975
American-born, Irish-educated Irish Volunteer and Commandant in the Easter Rising. Sinn Féin and Fianna Fáil politician during evolution of the Irish Free State, of which he was Prime Minister 1932–36, before becoming Prime Minister, or Taoiseach, of the sovereign independent Republic of Ireland 1937–48 and 1951–54.

General Alexander A. Vandegrift 1887–1973
Outstanding Commanding General of the First Marine Division of the US Marine Corps. Reinforced in the critical battle for Guadalcanal 1942, and the First Marine Amphibious Corps in the landings on Bougainville. Eighteenth Commandant of the US Marine Corps 1944–48.

Paul Verschaffelt 1887–1959
Civil servant, one of the early officers of the Public Service Commission established after the Public Service Act 1912. Played an influential role in developing an apolitical, merit-based, unified New Zealand civil service, based on cadet rather than graduate entry, before early retirement. (*DNZB* Vol. 4, p. 546)

Vice President Henry Wallace 1888–1965
Agriculturist and journalist who achieved fame as FDR's Secretary of Agriculture 1933–40. Served as Vice President 1940–44. Suffered FDR's brutal failure to endorse him at the 1944 Convention, which was in effect choosing two Presidents. Although Wallace initially led the vote, the Democratic machine swung the vote to the unknown Senator Harry Truman: the 'Missouri Compromise', viz David McCullough, *Truman* (New York: Simon and Schuster, 1993).

Fintan Patrick Walsh 1894–1963
Famous Head of Seamen's Union, President of the Federation of Labour, with intimate ties to the Labour Party. See C. Bollinger, *Against The Wind: The Story of the New Zealand Seamen's Union* (Wellington: NZ Seamen's Union, 1968). (*DNZB* Vol. 4, p. 55)

Sir Joseph Ward 1856–1930
Had a long career as MP for Awarua 1877–1919 and Invercargill 1925–30. Senior Liberal Minister who, with Pember Reeves, gave legislative form under Seddon to the Liberal era. Premier and first Prime Minister 1906–12. Wartime Coalition Deputy Prime Minister 1915–1918. Prime Minister for a second

time in 1928 until his death in 1930. See Michael Bassett, *Sir Joseph Ward* (Auckland: Auckland University Press, 1993), *DNZB* Vol. 2, p. 565.

Vincent Ward 1888–1946
Had a varied career in business and World War I. Private Secretary 1922–30 to his father J.G. Ward, who was very close to Vincent. Berendsen's account of him, as of Frank Thomson, will be one of the few records of such behind-the-scenes service.

Field Marshall Archibald Wavell 1883–1950
Distinguished British Army officer in the Boer War and the Great War, in the Caucasus and the Middle East. In 1937 he was appointed Commander in Chief, Palestine, and in June 1939 he became Commander in Chief, Middle East. Led brilliant campaigns in Libya, East Africa and Syria. Was forced against his judgement to send forces to Greece and Crete, opening the way to Rommel's successful offensives. He then went to India to become Supreme Commander, Far East, until fall of Singapore. Field Marshall and successful Viceroy of India 1943–48. Author of numerous publications, including *Allenby, a Study in Greatness* (New York: Oxford University Press, 1941), *Generals and Generalship* (London: *The Times*, 1941), *Other Men's Flowers* (London: Jonathan Cape, 1944), and *The Good Soldier* (London: Macmillan, 1948).

Beatrice Webb (nee Potter) 1858–1943
Fabian Socialist reformer, and partner of Sidney Webb, with whom she established the London School of Economics and Political Science in 1895. An expert in British trade unions and working class conditions. Author of *The Cooperative Movement in Great Britain* (1899), and *The Case for the Factory Acts* (1901); and co-author (with Sidney Webb) of *The Decay of Capitalist Civilisation* (New York: Harcourt Brace, 1923), and *Soviet Communism: A New Civilisation?* (New York: Scribner's Sons, 1936).

Clifton Webb 1889–1962
Followed Gordon Coates as MP in Kaipara. An early supporter of the United Nations, who became one of the 'big four' in the Holland Cabinet, as Attorney General and Minister of Justice 1949–51, and then Minister of External Affairs 1951–54. High Commissioner in London 1954–58. (*DNZB* Vol. 5, p. 548)

Sidney Webb 1859–1947
A founder of the Fabian Society in 1884. Married Beatrice Potter in 1892; together they established the London School of Economics and Political

Science in 1895. Professor of Public Administration 1912–27. Labour MP, Minister 1924–31 and Peer, as Lord Passmore.

Sumner Welles 1892–1961
FDR's Under Secretary of State 1933–43 who as Assistant Secretary of State had developed the US Good Neighbour Policy in Latin America.

Sir Thomas Wilford 1870–1939
Liberal orator and MP 1899; dynamic Mayor of Wellington responsible in 1900s for major development of the Wellington Harbour; Wartime Coalition Minister; Liberal party leader 1920–25; who failed to secure marriage of Liberal with Massey's Reform Party but became Minister of Justice and Defence in Ward Cabinet 1928–29 and High Commissioner in London 1929–33. (*DNZB* Vol. 3, p. 568)

General Charles Willoughby 1892–1972
German-born American soldier (with an American mother) Served in American Expeditionary Force in World War I and in many countries as US military attaché. Known principally as General MacArthur's Chief of Intelligence 1940–51. Author of *The Economic and Military Participation of the United States in the World War* (Fort Leavenworth, Kansas: Command & General Staff School Press, 1931) and *MacArthur 1941–1951* (New York: McGraw-Hill, 1954).

Hon. David Wilson 1880–1977
Dour Glaswegian-born influential Secretary of the New Zealand Labour Party 1936–40 for the landmark 1935 and 1938 elections; Member of the Legislative Council (MLC) 1937 and Leader 1939–44; Member of New Zealand War Cabinet; High Commissioner to Canada 1944–47; New Zealand Delegate to the General Assembly 1946 and other United Nations bodies (Mrs Wilson was asked to help in ensuring the small New Zealand delegation's coverage of the numerous United Nations Committees). Leader MLC 1947–49. Compiler of *History in the Making: a summary of the legislative and administrative actions of New Zealand's first Labour Government during its first year of office, November 27, 1935 to November 26, 1936* (London: Labour Bookroom, 1937).

J.V. Wilson 1894–1977
Erudite classical scholar, soldier, sophisticated international (International Labour Organisation and League of Nations) and New Zealand civil servant.

A key founding father of the New Zealand Foreign Service. Involved in drafting the United Nations Charter. Minister and first New Zealand Ambassador to France 1956–59. See Malcolm Templeton, *An eye, an ear and a voice: 50 Years in New Zealand's External Relations 1943–1993* (Wellington: Ministry of Foreign Affairs and Trade, 1993). (*DNZB* Vol. 5, p. 567)

Yoshida Shigeru 1878–1967
Notable Japanese diplomat and statesman, who advocated Japanese surrender. Appointed Foreign Minister and then Prime Minister 1946–47 and 1949–54; led rebirth of the Japanese economy and development of relations with the West.

Dick Collins was a prize captive in the early days of External Affairs, where he quickly became one of its stars. Early in the 1950s, he was sent to work with Berendsen at a UN General Assembly. That was a time when Berendsen regarded anyone from Wellington as an emissary from Satan. But he warmed to Dick, especially when he found that he was the son of Ginger Collins, whom he had known in the war years.

Then it was learned that the newly appointed Minister of External Affairs, Fred Doidge, was coming to New York. Berendsen commissioned Dick and Charles Craw to book a private room at a special restaurant and arrange a special menu that would please the great man.

Normally, Berendsen would keep almost hourly watch on what was being done to meet his wishes. But on this occasion, the dinner was only hours away when he asked what was planned. Dick said that the special course was Tripe a la Lyonnaise.

'What's that?" Berendsen snapped suspiciously. 'Sounds like tripe!'

'It is tripe,' Dick said. 'Very special tripe!'

Berendsen was indignant. 'By God, Collins, do you expect me to give my minister tripe? You'll have to change it!'

'No,' Dick said firmly. 'We can't do that. It's a special part of a special meal. It would spoil the whole thing!'

So the moment arrived. And when Doidge found he was to have tripe, he was ecstatic. 'I love tripe!' he declared.

'Yes, Minister,' Berendsen said. 'I thought you would.'

Tom Larkin

ILLUSTRATIONS

APPENDIX 1

NOTABLE SPEECHES

1. 'U.N. Charter Falls Short of Requirements: Veto Power a Negation of Equitable Democratic Principles' Sir Carl Berendsen, New Zealand Delegate to the United Nations General Assembly, 28 October 1946
2. 'Assurance Desired By N.Z. Violence Will Be Controlled' *The Dominion*, 27 November 1947, p. 7
3. 'Consideration of the Report of the Visiting Mission to Western Samoa' Ninth Meeting of the Trusteeship Council, 4 December 1947
4. 'Veto Seen As Threat To Security' *The Dominion*, 2 March 1948, p. 6H
5. 'Further Consideration of the Question of the Future Government of Palestine: Opening of the General Debate' Second Special Session of the General Assembly, First Committee 118th Meeting, 20 April 1948
6. 'U.N. Retrogressing Rapidly, Declares Sir Carl Berendsen' *The Dominion*, 10 July 1948, p. 7A
7. 'Japanese Peace Treaty: Statement by the New Zealand Delegate at the San Francisco Conference' *Documents on New Zealand External Relations* (Ed. Robin Kay) 1985, Vol. III, p. 1162
8. 'The ANZUS Pact and the Treaty of Peace with Japan' *Documents on New Zealand External Relations* (Ed. Robin Kay) 1985, Vol. III, p. 767
9. Editorial: 'The Best Use of Words as Weapons' *The San Francisco Examiner*, 15 September 1951
10. Speech by Sir Carl Berendsen at the Fourth Session of the United Nations General Assembly, New York, 22 September 1949
11. 'Allied Policy Towards Japan' Speech by Sir Carl Berendsen in the Far Eastern Commission, Washington, 11 December 1947
12. 'Question of the disposal of the former Italian colonies' Discussion of the report of Sub-Committee 17, Fourth Session of the United Nations General Assembly, New York, 4 November 1949
13. Extract from a statement by Sir Carl Berendsen on the veto at the Second Session of the United Nations General Assembly, New York, 20 September 1947

1. U.N. Charter Falls Short of Requirements: Veto Power a Negation of Equitable Democratic Principles

By Sir Carl Berendsen, New Zealand Delegate to the United Nations General Assembly 28 October 1946

'... My country is particularly interested in the question of trusteeship, not only because we have for thirty-two years been responsible for the mandated territory of Western Samoa, but also because of our long and increasingly happy association with their own indigenous fellow citizens, the Maoris, whom we all admire and respect. We can, I think, take some measure of legitimate satisfaction in the knowledge that all the Polynesian peoples for whom we are responsible are increasing rapidly in numbers and we believe that this fact is not without its evidentiary value as a test of successful administration.

Following upon the undertaking given . . . the New Zealand government, the first . . . to announce its intention to transfer an existing mandate to the new trusteeship system, prepared a draft trusteeship agreement . . . The agreement fulfills in our view the conditions of the Charter and we therefore hope that it will be accepted. . . .

In the discharge of their trusteeship responsibilities, the New Zealand government, one of the earliest advocates of this system, will make the welfare of the inhabitants their principal concern. And it is with this intention that we shall open our administration to the inspection of the United Nations. . . .

While warmly congratulating the Economic and Social Council on much that it has accomplished, we should like to sound one note of caution, indeed perhaps of criticism. We think there is some danger of over-elaboration in the organization of the United Nations. . . . [w] e look to the Assembly as the organizing center for new international institutions to give the best assurance of that high degree of financial and administrative integration which is so necessary in order to economize both money and effort. . . .

We are gratified that the Atomic Energy Commission began its work promptly and we hope that it will be able to proceed . . . with the utmost despatch. The main issue . . . is already perfectly clear. At the present moment, one State only is in possession of stocks of atomic bombs, and the knowledge of the full process of manufacturing them. That State offers to forego its enormous advantage on certain conditions. These conditions, and especially the right of international inspection, are by no means negligible. But are they unreasonable? The New Zealand government thinks not. . . . [S]ome organ must be empowered to make the necessary technical and administrative decisions without delay.

To delegate a sufficient degree of autonomy to the proposed Atomic authority, to save it from being paralyzed from any decisions of the Security Council, will, we realize, be a difficult matter. But here, of course, is the crux of any effective system of control. . . .

It is not the resolution of the Security Council which is to be feared, but its irresolution. . . .

I turn now to the question of voting powers in the Security Council which leads inevitably to consideration of the veto. The views of New Zealand on this matter have been stated from time to time by my prime minister, the Right Honorable Peter Fraser, and notably, during the course of the San Francisco Conference. Those views remain completely unaltered, and it falls to me today, merely to reemphasize those views and to add particularly in the light of what has since transpired. What are the qualifications . . . of a small country . . . to speak at all on this subject?. . .

What gives us this right? We have this right because we have established in our homeland in the southern seas, a true commonwealth, a home of liberty and of freedom where wealth is more evenly distributed, I believe, than in any other country in the world, where all can live a full and ample life, and all can strive as all do, to lay the foundations for a still better life for our children, and theirs. Have not we who have so much to lose, a stake in the maintenance of peace and the prohibition of war which would destroy all that we have done so much to create? Death or mutilation is just as stark and poignant a tragedy in my small land as it is in larger countries.

We have this right because twice in our time, isolated though we were, we in New Zealand have been involved in tragic war, the result of events at opposite ends of the world, freely, voluntarily pledging our all in the fight for international liberty and decency, which we recognized at once was our fight too.

We have this right, because in that cause we gave our best in blood and in treasure. The graves of New Zealanders throughout the whole world who died in defense of our beliefs, are a constant and eternal witness to the fact that our support of principles is not confined to words alone. If blood and tears, anguish and sacrifice, are the price to be paid for a voice, a proportionate voice in the world today, then we in New Zealand have paid that price.

We have this right: because the world today is one world; and there can be no lasting peace or prosperity in New Zealand unless there is peace and prosperity throughout the world.

And our demand for a voice is a modest one. We ask no veto; we ask no predominant or decisive voice. We ask for our proportionate voice in those councils which will influence the affairs of man as far ahead as man can see, a proportionate voice, no more, no less.

What now are the views of my country on the question of collective security generally. . .? It is just as much a disservice to the cause of peace to ignore the weaknesses as it is not to recognize the strength of the Organization that we have established for that great and high purpose. . . .

Now, in the first place, we . . . acknowledge at once that the Great Powers who played the predominant part in winning the war must similarly play the predominant part in winning the peace. . . . We agree therefore that some means must be devised to give to the vote and the voice of each Member of the United Nations such weight and authority as is proportionate to the size and the status of that Member. . . .

We agree, of course we agree, that the mere fact of the establishment of the United Nations, the provision of a public forum . . . is a real and substantial cause for universal satisfaction.

And we agree . . . with those provisions of the Charter which contemplate a determined and a long-scale effort to achieve a greater measure of economic justice as between nation and nation, as between man and man, and to provide for a more equitable distribution than exists at present of the good things that this earth can so abundantly provide.

And . . . finally we agree that what was achieved at San Francisco was the very best that could be attained at that time. . . . [a]nd . . . may still be the best that can be achieved now.

. . . . We, in New Zealand have never been able to understand

. . . why the Great Powers insisted on the right of veto on matters of peaceful settlement; but this with a much larger and more difficult question of the veto on enforcement action, was part of the price that the smaller Powers were called upon by the Great Powers to pay for the very existence of the United Nations. We agreed to pay this price. We thought it was a high price . . . . But we were not without a most earnest hope that in due course of time we should perhaps obtain a refund, that these Powers which had insisted on this privileged position would sooner or later – and sooner rather than later – find themselves able to agree to a modification of those principles.

I very much question whether anybody in the whole world today is satisfied with the transactions of the Security Council. . . . In taking resolutions on matters of substance, the Council is impeded by the veto. All the more reason why in the field where it is free from this incubus, namely in procedure, it should act with decision, and all the more reason why those Powers which have been granted these extraordinary privileges should see to it that those privileges are utilized with the fullest sense of the high responsibility of those five Powers to mankind.

We sincerely hope that the Security Council will . . . refrain from discussing at great length whether it should discuss a question. Let it use frankly and above all promptly its right to take a procedural vote on the establishment of agendas and others procedural matters.

Let the Security Council, . . . hampered as it is by the . . . veto, let the Security Council see to it that all due and proper care is taken, lest by frustration of its efforts to transact its vital business, lest by constant evidence of its futility, the Security Council should bring itself to stultification, and into public disrepute, lest it fail to win that priceless asset, the confidence of the whole world, which is essential to its success.

A second procedural matter of great importance is the participation in the Security Council discussions of Members of the United Nations not represented on that Council. We think there has been on occasion undue delay in inviting to the Council a State entitled to be represented under Article 31 of the Charter.

I turn now to a more fundamental discussion of the voting power of the Security Council and to the question of a possible revision of that power. . . . We dislike the veto as much as ever. We believe that side by side with the resolute effort to remove economic injustices, that [sic] there must be provided a completely effective system for the prevention of aggression, not at all to preserve the *status quo*, but certainly to prevent any alteration even of the *status quo* by individual national force.

We wish to see established an effective system of collective security, under which all contract that aggression against one is aggression against all and will be met and defeated as such. We believe that nothing short of this can, in the long run, be permanently effective; an agreement by all the right thinking peoples of the world that lawless force will always be met and defeated by lawful force wherever, whenever, with whatever justification, for whatever reason and in whatever circumstances an attempt is made to apply individual national force. Such a system properly and responsibly applied, with due regard to economic justice, would, we believe, achieve the desired end, but we also believe that nothing less can be permanently adequate.

. . . . I have already made plain how warmly we in New Zealand approve a provisional round-table for the public and detailed international discussion of differences. I did not elaborate that point nor did I say how warmly New Zealand approved the procedure established by the Charter for the peaceful settlement of international disputes and differences, but we do not believe that in the last resort the peace of the world can be permanently be preserved by words alone.

. . . [T]he Charter of the United Nations . . . clearly and properly contemplates provision of the use of force to repel aggression. . . . [H]istory accords abundant proof of the existence of predatory nations and predatory people who take advantage of the exigencies of the time to oppress and enslave their neighbours, and indeed, to seek the enslavement of the whole world.

Any attempt to rely on words alone to preserve world peace against a determined aggressor must lead inevitably to compromise with evil, to gross injustice to innocent and helpless people, and to that policy which has become known and properly despised, appeasement. And appeasement, in that sense, leads inevitably to war.

If then, words are not alone sufficient, as is clearly recognized by the Charter, how then does the Charter measure up to requirements? It failed in two important respects. In the first place, it failed because it provides no definite and inescapable pledge that aggression against one will be regarded as aggression against all and repelled accordingly. . . . [W]e will not have a completely effective Charter so long as this essential provision is absent.

The Charter fails, in the second place, by reason of the voting procedure established for the Security Council. . . . under which each of the five Great Powers reserve to themselves the right in every case, for any reason, however capricious, to decide whether it will or will not take part in any proposed resistance to aggression. . . . (and) to say not only whether it will take part, but whether the Organization as a whole can be allowed to function at all.

I pause here to compare this privileged position insisted upon for themselves by the Great Powers with the position of the Small Powers, who were asked to agree, and in fact did agree that they would be bound by the decision of the Security Council in all cases requiring action on their part. They were required to accept, and they did accept a provision that for all time to come they would apply force when called upon to do so by the Security Council acting, as it will, at an unknown time, in unknown circumstances, through unknown men, and to a substantially undetermined or unknown principle, a decision in which the smaller powers not only have no veto, they have no vote, and incredible as it may sound, no voice. I repeat – no vote, no voice, except for those of the lesser powers who happen, at the appropriate moment, to have been elected to a seat on the Security Council. . . .

Passing from this aspect, what have we now in this effort of ours to achieve collective security? We have a system that is not collective and is not security. We have an organization which cannot act against a Great Power, because of the veto. We have an organization which cannot act against a small Power, if that small Power is supported by a Great Power, because of the veto. We have an organization, then, which can act only against a small Power that is not supported by a Great Power.

What then is it that the world fears? Is it an attack on the peace of the world made by a small Power not supported by a Great Power? The question, of course, is derisory. If the five Great Powers are all agreed in the case of an attempt at aggression, then the world has nothing to fear. What we have established, then, is an organization that can be admirably adapted to crush aggression by a small Power, admirably adapted to take action in those circumstances where such an organization as this is almost entirely unnecessary, but largely precluded, by reason of the veto, from acting in those cases, and in those cases only, where mankind is in danger.

Indeed, I suggest to you that it is entirely essential that . . . as soon as may be – the nations of the world, and particularly the Great Powers, must consider whether an organization so limited as this can confidently hope to achieve its object.

Whoever heard of a fire department, each one of its five members of which reserved to itself the right to say whether he would go to a fire – even more, each one of the five members of which reserved the right to say whether the fire department could go to the fire or whether the fire would be allowed to rage unrestricted? Whoever heard of a police department, any one of five members of which reserved to himself the right to say whether he would attempt to arrest a criminal in the act of crime – more than that, any one of five members of which reserved to himself the right, not only that he would not attempt to prevent a crime, but to say that the whole police force cannot attempt to prevent a crime, and the crime would be allowed to be committed with impunity?

The Great Powers . . . must be prepared to venture some capital in this great movement to insure against war. They must be prepared to expend a little of their freedom to run their own affairs to suit themselves . . . to be guided by the public conscience of the world and not by their own unrestricted decision. Where success depends upon the contribution of all, all must contribute in due proportion. What the Great Powers are attempting to do is to have their cake and eat it too. . . .

Let me remind my colleagues. . . . The marriage of the veto to the Charter was a shot-gun wedding. If this matter had been left to the free and untrammelled vote of the delegates at that Conference, it would unquestionably have been defeated. . . .

The veto power . . . is not consonant with any law of logic or morality. . . . It is, in essence, the application of the false and pagan principle that might is right. It is a negation in the international field of principles of equitable democracy which are so dear to such a large section of mankind. It is an assertion of the indefensible principle that the Great Powers who, admittedly, comprise such a large proportion of the world's population and who, admittedly, have at their disposal an overwhelmingly predominant proportion of the material resources and the physical force of the world, are, at the same time, necessarily the repositories of all of the wisdom, all the determination, all the devotion that this great cause of peace demands. To merely state the proposition in these terms is to emphasize its essential fallacy.

Now we of the small nations happily are not alone in our doubts as to the effect of the veto in its present form. Apprehension, serious apprehension, has been explicitly expressed in recent weeks by more than one authority of unimpeachable competence and integrity. Among these, all have noted the recent comments on the veto power made by the Prime Minister of the United Kingdom, Mr. Clement Attlee. . . . [T]he United States Secretary of State, Mr. Byrnes, used this phrase: 'We must be willing to co-operate with one another, veto or no veto'. . . .

Now I challenge any person . . . to maintain the proposition that the veto, as such, is good of itself. . . . It is proper now to ask what can be done about this situation.

I do not pretend to know. Great Powers are, obviously, not at present convinced of the inequity and the dangers of the veto provisions. . . . And . . . it has been made quite impossible to amend the Charter without the consent of each of the five Great Powers. . . . [B]y this extraordinary provision, combined with a veto, this infant organization has been brought into the world with its hands manacled and its feet fettered. . . . though we are not without hope that some gradual progress can be made, perhaps along the lines of the Australian proposal.

What further can be done? I suggest at the moment, very little. . . . [A]ll that men of good will . . . can do in present circumstances is to pursue the object . . . a system of collective security which can indeed be relied upon to preserve mankind from the horrors of war, intensified a million fold, as they have been by recent scientific invention.

Secretary of State Bynes in his recent speech made the following comment: 'We must co-operate to build a world order; not to sanctify the *status quo*, but to preserve peace and freedom based upon justice and we must be willing to co-operate with one another – veto or no veto – to defend with force, if necessary, the principles and purposes of the Charter of the United Nations.' . . . We, in New Zealand are in full agreement . . . with that policy. That; that is the objective that we must pursue with patience, with firmness and with determination. That; nothing more. It is that, which we must in time achieve, if we are to fulfill our high and onerous responsibility to men and women of good will throughout the world today; to carry out that great trust that rests upon us, for our children and our children's children, as far ahead as the mind can reach; to preserve them from the horrors of war. That; and nothing less.'

2. Assurance Desired By N.Z. Violence Will Be Controlled

The Dominion, 27 November 1947 (p. 7)

'The New Zealand delegation stands for partition, but as I have already explained to the committee, the New Zealand government entertains apprehensions, serious and grave apprehensions, as to the adequacy of the proposal in respect of enforcement and implementation,' said Sir Carl Berendsen in a speech immediately before the United Nations committee voted on Palestine on Tuesday, a report of which has been supplied by the Department of External Affairs.

'I do not intend to repeat what I have already said on this subject. We wish to vote for partition, and we most solemnly and earnestly urge that the woefully weak provisions relating to enforcement and implementation be strengthened to the utmost extent that is now possible. It would, in particular, greatly help us in our very earnest consideration of this matter if we could have some understanding, some undertaking, some pledge from all the members of the United Nations, and particularly and especially from the permanent members of the Security Council, that if that contingency which we fear but which we most fervently hope will not arise, namely, disorder and bloodshed in Palestine, should in fact occur, then all will join at once in a united and concerted effort to suppress violence and implement the plan for partition by means of an international force to which all members of the United Nations will contribute in proportion to their strength.

'We urge this most earnestly as a duty which the United Nations owes to itself and to the people of Palestine, Arab and Jew alike. Such an undertaking would go a long way towards removing the doubts which we entertain. We hope that this appeal will not be ignored by the Great Powers especially, and that they may be able to make some statement on the matter at the meeting of the Assembly.

'In the meantime, my course in the committee decision is clear, and in the final vote on the partition proposals put forward by the first sub-committee. I shall abstain from voting without prejudice to the vote I shall cast on the matter when it finally comes before the assembly.'

3. Consideration of the Report of the Visiting Mission to Western Samoa

Ninth Meeting of the Trusteeship Council, 4 December 1947

'. . . . Let us start with the postulate that for a period of years the New Zealand Government has been convinced that some substantial further step could be taken in the direction of increased self-government for the Samoans. Well, we have been engaged in a war, a war of survival. During the period of the war, I think all my colleagues will agree, it was not practicable to take any steps in that desired direction. The only steps we were able to take with reference to our Samoan friends was to protect them from any ill effects as the result of the war, and that we did. When the war was over, we had the aftermath of war – the cleaning up after the war, gathering ourselves together and resuming our devastated economy. During that period it was not possible to take any effective steps. As soon as that period was over, we had the San Francisco Conference, the establishment of the United Nations, and with it the establishment of the Trusteeship System.

As a good Member of the United Nations, with a very sincere sense of our responsibilities to these magnificent people of Samoa, we considered it to be our duty to bring that former mandated territory under the Trusteeship System. We took the necessary steps to do that, and that is now being brought about. What was the first reaction of these people in Western Samoa? You all know. They produced a petition asking not for trusteeship status but for self-government under the protection of New Zealand. Obviously that petition had to be considered . . . and we felt it our duty to invite the Trusteeship Council to send a mission to Samoa to ascertain the facts on the spot. . . .

It was a source of great gratification to us to find that the lines upon which we were thinking and those upon which the Mission has reported were to a very large extent parallel. We were then faced with this dilemma, and this is the point which I really wish to explain to my colleagues as carefully as possible. If we let the report of the Mission take its normal course, what happens? The report comes to the Trusteeship Council, and we all agree that it has no effect whatsoever unless and until it is approved by the Trusteeship Council. Nor, indeed, will the decision of the Trusteeship Council have any effect unless and until it is approved by the General Assembly.

Now let us look at the time factor. . . . The Trusteeship Council cannot bring into effect any proposals whatever, nor can the General Assembly; it must be done by the New Zealand Parliament. The New Zealand Parliament meets from the end of June until, normally, early in November. If we wait for these recommendations – which, I repeat, are closely parallel to what was intended by the New Zealand Government, the only authority that can act – to go through the normal course, how long does that take? The report comes before the Trusteeship Council, but the New Zealand Parliament . . . is now out of session and will not meet again until next year. Thus, if the Trusteeship Council were to approve the report of the Mission – and since it is a body of very sensible men it certainly will – nothing could be done by the New Zealand Parliament this year, if we waited for the normal course of events.

But that is not all. The report of the Trusteeship Council must go before the General Assembly. It cannot go before this year's session of the General Assembly because this General Assembly has now completed its business. Therefore, it must go before the next General Assembly, which begins in September 1948. By the time that General Assembly has approved the Trusteeship Council's report, as of course it will, the New Zealand Parliament will have risen again and we should have a delay . . . of two or three years. . . .

I ask you gentlemen, what you would do, and I venture to throw out a little challenge that . . . there is not one of you . . . who would not have done what we did. We acted; it is our function to act. You still retain the same functions that you will always retain. You can either approve this report or disapprove it. . . . The New Zealand Government, as a good Member of the United Nations, would give the most earnest and careful consideration to such a decision. In the meantime, however, we should have lost two years and perhaps three. How could we explain that to the Samoans? How could you explain it to the Samoans?

I shall agree at once that there is something unorthodox . . . in our having acted. However, it was our right to act. . . . to save two or three years. . . . You can still say, if you are so unwise as to say it, that the Mission's report is wrong; and I undertake to say that my government will give the most earnest consideration to anything that this Council and the General Assembly may say.

The choice was between acting, as we were entitled to act, in the best interests of these people, and putting the matter back for years – and I challenge anyone to say that we should have put the matter back for years.'

4. Veto Seen As Threat To Security

The Dominion, 2 March 1948 (p. 6H)

'In United Nations we have an organisation magnificent to crush a prowling mouse, but helpless to fight a marauding tiger.' In these words the New Zealand Minister to the United States and New Zealand representative in the United Nations, Sir Carl Berendsen, in an address in Wellington last night, illustrated the effect of the veto on the power of United Nations to prevent war.

Any one of the five Great Powers could veto discussion or action by the Security Council against any aggressor it might support, he said, but any small nation which might be an aggressor could not prevent action to curb its aggression.

Sir Carl characterised the veto as 'a crowning and monumental piece of human folly' as a result of which the organisaton had entered the world 'with its hands manacled and its feet fettered.' It was not an adequate system of collective security and would not be so long as the veto was retained.

'Given time – if God gives us time – we can get a proper organisation if men will reason, and not fiddle,' he added.

What should be aimed at was a situation in which unlawful force was met by lawful force. Until that was attained there would be no collective security.

What was needed was a body which could establish international law, a body which could interpret international law – that had been established – and a body for enforcing international law.

'The first international law should be "Thou shalt not wage war," declared Sir Carl.

New Veto Suggested

Sir Carl said he would like to see the present single power of veto abolished and replaced by a veto of any two of the five Great Powers. It was not right that the vote of New Zealand, with about 2,000,000 inhabitants, should equal that of the United States, with many times the population, but he would like to see some system of weighted vote – which would take in other things than population – production, willingness to help in world affairs, and so on.

'If enough well-thinking members agreed to attack any nation which became an aggressor, I am convinced we should never have an aggressor,' he said. 'That is a serious risk, but we must take that risk.

'The alternative the world needs is not resolutions. It is resolution. If we have resolution, we shall never have to use it.

'It may well be we are approaching a new climacteric in the affairs of men. There is a cleavage between those who believe in the secret ballot and those who believe in the secret police.'

The difficulty at the moment was the heated passions on both sides. The only way to overcome this was infinite patience and determination – the determination to hold fast to principle.

'If we won't have either, I fear the worst,' said Sir Carl. 'I believe the problem to be solved is a moral one. The League of Nations failed for a moral reason, because its members had not the courage to do right.

'Twice in our day the transgressor has made a raid on civilisation. Twice democracy was unready and had to buy time with the flower of its youth. That cannot happen again in these atomic days, when the first blow may well be the last.'

The remedy in the first place was collective security. Then the distribution of the world's good things must be equalised, even if in so doing they had to give up some of their good things to the less fortunate of mankind. And thirdly, they must approach problems not with the consideration of what was good for them, but with a consideration of what was right.

'Nothing is politically wise unless it is morally right. There must be no compromise of principle.

'The alternative is a relapse to the old power politics. Enlightened, determined, public opinion alone will ensure the success of the great and noble undertaking. In our trembling hands today we hold nothing less than the fate of man.'

5. Further Consideration of the Question of the Future Government of Palestine: Opening of the General Debate

Second Special Session of the General Assembly, First Committee, 118th Meeting, 20 April 1948

SIR CARL BERENDSEN (New Zealand). . . . wished to make some general observations on behalf of his Government. The tragic situation leading to their meeting had laid a heavy responsibility on all Members and laid upon all Governments the duty, as well as the right, to set forth their views plainly. During the previous November the problem before them had been admitted to be difficult and intractable. The situation then was the cumulative result of many events in the past and in particular of the Balfour Declaration in 1917. That, like most international documents, was open to various constructions. . . . The United Kingdom had been given the Mandate for Palestine with the approval of many of the nations now present, and had administered the Mandate with high motives and with some degree of success. . . . [T] hey had tried to reconcile the irreconcilable, but neither Arabs nor Jews would compromise. There had been periodic bloodshed, involving on many occasions not only the two contesting sides but also the British. The latter had a thankless job and had at last decided that they could no longer bear alone the odium of what was clearly an international task, while others were free to criticize without accepting responsibility. Moreover, the United Kingdom had devoted itself completely to the war for liberty and, as a result, was in a difficult position. Because of its temporary weakness brought on by sacrifices in blood, treasure and repute, the United Kingdom found its thankless task too great, and had passed it to the United Nations as a world problem. . . . [N]o nation, even if one had been willing could have done better. . . .

After mature and anxious consideration, the (second regular session in November 1947) Assembly decided . . . by a two thirds majority, that the best available course was partition with economic union. An imposing list of States had supported this plan, and it would interesting to find out how many still held those views. He did not suggest that any State then favouring partition with economic union thought the solution to be perfect, for any decision would necessarily impose some measure of hardship and injustice. It represented, however, the best that could be done in the circumstances with the least injustice and departure from principle.

The New Zealand government believed . . . that partition with economic union offered the best solution. He believed that the Assembly had decided to do the right thing, but in the wrong way. He had pointed out in November that the partition plan was good but that if the Assembly assumed the right to divide the State, it should also assume the duty of implementing the plan in a peaceful and orderly manner. He had expressed his anxiety as to the success of the plan if there were not provisions for enforcement. . . . The Assembly, however, had preferred to gamble on the issue and had lost, but the losses were being paid by the people in Palestine, mainly by the Jews and the Arabs, but also by the British. The Assembly's disgrace was that it had not faced inevitable facts. Many had naively professed to believe that enforcement was unnecessary, despite the seriousness of the Arab warnings and pleas. It was hard to understand how anyone could have thought a peaceful solution was possible since the problem admitted of no perfect solution. Nevertheless the plan could have been effective if the proper steps had been taken.

Other representatives last year had appeared to think that, although force was needed, it had been provided for from two sources. There were to be both Arab and Jewish militias which were to keep order and, moreover, the Security Council would ensure enforcement. The former concept was again very inadequate and as for the latter they need only consider the existing situation. Out of this error of judgment had arisen the present situation where murder and outrage were rampant. A further result was the risk that the General Assembly would lose the public confidence upon which its authority depended.

. . . . Unless the Assembly could offer steady and consistent leadership it would lose its following and confusion and dismay would ensue. This did not mean that policies should remain immutable when circumstances changed, but the New Zealand delegation believed that if partition with economic union was right in November it is right today. The circumstances have not changed since the matter was so carefully considered and debated in November. The only new factor in this case was a series of murders and outrages on both sides. Neither the Jewish nor the Arab actions could be defended or explained; both should be strongly censured and both called for repression by lawful force. Whether the actions were alleged to be for or against partition, outrages remained outrages.

Nothing, or at least very little, had been done . . . to further the November decision or take counter-measures against the known opposition. Yet, it was not alleged that partition had become impossible because of a series of outrages. These acts should have been foreseen and, further, they were no excuse for abandoning the Assembly's decision. The Assembly would be taking a very grave responsibility if it allowed its resolution to be stultified by illegal violence. As to the force required by the General Assembly to implement partition, he doubted that it would be any greater than that needed to impose a trusteeship at the present time. If the Members would accept a share of duty in order to implement trusteeship, they should equally do so to in order to implement the decision of last November. The New Zealand policy for the present Assembly was that it should enforce its decision on partition, undeterred by violence, since the plan was the best available under the circumstances. He urged very earnest thought before any abandonment of principle because of outrages which had been foreseen. Otherwise he thought that a tragic blow against the United Nations might be struck. They should not capitulate to threats and violence and ought to realize that they could not maintain order in the world by words alone.

New Zealand would continue to urge the enforcement of partition but would examine any proposals which could achieve a just and reasonable truce, and would indeed welcome them warmly. He believed the problem amounted to a test case for the future of the United Nations. What was required was not resolutions but resolution. They should not add to the irresponsibility of their November decision for partition without provision for enforcement, the further and perhaps the final irresponsibility of surrender to illegal force.

6. U.N. Retrogressing Rapidly, Declares Sir Carl Berendsen

The Dominion, 10 July 1948 (p. 7A)

Speaking up for many a smaller Power, Sir Carl Berendsen (New Zealand) voiced fear today that the United Nations was retrogressing rapidly. He told the Little Assembly that the only way to keep world peace was to abolish the veto and adopt real collective security.

The Philippines and Argentina also called for elimination of the veto instead of partial abolition, which was approved yesterday.

The Little Assembly yesterday recommended the Big Five to agree to drop their veto on cases involving the peaceful settlement of disputes, on applications for United Nations membership, and on decisions whether issues are vetoable. Sir Carl Berendsen said he accepted yesterday's decisions but termed them 'chickenfeed'. The Security Council, with its veto tangles, had been a 'deplorable failure' and the General Assembly itself had put up some dismal performances.

'The world faces an unfortunate and menacing cleavage – a cleavage between East and West, between those who believe in the supremacy of the State and those who believe in the supremacy of the individual, between those who, as a distinguished American has said, believe in the secret ballot and those who believe in secret police,' he said. 'Removing the veto would not affect this menacing situation; collective security is a thing of the spirit. It depends on the determination of mankind to do right and resist wrong. But until the veto is removed you cannot establish collective security through this organisation. If the veto is removed you have a chance – depending on your spirit, courage and determination.'

7. Japanese Peace Treaty

Statement by the New Zealand Delegate at the San Francisco Conference, 6 September 1951

'Mr President, Delegates, it is an historic occasion upon which we are gathered together and an historic and a friendly city in which we meet. . . .

It is our purpose at this conference to bring to an end one among many – agonising and tragic – of those fatal paroxysms which from time to time seem to carry a nation to madness and to evil. We are met here today formally to terminate the conflict that was forced upon us by the unprovoked aggression of Japan; to bury, we hope for all time, our just resentment, our righteous indignation at wanton aggression, our horror and revulsion at the atrocities with which this aggression was perpetrated. We are met here to welcome once more to the comity of nations a great people – a great people – who until, possessed of demons, they chose the path of evil two decades ago, had deservedly won the honour, the respect and the admiration of the whole world. Today we put the sad past behind us; today we extend the hand of fellowship to the Japanese nation and the Japanese people.

This is indeed an unusual conference. . . . because . . . it has not been possible to discuss in the customary fashion the terms of the engagement into which we are about to enter. The sad fact is that one group of peoples has been determined in this, as in every other, matter to have their own way or disrupt, confuse and divide as best they may. . . .

And the conference is unusual . . . in that this peace settlement has been deferred for an unusually long time. . . . [T]here is at least one real and substantial advantage in the delay . . . inasmuch as high and outraged indignation has had time to cool and thus render it possible to produce such a peace as is now contemplated today – a good peace; a peace of reason, a peace of hope. But the time has clearly arrived when there must be a clarification and a settlement; when Japan must be accorded once again that full sovereignty which is Japan's right and without which Japan can never recover its proper and useful place in the world of today.

No one, I think, will suggest that the treaty we are about to sign is satisfactory to all. . . . [I]n its entirety it does not completely satisfy any country represented here. . . . [I]t does not entirely satisfy New Zealand . . . in respect of security we would have welcomed some reasonable limitation of Japanese offensive armaments, some greater measure of assurance that that struggle which was so brutally forced upon us, that savage attack which was so narrowly beaten back, could never occur again in our time.

For our part we wish the Japanese well; we have no desire to hold Japan in bondage nor to reduce a proud, energetic and capable people to a status of inferiority. But geography has determined that Japan and New Zealand alike must live in the Pacific, and at no great distance as the airplane flies today. For four long and harrowing years, recklessly and wantonly, Japan made us struggle for our very existence, and the might and power of our friendly allies and the heart-rending sacrifice of our own blood and our own resources barely and narrowly sufficed to save us from slavery or extinction. It is but natural that there should linger in New Zealand some misgivings as to the shape of things to come in the Pacific, some concern as to . . . the policy and the disposition of the Japan of the future. Our one concern has been security. As prudent men responsible for the safety of our country in the years, in the decades and the centuries that are coming, we have felt that we must be guided in some degree, in our hopes and apprehensions for the future, by our perils and our sufferings in the past.

A number of considerations . . . have influenced our thinking . . . on this particular question of security. On the one hand, we have felt that the conventional method of the past for providing against a recrudescence of aggression – the system of physical limitations, controls and penalties – has not, on the whole, proved successful, and even when it has been successful, it has seldom been successful long. Furthermore, two additional considerations have weighed heavily on our minds. . . . Firstly, and indirectly, are those democratic reforms which have been instituted in Japan during the . . . occupation. It is of importance to us, to our security and to the security of the Pacific, that these reforms be maintained and consolidated, because it is to our interests, as well as our earnest desire, that the Japanese people should enjoy political, economic and democratic progress, that they should become a contented people looking forward from generation to generation to a life of reasonable comfort and proper achievement; that, we feel, will help us as well as the Japanese.

And more directly to remove our apprehensions we have been privileged last week to enter into a tripartite security treaty with the United States and Australia under which each of the three parties agrees to regard an attack on one as a danger to the others and to act accordingly through its constitutional channels.

From another point of view, Japan's capacity for future aggression, . . . is of course, in accordance with the terms of the treaty, substantially reduced by the removal of territories outside of the Japanese mainlands and by Japan's now limited economic resources.

And finally, in these days of a world-wide attack by a ruthless dictatorship on the freedom and liberty of the whole world, it would not . . . be wise to leave . . . a "power vacuum" in such a critical locality as Japan. So there we have our choice – either to leave Japan an easy prey to Communist aggression or to take the risk . . . of abandoning restrictions on Japan's power to rearm for defence.

It is the latter course that we have chosen. And if it is a risk it is a risk that we in New Zealand have taken with our eyes open as an earnest of the intention of our small country to play its part as a good neighbour in the Pacific. The onus is on Japan to fulfil this trust as we hope and believe Japan will fulfil it.

For the rest, in the words of that distinguished American who, more than any other man, is to be honoured as the architect of this treaty; in the just phrase of Mr John Foster Dulles "each nation has voluntarily subordinated some special interest so that a broad basis of unity might be found". A broad basis of unity has been found and the document now before us represents, we believe, the highest common factor of differing interests and desires. It is a just peace that we are about to sign, a peace of generosity, of forbearance, of reconciliation, and of renewed faith in mankind. Absent entirely are those heritages of the past, the "war guilt" clause, the machinery for control and supervision, the imposed penalties, the continued occupation, the huge and crushing bill of costs and reparations. This is a peace that contains no elements of revenge or of a justifiable resentment; it is a peace of good hope and good will.

And what are we to say of the objections . . . by the Soviet Union and its satellite supporters? Merely this, that these objections are entirely in line with the disruptive policies in international affairs that are consistently being pursued by this group of totalitarian countries. These people have not come here with any intention of assisting Japan or of advancing the cause of peace. They have come here to do mischief. If the representatives of the Soviet Union had any idea of co-operation they could have shown their good faith . . . by discussing with the United States . . . the details of the draft which is now before us. If they had been sincere in their approach . . . they would have proffered their detailed proposals, as did all other countries, at the proper time. . . . If they had wished to provide another earnest of good faith they could most certainly have done so, by lifting the mystery of those hundreds of thousands of Japanese prisoners of war in Siberia of whose fate, six years after the termination of hostilities, nothing whatever is known.

Having regard to the benevolent nature of the treaty we sign, the epithets thrown by the Soviet group do not disturb us. Allegations of the "dictatorship" of the United States leave us unperturbed. Mr Secretary, your name, the name of your country, conveys no terrors to us. We who live in the Pacific are sensitive indeed to any threat of dictatorship. We know the record of the United States, however, and we have no apprehensions whatsoever in that connection. But we know the record of others, also, and it is the threat of dictatorship by others which arouses our apprehension, our alarm, and inspires our necessary and moderate precautions to protect ourselves.

Nor do we see any objection to the proposal that United States troops should, at the request of the Japanese, remain in Japan for an agreed period. . . . For our part we would welcome such a proposal, as a necessary precaution for the security and the stability of the area and as a deterrent to aggression from the Asian mainland

Nor have we been impressed by the Soviet contention . . . that the Japanese peace treaty, to be legitimate and to be effective, must be the product of the larger powers alone. That is a thesis which neither we nor any other self-respecting small power can possibly accept. . . . [T]he best way for the Soviet Union to assist in reducing tension is to cease from creating tension; . . . the best way for the Soviet Union to achieve peace, if indeed it desires peace, is to make peace. . . .

The United States, with the full co-operation of the United Kingdom, Australia, New Zealand and other members of the British Commonwealth, fought the Japanese for four years; the Soviet Union fought the Japanese for six days. . . . It ill becomes a country which by the looting of Manchuria and the occupation of the Kuriles has profited so greatly, to cavil at the honest, careful and moderate attempts of the United States and others finally to dispose of the difficult and intricate questions involved in making a peace with Japan.

It is the intention of the New Zealand Delegation to sign the draft treaty now presented to us. It is a grave, a great and a noble experiment in humanity that we make; we make it in good faith, in the hope that good faith will in turn evoke good faith, and it is our earnest and fervent prayer, as it will be of right thinking people the world over, that history will justify and sanctify what we do here, that the nations may learn that good faith and good will offer stronger hopes for the well being and prosperity of mankind than any recourse to power or evil. It is our hope – and our belief – that what we do here will lay a firm and sure foundation for the peace, prosperity and happiness of Japan, the Pacific and the world.

8. The ANZUS Pact and the Treaty of Peace with Japan

Statement by Sir Carl Berendsen at the Signing of the Treaty, San Francisco, 1 September 1951

I sign this treaty on behalf of my country with a deep sense of the privilege that is mine and with a firm confidence of real and lasting achievement. We in New Zealand are not of those who ask what we are not prepared to give; we are not of those who demand help which we are not prepared to accord; we are not of those who are content to leave to others burdens which we should ourselves assume. In our short history we have always been ready to give what we have been ready to ask. Man for man we have played, and are playing our full part – sometimes, in legitimate pride, we think more than our full part in those great struggles of our time which have called for the co-operation of all right-thinking peoples. And the pact we sign today is one of co-operation, a joint offer and assurance of aid, real and immediate, should aid be needed. In this treaty the three signatories accept the same, and a common, duty. It is not a guarantee of the security of New Zealand by the United States and Australia, of Australia by the United States and New Zealand, of the United States by Australia and New Zealand. It is a common undertaking to regard a danger to one as a danger to all, a common assumption of formal duty – the same identical duty – by each of the three parties. It is a reaffirmation, especially heartening and encouraging at such a time as this, that these three countries, which have fought together in two great wars, have established a true and lasting comradeship and goodwill, and a common trust and confidence. And it is more than a pious and friendly expression of such sentiments.

Each of the parties has proved not only its fidelity to its pledged word but its ability and its determination, if and when the dread need arises, to turn from words to acts, and to prove, by its courage and its resolution, its ability to fight, when fight it must, to preserve its liberty and its way of life. In this treaty the three parties serve notice, clear and unequivocal, that, in the words of the treaty itself, 'no potential aggressor could be under the illusion that any of them stand alone in the Pacific area.'

The treaty therefore rests upon the solid basis of common interests and ideals, upon the regard and affection of the respective peoples, upon their common desire for peace and upon their common determination to resist aggression. It reflects also the inescapable facts of geography on the one hand and on the other the especial perils to which the Pacific may be exposed in the course of this world-wide conflict between liberty and slavery with which the whole of mankind is today oppressed. And the reassurance which this treaty affords us enables us to approach with an easier mind and a fuller confidence, the task that lies before us next week the completion of a treaty of peace with Japan; a treaty of generosity, of forbearance, of reconciliation and of renewed hope for the future.

Nor is the treaty isolationist in its nature. We in New Zealand have no reason to fear any suggestion, malevolent or ignorant, of selfish or isolationist intentions. Our history – the history of two world wars and New Zealand's armed and active participation all over the world in those causes which we have believed to be just – is the answer. We believe, and our acts and our policies have implemented that belief, that a true democracy must be willing to serve wherever democracy needs to be defended.

And accordingly this treaty does not restrict itself to its parties alone; it contemplates close and constant consultation with others of like interests or in like peril. By creating an area of stability in the Pacific this treaty may be expected to reduce world tensions and thus to prove a reinforcement of, and a contribution to, the general system of international security which is today slowly – but we hope surely – being erected. By providing directly a strong measure of defense against attack in the Pacific it does at the same time, in so doing, make it possible for its parties to play their part elsewhere; because the problem that the free world is facing today is a global problem – it is merely the manifestations of that problem which may from time to time appear to be local.

And, finally, the treaty has no effect whatsoever unless and until one of its parties is attacked. It is purely and solely a measure of self-protection against the perils with which today all freedom-loving countries are menaced. It is defensive in purpose and in effect, a threat to no one, and no country, the wide world over.

While in its explicit terms it is primarily a reassurance, an affirmation, an undertaking that in case of need none of its parties will stand alone, in its potential effects it might prove of even greater – perhaps of decisive – importance. The notice that is served today upon any evildoer might, indeed, have the effect of eliminating for all time that very aggression which alone can bring this treaty into practical application. There lies our hope – and our belief.

From this – and every other – point of view the treaty is clearly, demonstrably and entirely in conformity with the aims and the principles of the United Nations and with the hopes and ideals of people of good will everywhere.

Today we sign this treaty, which offers such great hope to all of us, here in the Presidio, a centre of great historical significance, the repository of a wealth of memories and traditions; today we make a new tradition, create a new memory, of something which, if God pleases, we will find to be good and prove to be enduring. Here at the Golden Gate we sign today a beneficent pact which, I believe, may itself open a golden portal to the peace, prosperity and happiness of the Pacific and of the future that lies before us.

9. The Best Use of Words as Weapons

Editorial in The San Francisco Examiner, 15 September 1951

The most effective and the most popular speaker at the San Francisco Conference was New Zealand's skilful and personable ambassador to the United States, Sir Carl Berendsen.

The masterful use of words as weapons by Sir Carl was utterly devastating in its effect upon the positions of the Soviet Union and the Communist satellite nations before the conference, making their position not merely untenable but ridiculous.

It had been the purpose of the Communist delegations to prolong and confuse and eventually to disrupt the conference, as Sir Carl so succinctly put it, TO DO MISCHIEF.

Everybody else knew why the Russians and their puppets were there, and the Russians of course knew it better than anyone else, but it was left to the forthright New Zealander to set up the barrier of words essential to the defeat of that purpose. . . .

The potentiality of the Russians for disturbance and disruption of the San Francisco conference, which had never been very far above the point of diminishing returns, reached the vanishing point with the straightforward speech of the good natured and good humoured New Zealand statesman who earned a permanent and honoured place in the esteem and affections of all Americans.

10. Speech by Sir Carl Berendsen at the Fourth Session of the United Nations General Assembly

New York, 22 September 1949

It had not been my intention to take part in this general debate, but this is our annual stocktaking, our periodical survey of our achievements and our failures, of value not so much perhaps to us here, who know full well not only what we have done but what we have not done, as to the millions of right-thinking men and women in the world who pin their highest hopes on the success of this Organisation. From that point of view, it seemed to me and to my colleagues of the New Zealand delegation to be our duty to express, as shortly and as succinctly as may be, our general views on the progress of the United Nations, its successes, its failures, and its prospects for the future.

There is much – and it is well to place this fact in the forefront of any appraisal of the work of the United Nations – on which we can congratulate ourselves, much for which the world should be truly thankful. That the Organisation exists at all is in itself a matter of great and happy moment to mankind; whatever the merits and defects of our Organisation today, there must be such an organisation as this if man is to discuss man's problems in a manly and sensible way. And even in the matter of achievement, there is much that is gratifying, much without which the world would be less happy, less secure, and less hopeful.

Let us glance for a moment at this aspect. We can all agree that one substantial buttress of peace would be the removal or alleviation of the admitted economic and social injustices and inequalities which are so prevalent throughout the world today; that if we could make a determined, and enduring, and a successful effort to level up in the international field the distribution of the material resources and the amenities of life which are possessed in such full measure by the more fortunate of the nations, then one potential cause of conflict would be removed or greatly reduced. It was to rectify or alleviate this sort of injustice – and this is indeed within the power of man – that the Economic and Social Council was established. There is much – very much – in the work of that Council that gives ground for encouragement, and my

Government feels that the steady consistent work of international co-operation in the economic and social field is one of the most hopeful measures of the success of the United Nations.

My own country, New Zealand, has had a very special interest in the Economic and Social Council during the present year – its final year as a member of that body – because one of its representatives has held the office of President of the Council. The work of my colleague Mr Thorn in this office has been a matter of great pride and satisfaction to the people and the Government of New Zealand. Another New Zealander, Dr Sutch, has been Chairman of the Council's Social Commission. Those intimately associated with the Council's proceedings will agree that it is indeed overcoming many of the weaknesses apparent in its early stages, and in particular that it is now – and very properly – endeavouring to concentrate on measures of a constructive character.

Here may I pause to call attention to a very serious difficulty? We must not allow our hearts to run away with our heads; we must not allow our anxiety to achieve results as quickly as possible over as wide a field as possible to lead us too far and too fast. We do now run a risk of so dissipating our energies and our resources in endeavouring to do too much too soon that in the long-run we may fail to do enough. There can be few of us who were not shocked and astonished at the figures quoted by our colleague from Brazil as to the number of meetings held under the aegis of this Organisation. When one hears of between 3,000 and 4,000 meetings annually under this Organisation alone, one wonders how such meetings can possibly be adequately manned, how the cost of such meetings can possibly be met. It is quite clear that if meetings go on multiplying at this rate, many members, and certainly the smaller countries, will be unable effectively to cope with these demands. I suggest that we must pick and choose; first things first.

The recent session of the Economic and Social Council in Geneva was distinguished by the consideration given to the highly important question of technical assistance to underdeveloped countries. There are hundreds of millions of the inhabitants of this globe – our fellow human beings – who do not have enough to eat, do not have enough to wear, do not have the tools or the skills which can assist them to improve their living standards. These peoples – I repeat, hundreds of millions, mainly in the underdeveloped countries – can indeed be assisted by those nations here represented who are fortunate enough to have more fully developed economic systems. My Government lays great stress – very great stress – on the necessity for the economically strong to assist the economically weak, and, as we have already announced in the Economic and Social Council, when the scheme of technical assistance for economic development comes into operation New Zealand will make a full contribution to this inspiring means of international co-operation.

My Government earnestly hopes that the scheme for technical assistance for economic and social development will be quickly worked out and put into practice. In fact, my country has, to the extent of its capacity, already been assisting in international work in economic and social development. We, of course, made our contributions to UNRRA and to the Children's Fund, and, in addition, there is other work which New Zealand shares with countries with interests in the South Pacific – I refer particularly to the South Pacific Commission, where the countries concerned have agreed to a joint programme designed to raise the economic and social standards of the islands of the Pacific which come under their care. My Government has already made substantial commitments in this field of international assistance. And it would be proper here – I am sure that every one of my colleagues would agree with me – to pay a tribute to the spirit animating President Truman's "fourth point" and to the activity of the United States Government, which is endeavouring so strenuously to give reality to the proposals now under consideration. This, indeed, is one way in which the sufferings of a large proportion of mankind can be relieved, provided – and this condition applies to many of the matters that are discussed in the United Nations and its subsidiary bodies – that our activities are translated into deeds. I should be the last to minimise the usefulness of words, but words, however noble, are not enough. Fine words butter no parsnips. Fine words fill no stomachs. Fine words prevent no wars. Amongst the greatest, and I suggest to you, most common fallacies of our time is the apparently unshakable belief that, once you have passed a resolution, you have done something. Believe me, there is something quite fundamental there. The belief in words, and in words alone, can indeed bring to naught the noblest of intentions. The aim of this Organisation clearly must be words followed by deeds.

The New Zealand Government notes with interest and with warm approval the importance that is attached by the Economic and Social Council, and by very many members of the United Nations, to the adoption of policies calculated to lead to full employment everywhere. This seems to us to be a fundamental requirement, and it has been an essential policy of my Government even before this Organisation was established. Success will require co-operative action in many spheres and by many of the specialised agencies, and all this work must be co-ordinated by the Economic and Social Council and supervised by the General Assembly. We feel that this is a work of real importance, of real urgency, and we are hoping to play a full part in committee discussions on this subject. The emphasis, however, must now be put on the examination of the numerous problems to be solved before we can make full employment policies on an international level effective.

I should like now to refer in passing to those very important proposals that have been drafted in respect of genocide and human rights. These do, indeed, mark an important step forward in man's development. But again, let us not deceive ourselves. The drafting of conventions does not in itself effect anything; it merely points a way. The conventions in practice will mean little or nothing unless and until the nations of the world adopt them – and, even then, they may be largely ineffective unless the nations of the world implement them. It can scarcely be suggested, for example, that a people who could sink to such a depth of turpitude as to be guilty of genocide are likely to attach any meticulous importance to their pledged word in a convention. It could scarcely be suggested that they are likely to shrink from a breach of their word. The mere signature of a convention does not – unless we are determined to see that it does – necessarily lead to the elimination of this horror of genocide. Nor, of course, are human rights for all times to be preserved merely because the nations declare that they should be.

And we must not lose sight of the fundamentally important functions exercised by the United Nations in the promotion of understanding among its members and in the field of conciliation. It is of the utmost importance to mankind that the world should possess a forum such as this, a table around which all the nations of the world can gather to discuss their mutual problems and to endeavour so to adjust matters that the common welfare of all may be achieved. If time permitted, I should welcome the opportunity of recording many instances of successful conciliation which have, in some cases, removed a threat of conflict and, in others, greatly reduced such a threat.

Now, all those things are good. They are, I think, better than the man and the woman in the street fully realise. They are unquestionably and incontestably sufficiently good for the United Nations to deserve, to demand, the fullest encouragement and support from every honest citizen in every country in the world. That support must be accorded, must be continued, must be increased. And I could stop here, with great satisfaction to myself and without having stated one thing that is not completely true.

But I should not have told the whole truth. These things, I say, are good; they are very good, but they are not good enough. Unless now, and in the years immediately to come, we are successful in preventing war, the soaring hopes of mankind will fall broken to the ground. The preservation of peace, the prevention of war, is the first and most fundamental problem upon the solution of which depends everything else. This Organisation was established to prevent the unlawful use of force. The primary purpose of this Organisation was the establishment of a system of collective security. In that primary purpose – and there should be no attempt to conceal the fact – we have not been successful. I suggest that it is a disservice to the United Nations, a disservice to the cause of peace, to pretend to ourselves that we possess in the United Nations an effective system of collective security. Every informed man or woman knows by now that we possess no such thing. It is true, most regrettably true, as the representative of Brazil pointed out to us in his opening speech, that this Organisation has been singularly unfortunate in the international climate in which it has had to operate, and that the world-wide clash of ideologies between those on the one hand who believe in the supremacy of the individual, and those on the other hand who believe in the supremacy of the state, between democracy as we know it and authoritarianism, between those who desire to implement the principles and objects of the Charter of the United Nations and those who have too often appeared to desire the stultification of that body, has placed a strain – not clearly foreseen – on a young organisation which has proved beyond its strength. No doubt much of this is true, but the plain fact of the matter is that the structure which was approved in San Francisco was never adequate to support an effective system of collective security.

I do not intend to inflict upon the General Assembly another exposition of my country's views on the veto power which has so crippled this organisation as a means of preserving peace. But those views remain unaltered and I must repeat what I have said so often from this rostrum – namely, that while each of the five great powers insists on retaining to itself not only the right to say whether it itself will take action, but, incredible as it may sound, the right to prevent the organisation from taking action, even if that one great power is in a minority of one – while this blot on the Charter remains we can never have an effective system of collective security. I do not presume to say to the five great powers that they should relinquish this great and pregnant privilege. That is their business. But I do say that unless and until they do relinquish that privilege there never can be an effective system of collective security.

That what I say is true will, I think, be widely admitted, and I suggest that it is proved by the necessity of the establishment, for purposes of self-defence, of two separate and limited systems of collective security, one on this continent, the other the Atlantic Pact. I have nothing whatever to say against those thoroughly justifiable and non-aggressive agreements for self-defence. They are – most unhappily – essential in circumstances as they exist today. They are incontestably justifiable if and so long as they meet, as they do at present meet, the following three conditions – namely, that they do not represent any threat to to any peace-loving state, that they are for the parties a real and not merely a verbal reinforcement of security, for the smaller countries in the group as well as for the greater, and – which is of primary importance to a country such as mine – that they are not regarded as an excuse for non-participation in more general action by the United Nations in the case of acts of aggression or threats to the peace which are not covered by the terms of the particular arrangement. But no one can possibly suggest – and no one, I think, has attempted to suggest – that the peace of the world can, in the long-run, be maintained by such limited and partial arrangements. I could not agree more fully with what the representative of the United States said in his address – namely, that the problem of peace is a universal problem which cannot be solved except on a universal basis.

The long and the short of it – as sensible men and women throughout the world should always remember – is that while we have in this organisation something that is very precious indeed and something that is worthy of all support, nevertheless, we do not have the one thing, the means of defeating aggression, which in the long-run man must achieve or perish.

I am one of those who believe that if the world has the good fortune to enjoy a long enough period of peace, the United Nations will prove itself able to preserve the peace; that if we have sufficient time we shall find means to free ourselves of the shackles of the veto and to establish an effective Organisation of all peace and liberty loving countries determined to protect themselves, all for one and one for all, against any aggression. But have we the time? I do not know and you do not know. This much is certainly abundantly clear: the problem is not only fundamental and vital, it is insistent, it is urgent, it is on our very doorsteps, it is in our every home. Man must solve this problem – and solve it in time – or man will perish.

11. Allied Policy Towards Japan

Speech by Sir Carl Berendsen in the Far Eastern Commission, Washington, 11 December 1947

Of course, we realise that it is entirely natural and understandable that an occupying power holding such a predominant place in Japan as does the United States should earnestly desire to avoid any unnecessary complication of its difficult and delicate task. It is also true that it is difficult to build a democratic country out of a hungry people. These things are plain and undeniable.

But there is another principle involved. If there is to be hardship, and if at a time like this when there is not food enough to go around, anyone has to go short, then clearly, as we see it, the shortage and the suffering should fall upon the aggressors and not upon their victims. There does not seem to be any reason whatever, in logic or in equity, why for example, the people of China, or Malaya or the Philippines or India or Burma, or, indeed, any of the peoples of the world who are suffering from hunger as a direct result of Japanese aggression, should be allowed to go short of food in a time of desperate need while the Japanese, the substantial cause of their miseries, are supplied with food in greater proportion. The paper before us acknowledges this general principle, the validity of which, of course, is unquestionable, but the paper provides an important exception, in that the Japanese may be permitted to receive more food than their former victims if such extra food is necessary to prevent such starvation and widespread disease and civil unrest as will endanger the safety of the occupation forces. This is an exception, sir, which may become both unjust and dangerous.

It may become unjust because it can lead to a violation of that general principle I have referred to, and it may become dangerous because it leaves the way open for the Japanese, by deliberately fomenting internal disorder, to induce SCAP and the United States Government to allow more food. But, of course, in the proper discharge of the Commission's responsibilities, it is clear to all of us that such an exception must be inserted in the policy paper. In the circumstances we couldn't possibly do otherwise, but I do suggest that we should act with our eyes open. It is, therefore, obviously the duty of all concerned to minimise both the possibility of injustice and of danger, and to take all necessary steps to insure that the amount of actual food required by this exception is as small as possible. The Japanese food problem is only one part of a world-wide problem, as it recognised in the statement of the United States member in the document recently filed, FEC 248/4, and the more the Japanese can be got to see it in this light, and together with their own part in the history of its development, the less is there likely to be unrest and the more co-operative will the Japanese become and the lower will the level of food required to prevent danger to the occupation forces also be. In a previous food paper before the Commission, that is, FEC 026/12, there was a very significant paragraph which doesn't appear in the present paper, and I should like, with your permission, sir, to quote that paragraph. The paragraph reads as follows:

> The Supreme Commander should make it clear to the Japanese people that:
>
> 1. Many countries are suffering from a dire shortage of foodstuffs largely due to Japanese aggression and in many of the countries devastated by the Japanese the diet of the people is inferior to that of the Japanese.
>
> 2. The Supreme Commander assumes no obligations to maintain, or to have maintained, any particular standard of living in Japan, and
>
> 3. The Supreme Commander assumes no responsibility to the Japanese people to import foodstuffs to meet any deficit arising from the failure of the Japanese Government and people to assure the just and impartial distribution of their indigenous foodstuffs.
>
> 4. The standard of living will depend upon the thoroughness with which Japan rids itself of all militaristic ambitions, redirects the use of its human and natural resources wholly and solely for purposes of peaceful living, administers adequate economic and financial controls and co-operates with the occupying forces and the governments they represent.

Now, sir, in the course of the food discussions, which, of course, were very prolonged in the Commission and in the committee, the New Zealand delegation fully understood the reasons for most of the arguments which were adduced by the United States, although, of course, on occasions we contested their validity, but we never did understand the reason for the flat United States rejection of sub-paragraph (1) in the abstract of the paragraph which I have just read. That is the sub-paragraph which suggests that the Supreme Commander should make it clear to the Japanese people that many countries are suffering from shortage of foodstuffs largely due to Japanese aggression. The remainder of the paragraph that I quoted was fully accepted by the United States delegation. Now my Government attaches great importance to this matter being understood in its correct perspective, and being so understood by the Japanese, and it has at times felt doubtful whether this was the situation or even whether SCAP was doing what could be done in this respect. And the attitude of the United States upon that sub-paragraph (1) I have referred to didn't help very much to remove the doubts. But it does appear that comparatively recently something has been done to put the matter to the Japanese in the proper light. I refer to the two papers that have been filed in the Commission – FEC 248/5 and 248/6 – and I refer also to a press report to the effect that the Japanese miners have been informed that they were getting twice as much food as the European miners but that they were only producing one-fourth as much coal. Now that is the sort of thing which ought to be told to the Japanese, but here again in the statements that were made by SCAP officers at their press conference, the two statements that are filed as of record in the Commission, I note that the SCAP officers gave a reasonably good picture of the world food situation but there was no significant mention of the one big fact which must be brought home to the Japanese – that their own career of wanton aggression throughout the food-producing lands of South-east Asia has been and still is a major cause of the world shortage of rice. We should like to see this fact hammered home to the Japanese until every man, woman and child in Japan had at least some appreciation of the grave extent of Japan's own responsibility in this matter. I repeat that the information at our disposal may not be complete, but in any case, I would suggest to the United States representative that possibly his Government might profitably look again at the whole paragraph that I have referred to, that is, the paragraph that was in the previous document, and carefully consider the advisability of implementing it so as to attain the two objectives: (a) The maximum possible co-operation from the Japanese, and (b) The reduction in the amount of food required to keep safe the occupation forces.

12. Question of the disposal of the former Italian colonies

Discussion of the report of Sub-Committee 17, Fourth Session of the United Nations General Assembly, New York, 4 November 1949

Sir Carl Berendsen (New Zealand) said that his country had a special interest in the problem at issue not only as a Member of the United Nations, but also on account of the substantial part that New Zealand forces had played in the liberation of North Africa. The New Zealand delegation had voted for the proposals presented at the previous session, but had not done so without great doubt and anxiety. Since those proposals had been rejected, it was now possible to emphasize the principal cause of his delegation's reluctance to approve them, namely that they had appeared in a large measure to disregard the wishes of the inhabitants. Those wishes, however, need not be the decisive consideration if the General Assembly considered them premature or ill advised; nor was it always possible to ascertain what the exact wishes of the inhabitants were. Examining the nature of the evidence as to those wishes, and speaking in the most general terms, with a clear recognition that in every instance minorities existed holding the strongest of opposing views, he considered that the majority of the inhabitants of the territories had been and were clearly opposed to any return to Italian control in any kind of form. Therefore, it would not be wise, or in the interests of the world, of Italy or of the inhabitants themselves, to force such a return upon them.

In that respect, the present proposals marked a substantial and welcome improvement over those submitted at the previous session, and he was particularly happy to recognize that Italy had now come forward in support of proposals for an independent Libya. While the present proposals represented an improvement, however, his delegation did not find them in general acceptable, for the same reason to which he had previously referred, namely that those proposals paid insufficient regard to the wishes of the inhabitants in so far as those were known. While the members of the Sub-Committee might have arrived at different conclusions regarding the wishes of the inhabitants, or while they might have thought that heed should be taken of considerations other than those wishes, it did seem to his delegation that those wishes as it understood them had once again been overridden. He was unable to understand how so many Members of the United Nations who, in the Fourth Committee and the Trusteeship Council had been such vehement and undeviating supporters of the rights of non-self-governing peoples and the principle of self-determination, could possibly have felt that the proposals laid before the Committee, both now and at the previous session, were in accordance with the wishes of the inhabitants.'

Sir Carl suggested that it would be a grave mistake to insist that acceptance of any one of the Sub-Committee's proposals should depend upon acceptance of the others. Entirely separate considerations applied to the various areas and peoples, and in order to arrive at a decision, each area and people must be examined separately and individually. The proposals which had received the largest amount of support at the previous session had been based on the assumption that the peoples of Libya were not yet ready for self-government. The present proposal, presented only six months later, assumed the contrary to be true. It might well be that neither was completely right, and he was far from convinced that it was in the interests of the peoples concerned to postulate premature self-government. However, it was better to err on the side of freedom that on the side of control, and his delegation would accept the general principle of the early independence of each of the three constituent portions of the area known as Libya. While he further agreed that a united Libya would be the best solution, it seemed quite improper to impose upon the people of Libya or on any of the three divisions of Libya, a unity which they might not desire. In that respect the General Assembly should assist and not insist. The impression left in his mind by the statements of the representatives of Cyrenaica had been that while the latter did not insist or ask for a united Libya, they would be prepared to accept a united Libya on condition that the country be united under the leadership of the Emir of the Senussis. He had understood that those representatives opposed a united Libya unless that condition were met. It was clear that, in so far as their wishes were known, the inhabitants of Cyrenaica did not desire a united Libya in the form recommended by the Sub-Committee, and, until his delegation was convinced that the people of Cyrenaica did desire a united Libya in that form, he could not support the proposal now before the Committee.

Sir Carl said that having had lengthy practical experience in administration, he could not imagine anything more likely to create confusion and distrust than the Sub-Committee's proposal to appoint a commissioner and a council comprising ten members to advise that commissioner. He considered that proposal to be a practical mistake and suggested that the Committee reconsider it seriously with a view to its elimination.

New Zealand was among those holding that Ethiopia, which had suffered so grievously under the aggression of fascist Italy, was entitled to redress and to an assured access to the sea. His delegation also agreed that where people of the same or a kindred race desired union with Ethiopia, it was not for the Assembly to place any obstacle in the way. However, in view of the difficulties created by the existence of large bodies of extraneous peoples and the doubts that had been expressed as to whether Ethiopia was in a position, unassisted, to develop those territories successfully, if such a proposal were adopted, specific undertakings should be entered into by Ethiopia to safeguard the rights and interests of those substantial and economically developed minorities. As for the suggestion that the remainder of Eritrea be included in the Anglo-Egyptian Sudan, where the people would find themselves united with a people of similar characteristics, while he could understand the reluctance of those apprehensive as to the wisdom of that proposal, he would be prepared to accept it as practical solution in certain circumstances. On the information available, it did not seem that Eritrea by itself was, or in the foreseeable future could be made, a viable independent entity. Nor did he think that those desiring union with Ethiopia should be deprived of their wishes in order to permit a dubious solution for the problem of those who did not desire union with Ethiopia. There was much that could be said for a federal solution if that should be acceptable to the parties. Though he would wish to see the just claims of Ethiopia recognized and satisfied without delay, he was prepared to support the Sub-Committee's proposal that further inquiries should be made on the spot by a United Nations Commission before a final decision was arrived at.

Sir Carl thought that, with regard to Somaliland, the Sub-Committee was making the same mistake as had been made previously, that of paying inadequate regard to the wishes of the inhabitants. While he agreed that the comments heard from the representatives of the people of that territory had been gravely contradictory, it seemed to be true that the majority of the people of former Italian Somaliland did not wish, and indeed would resist, the return of Italian control in any form. That judgment was confirmed by the conclusions arrived at by the Four-Power Commission of Investigation. While the cause of those people had been gravely jeopardized by recent riots in the territory, and had not been assisted by the clamourings of the Soviet group in that respect, in theory there would appear to be much to be said for a United Nations trusteeship. There would be much more reason for such a proposal had it not been for the behaviour of certain Members of the Organization who had gone so far in endeavouring to stultify the latter's work as to render, in the opinion of many, such a trusteeship quite impossible as things were at present. He was not prepared to go that far, however. A system of United Nations trusteeship would ensure that the people of Somaliland were brought forward to self-government as rapidly as possible and that no opportunity was lost as time passed of re-uniting all Somalis under one administration. Such a solution would also afford the Assembly and the Trusteeship Council some practical experience, but he did not wish to form or express any final opinion on the matter at present.

The Sub-Committee's proposal almost necessarily implied that in ten years' time Somaliland would be declared independent, since it seemed unlikely that the General Assembly would decide by a two-thirds majority that independence was not to be conceded to any country, whether it was ready or not. Ten years was a short time, and it was probable that at the end of that period the territory would be a little more ready for self-government than it was at present. In that connexion, Sir Carl drew attention to the fact that because of the sacrifices and efforts of the United Kingdom, which had administered the territory at a cost which it could ill afford, the administrative and educational language in Somaliland for the last decade had been English. While it was a minor point, the disruption and delay that would result from a sudden reversion to Italian should not be ignored.

He did not believe that the people of Somaliland desired Italian trusteeship or that the benefits the territory would receive from such trusteeship were so obvious and overwhelming as to warrant overriding the wishes of the population. If the purpose was either explicitly or implicitly to give trusteeship over Somaliland to Italy as a kind of consolation prize, he must say that such a proposal was unworthy of the Assembly and of the problem entrusted to it and was most unlikely to be welcome to a great nation such as Italy. However, he did not wish to express any final conclusion and therefore suggested the desirability of extending the activities of the proposed commission for Eritrea to include Somaliland. If there was any support for that suggestion, he would be prepared to submit a formal proposal to that effect.

In conclusion, Sir Carl said that the people of the territories were entitled to expect from the General Assembly the most careful and earnest judgment based on the universal principles of equity, justice and fair dealing. There should be no dispute on the matter except as to what was indeed in the interests of those peoples.

13. Extract from a statement by Sir Carl Berendsen on the veto

Second Session of the United Nations General Assembly, New York, 20 September 1947

. . . It is the duty of all right-thinking people to consider and to consider with anxious and earnest care the situation in which we find ourselves today and its causes. I agreed once that what was achieved at San Francisco, inadequate as many of us believed and believe it to be, was, in fact, the best that could have been achieved at that time in the circumstances as they existed. It may well be that this, unhappily, may prove to be the best that can be achieved now. I have no suggestions to make at present as to how to overcome the stultification which has arisen as the result of the provisions of the Charter prescribing the voting powers in the Security Council. It was, in fact, at San Francisco, and it appears to be a fact now, that certain of the five great powers, and not only one of them, insist on their right to veto. They are clearly within their rights, if they choose to exercise them, in insisting upon maintaining the arrangements that were agreed to – agreed to because nothing better could be achieved at San Francisco.

But while the great powers, or any of them, continue to insist upon their power of veto – and the General Assembly has already heard with deep appreciation the offer of one great power to forgo at least a portion of that right – there is little that can be done to better the unhappy position in which the Security Council finds itself today.

To the great powers I say that in insisting upon the right to veto, and so long as they continue so to insist, they are rendering it completely impossible for the world to achieve its highest objective – namely, an effective system of collective security against war.

Now, I must not be misunderstood. Clearly no charter, even in the most perfect form, can, of itself, create an effective system of preventing war. That must depend in the final result upon determination to do the right and to unitedly defeat the wrong. It is a matter of spirit. But the negative is true – that the Charter presently operating does, in effect, prohibit any such possibility. There can be no effective system of collective security while each of the five great powers retains the right of vetoing any action. The utmost the world can expect from an organization so afflicted is, on the one hand, a mechanism for suppressing small uprisings against the peace, for which purpose an organization such as this would, of course, be unnecessary if the only contingency upon which the United Nations can under any circumstances operate the Charter is that the five great powers are in unanimous agreement. On the other hand, a means of discussing situations as they arise and of endeavouring, by the use of reason and discussion, to prevent the outbreak of conflict. Such a means we certainly have – if not in the Security Council, then, at any rate, in this body. And those who believe that such limited measures are adequate to prevent war will no doubt consider them sufficient. But I assert that those who believe in the adequacy of words and words alone to prevent war are hiding their heads in the sand – they are flying in the face of history – and of recent history at that – history that has been and, God forbid, may again be. Indeed, let us not lose sight of the fact that those people were not among the authors of the Charter. The Charter is based on the completely impregnable principle that we cannot permanently ensure the peace of the world unless and until we are unitedly prepared to enforce it. That is the principle upon which the Charter is built. And the veto power is destructive of that principle. Again I say, the great powers cannot have their cake and eat it too. They cannot retain their right to take their own course in all circumstances and expect the United Nations as presently established to be competent to enforce peace. The two propositions are mutually exclusive. The great powers or the small powers cannot obtain insurance against war. No power, great or small, can obtain insurance against war without paying the inescapable premium. That premium is submission in the last resort to the combined judgment and conscience of the world. I will agree at once that the great powers who played such a predominant part in winning the war must be allowed, indeed assisted and encouraged, to play a predominant part in winning the peace. There must be some means established of giving to those great powers their proportionate voice in the great and age-long struggle of mankind.

But the veto, which is – and has proved itself to be – completely stultifying, is not the way. Many means of achieving this desirable objective have been suggested. A system of weighted voting, though difficult to devise is not impossible, and it might be worthy of consideration. A workable compromise in the meantime might well be a veto for any two, not any one, of the great powers. My country would agree at once to eliminate the veto altogether in respect of matters of peaceful settlement. This would obviously be a most useful advance.

It is necessary, in this connection, to consider with the utmost care the very welcome suggestion to this effect made in the course of the debate by the representative of the United States. The New Zealand delegation most warmly welcomes this proposal, but the proposal would unhappily leave the veto in full operation in respect of matters of enforcement. This would fail to remove the principal bar on the veto on action for the formation of an effective – and a fully effective – system of international security.

Nevertheless, if that proposal could be achieved, it would mark a magnificent step forward. All will recognise, of course, that if it is proposed to obtain this objective by means of an amendment to the Charter, then any one of the great powers, by the simple provision which was inserted in San Francisco requiring their ratification of all amendments, can indeed effect the elimination of the veto. An amendment to the effect suggested can obviously be achieved only if the five great powers agree. If, alternatively, it is proposed to obtain this end within the present terms of the Charter by means of a gentlemen's agreement, then clearly such an agreement can be arrived at only if the gentlemen will agree and continue to agree.

Whatever the difficulties are in the way of taking this great step forward, the fact that the United States has found it possible to make such a suggestion is of the greatest import to the world. The New Zealand delegation will support the proposal in every way possible. Of course, if in any case the Security Council has found itself unable to fulfil its high functions, then it is clearly not only the right, but the bounden duty, of the Assembly to take that case under consideration.

What is the alternative? If, in any case, for reasons good or bad, the Security Council is unable to solve a dispute or resolve a situation, is it suggested, and can it be suggested, that those members of this organization who do not possess seats on the Security Council – and they are the great majority of the members of this body – are to stand by idly twiddling their thumbs? Nonsense. A second proposal made by the representative of the United States might well prove of material assistance in this connection.

If the use of the veto is bad – and I assert it is – the abuse is worse. That there has been such abuse seems unquestionably to be a fact. My country will gladly support any proposal which is calculated to eliminate or reduce the possibility of abuse. And surely no sensible person in the world over can defend a contention that any one member of the United Nations, however great, however powerful, should be able to veto the admission of a proposed new member on grounds other than those specifically prescribed in the Charter.

Let no one imagine that the present situation can continue indefinitely. The United Nations must get better or it will get worse. What then can be done now? Obviously, having accepted the Charter as we all did, we must honestly operate it until we can improve it. We must make the best of what we have until we can make it better. We must nourish and sustain, pay for and pray for, this organization that we have established, whatever its defects. But at the same time we must patiently and consistently pay due and earnest regard to the weaknesses that exist today. We must endeavour, as best we may, to alter or remove those provisions which have had such a stultifying effect. We must take each opportunity as it arises to improve both the constitution under which we operate and the practice and procedure that we have established.

The views of my small country on this matter have never altered. They were expressed by my Prime Minister at San Francisco. They have been expressed from time to time at the meetings of this great body, and they will continue to be expressed in the future. Realising, as we do, most fully and most regretfully, all the difficulties that must be faced and overcome before we can hope to achieve any mitigation of this crippling veto power, we shall nevertheless feel compelled to vote as we have voted in the past, with that moderation and understanding of the problems of others which is, I hope, characteristic of New Zealand, and to support any proposal which tends toward the moderation or the elimination of the veto power, a privilege to five of the nations of the 55 members of the United Nations, which, however necessary they may feel it to be for their own purposes – whatever their position in the world – is nevertheless completely inconsistent with any possibility of establishing that permanently effective system of collective security without which mankind can never be free from the nightmare of war.

There is little that the lesser powers can do to solve this problem. The problem was created by the great powers, and its solution lies with the great powers and the great powers alone. That problem, that issue, is squarely before them.

When Charles Craw was working in the New Zealand permanent delegation to the United Nations, Berendsen and his driver Hunter would pick him up at an agreed time outside the New York office. When Chinese troops intervened in the Korean War, Berendsen held that China should be designated an aggressor and was eager for instructions enabling him to say so. They were slow to come and he was fretful about that.

It was in these circumstances that Charles was about to leave the office as a telegram was coming through. He waited to see what it was about and then joined Berendsen, who immediately upbraided him for being late and brushed aside his explanation.

A day or two later, when Berendsen's anxiety for instructions about China had grown still further, exactly the same situation arose. On this occasion Charles left and joined Berendsen on time.

Berendsen was in a good mood. 'Everything all right? Anything going on in the office?'

'Nothing much,' said Charles. 'There was a telegram coming in, that's about all.'

'Oh? And what was it about?'

'I don't know,' said Charles. 'I left so as to be on time.'

'You don't know? Why, it'll be about China of course! Hunter, get back to the office!'

So with difficulty, the car returned. Charles obtained the telegram and Berendsen read it.

It wasn't about China.

Tom Larkin

APPENDIX 2

PERSONALITY IN FOREIGN POLICY: SIR CARL BERENDSEN IN WASHINGTON

BY ANN TROTTER

In 1944 when Sir Carl Berendsen became New Zealand's minister in Washington, New Zealand policy-makers were taking a hard look at what New Zealand interests really were. The simple proposition of relying on the British for New Zealand's security was clearly no longer enough and, although there was still a strong feeling in the public and politicians' minds that Britain's security and that of New Zealand were somehow linked, it was clear that new relationships, primarily with the United States, would have to be worked out. The war in the Pacific had demonstrated to New Zealanders that their country, on the southern fringe of the Pacific, must necessarily have some security requirements that differed from those of Britain, on the fringe of Europe.

The legacy of New Zealand's long association with the British imperial system, however, was an attitude and a psychology unexpected in a country of New Zealand's geographical position and size. Not only were New Zealanders accustomed to being part of a team, and one which they perceived to be powerful, capable of winning games and held in some awe and respect by outsiders but, as one of the old white Dominions, they regarded themselves as members of the club's board of management with, therefore, some useful executive experience.

Although New Zealanders had the reputation of not rocking the boat in imperial conferences and although New Zealand had no interest in the constitutional niceties of the imperial relationship, its ministers did not hesitate to speak out on the issues on which they felt strongly. Their loyalty was neither dumb nor blind.[1] New Zealand thus regarded

1 See F. L. W. Wood, 'The Anzac Dilemma', *International Affairs*, XXIX, 2 (April 1953), p. 183 and F. L. W. Wood, *This New Zealand*, Hamilton, 1952, pp. 152–61.

itself as part of the world, and as having a voice in world affairs to a degree to which its geographical position and size might not otherwise have entitled it.

New Zealand too was accustomed to following a cause. From 1935, to the imperial ideal was added the cause of collective security. The New Zealand Labour Party which became the government in that year had long argued that collective action through the League of Nations was the only means of securing just and lasting peace. In 1936 New Zealand submitted at Geneva a 21-point programme for strengthening the League covenant and, in the cases of Spain, China and Abyssinia, New Zealand condemned aggressors and urged stronger League action.[2] There was an increasingly high moral tone in New Zealand's voice in international affairs and, at home, there was satisfaction in the grand, independent, and inexpensive gestures that won the country a certain notoriety. The Deputy Prime Minister, Peter Fraser, said in 1938 of New Zealand's stand in the League: 'It was time somebody spoke – the country has to make up its own mind on international problems as a sovereign country . . .'[3]

This attitude in the League was accompanied by opposition to the policy of appeasement being followed by the British government. The Prime Minister, M. J. Savage, is reputed to have shamed the Imperial Conference in 1937 with his refusal to accept the notion of peace at almost any price.[4]

Thus the established tenets of New Zealand's pre-war policy can be seen to be acceptance of, and some pride in, the imperial link, accompanied by some suspicion of the deeds and motives of the British politicians and their advisers; belief in the right of small countries to a voice in world affairs and readiness to make the grand gesture on behalf of that voice; belief in collective security as the best hope for world peace and suspicion of the machinations of the great powers in world bodies; belief that force must be opposed whenever it occurred and a consequent hatred of appeasement.

2 See W. David McIntyre and W. J. Gardner, *Speeches and Documents in New Zealand History*, Oxford, 1971, pp. 358–61.

3 See J. V. Wilson, 'New Zealand's participation in International Organisations' in T. C. Larkin, ed., *New Zealand's External Relations*, Wellington and London, 1962, p. 70.

4 Carl Berendsen, Unpublished memoirs, manuscript in the possession of the Berendsen family (hereafter Memoirs), Personalities: M. J. Savage.

These are the ideas and attitudes which Berendsen took with him to Washington and expanded there. In doing so he was not simply reflecting the policy of the New Zealand government; he was expounding policy positions which were in fact his own. From 1926 until 1943, when he went to Australia as New Zealand's first High Commissioner there, Carl Berendsen was single-handedly the draftsman of New Zealand policy, literally from a cramped backroom.[5] From 1926 to 1935 he wrote the papers for Imperial Conferences and replied to Dominion Office telegrams for conservative prime ministers whose relative lack of interest in external affairs reflected the attitude of most New Zealanders.[6] In 1935 he took on board and articulated Labour Party ideas about collective security at a time when he had become convinced that world conflict was otherwise inevitable.[7] Berendsen was the author of the 21-point statement, designed to give the League Covenant some backbone, which New Zealand deposited in Geneva. He responded to the crusading spirit of Labour's policy with a passionate moral fervour fuelled by his own clear and relatively simple ideas of right and wrong.

For seventeen years, Carl Berendsen as Imperial Affairs Officer (1926), Secretary for External Affairs (1928) and Head of the Prime Minister's department (1932–43), was a back-room man and a one-man band formulating and articulating New Zealand policy not just towards Britain, the Empire and Commonwealth, and the League, but also towards Samoa, New Zealand's mandated territory, for the administration of which he was responsible. On the long sea voyages which in those days brought New Zealand prime ministers and their advisers to imperial conferences he provided information to the prime minister of the day and helped to shape his ideas.[8]

In 1944, Berendsen had two tasks. He had to stamp New Zealand's

5 A. McIntosh, 'The Origins of the Department of External Affairs' in F. L. W. Wood, ed., *New Zealand in World Affairs, I*, Wellington, 1977, p. 16.

6 Angus Ross, 'New Zealand and the Commonwealth to 1939', in *The Commonwealth Past, Present and Future*, papers delivered at a seminar of the Christchurch Branch of the New Zealand Institute of International Affairs, NZIIA, Wellington, 1972, p. 7.

7 Berendsen, Memoirs, Personalities: Savage.

8 See McIntosh, p. 12–17. I am grateful to Professor Angus Ross, Dunedin, for information of his interview with Sir Carl Berendsen. In this Sir Carl mentioned how valuable he found the long voyages on which he and the prime minister of the day would work every morning and discuss the topics they expected to come up at Imperial Conferences.

presence on the consciousness of the politicians in Washington unaccustomed to concerning themselves with the views and security requirements of lesser communities sited in strategically unimportant areas of the South Pacific. On the face of it, New Zealand was not potentially of much interest to the United States. His other task was to make New Zealand's presence felt in the new world organization, the United Nations, for which he and the New Zealand Labour Government held great hopes, seeing it as the basis of future world peace and security.[9] Berendsen relished the challenge. After years of silence and relative obscurity he had a platform at last and a captive and influential audience.

Berendsen arrived in Washington with the confidence engendered by his long experience of making policy and handling politicians, by his wide experience of international meetings and his knowledge of the skills required to operate as an effective delegate at such gatherings, and by his established acquaintance with leading British civil servants and a number of old Geneva hands. Berendsen was not only New Zealand's Minister in Washington – the Legation was raised to an Embassy in 1948 – he was also New Zealand's chief delegate to the United Nations. This unsatisfactory arrangement meant that Berendsen spent a great deal of time in New York while the day-to-day essential and less glamorous political work was carried out by junior officers in Washington. The difficulties were compounded by the fact that, especially in the early years, the Embassy staff, and of course the staff of the New Zealand Department of External Affairs as a whole, was small.[10] As was demonstrated by his failure to build up a professional administrative service for Samoa in the period from 1928 to 1943 when he was responsible for the administration of that territory, and his refusal to lay the ground work and establish the nucleus of a professional department of external affairs in New Zealand before 1943,[11] Berendsen was not an organization man. He was himself hard working, tremendously able, extremely well informed in matters of

9 See Fraser's statement on the Commonwealth Prime Ministers' Conference 1944 in *New Zealand Foreign Policy Statements and Documents 1943–1957*, Wellington, 1972 (hereafter cited as Statements 1943–1957), p. 71.

10 I am indebted to Sir George Laking, Mr. Frank Corner and Mr. Charles Craw, interviewed in Wellington, October 1985, for this information.

11 J.W. Davidson, *Samoa Mo Samoa*, Oxford, 1967, p. 135–58; McIntosh, p. 17.

New Zealand policy, vastly more experienced than anyone else in the New Zealand Legation and delegation to the United Nations, and a prima donna. None of this made it simple to work with him.

Berendsen plunged into American life with great enthusiasm. The freedom, easiness and generosity of the United States appealed to him, just as his open, hearty and no-nonsense approach appealed to the Americans. 'He was the sort of chap,' said one former colleague, 'who didn't require great formality.'[12] All the same he loved being Ambassador, rubbing shoulders with the great, and conscious of the dignity of his office. 'An ambassador,' he wrote, 'cannot afford to be made to look ridiculous. He carries the dignity of his country and his monarch with him wherever he goes . . . I have never allowed myself as an Ambassador to be ignored or directly or indirectly insulted or imposed upon without insisting upon the dignity of the country I had the honour to represent.'[13] Very often this meant that, though he rated matters of personal comfort highly, an inadequate railway carriage or an uncomfortable bed was represented to the unfortunate menial who had to face the famous Berendsen wrath as an insult to the Crown.[14]

Berendsen has variously been described as forceful, pugnacious, dogmatic, aggressive, obsessive, passionate, active, self-confident and voluble.[15] Socially he had a bluff, hearty, hail-fellow-well-met manner and he was soon well-known in the Washington and United Nations scene; but he seems to have had few, if any, friends in the United States, or indeed in New Zealand. If there is a New Zealand personality, passion, emotion and obsession are not usually associated with it.[16] Berendsen was, of course, an Australian who had come to New Zealand with his parents in 1900 at the age of ten. It may be that some of his vitality and showmanship came from these Australian origins. Perhaps they arose simply in response to the difficulties and uncertainties of a childhood that was peripatetic and always financially insecure.[17]

12 Interview with Sir Guy Powles, Wellington, 7 October 1985.

13 Berendsen, Memoirs, Book III 1944–1952, Chapter xvi.

14 e.g. ibid.

15 Prime Minister's Press Statement, 13 December 1973; interviews with Mr. Frank Corner, Wellington; Mr. Tom Larkin, Wellington; Mr. Charles Craw, Wellington; Mr. Jim Weir, Wellington; Professor Angus Ross, Dunedin.

16 See Gordon McLauchlan, *The Passionless People*, Auckland, 1976.

17 I am indebted to Mr. Tom Larkin, Wellington, for information about Sir Carl's childhood and education.

Rather surprisingly, working with Berendsen seems to have been, if not fun, at least not unpleasantly exciting. Sir Guy Powles said: 'He was comparatively easy to work for as long as you got over the initial fright and distress at being up against such a powerful personality.' Powles said that it was always stimulating to have an interview with Berendsen no matter what the subject was.[18] His rages were certainly stimulating, terrible to behold and to endure. His remorse, if he found or felt himself to be in the wrong, was apparently equally dreadful and even harder to bear. He had a huge rasping voice which boomed around the New Zealand office and everyone knew when a speech or despatch was being dictated. Unfortunate secretaries charged with the task of taking down the cascade of words were frequently reduced to tears. Absolute punctuality was demanded of all staff, and political officers obtained perforce a rigorous training in the rapid production of lucid reports – the account of the three-month-long deliberations of the General Assembly had, for instance, to be produced within three days.[19]

Nevertheless Berendsen's staff seems to have enjoyed the sense of being in contact with a rather special personality and, in spite of the tribulations, to have appreciated the basic integrity of the man. They knew that Berendsen was convinced that what he was doing was right and would not do anything he thought was not right, so to that extent he was predictable, even if one did not agree with his concept of right and wrong. Berendsen was an extremely decisive man who could not bear shilly-shallying. He believed things were black or white and he reputedly said: 'If you look at a thing and it's 51% black and 49% white then for Christ's sake it's black.'[20] His views on some other matters were equally primitive. He said he would stand up for his staff right or wrong, and he did so, winning thereby loyalty which might not have been inspired by his otherwise bullying behaviour.[21] He seems to have feared no man and dressed down visiting New Zealand politicians who did not meet his standards with as much facility as he did the staff

18 Interview with Sir Guy Powles, Wellington, 7 October 1985.

19 Interviews with Sir Guy Powles, Mr. Charles Craw, Mr. Jim Weir, Wellington, October 1985.

20 Both Mr. Frank Corner and Mr. Charles Craw, who worked with Sir Carl Berendsen in Washington and New York respectively, related this Berendsen maxim.

21 Both Sir Guy Powles and Mr. Charles Craw related episodes in which Sir Carl's trust in, and support of, his staff were demonstrated.

of the Embassy.

He could also be very funny and had a great comic command of language. He was, of course, an actor, although it is also true to say that, throughout his Washington years, he played to the hilt only one character part.

Berendsen liked to speak impromptu, composing with great fluency as he went, and he prepared his own set pieces, shutting himself up to think about them and emerging to dictate the entire speech. At best his speeches and despatches were masterpieces of magisterial prose which seemed to owe something to Gibbon, Macaulay and Burke; at worst, particularly in his later years in Washington, his style was so florid as to be embarrassing. Huge episodic sentences full of brackets, dashes, parentheses and semi-colons went on for nearly a page. Here is an example from 1950. His subject is the plague of communism:

> Wherever there are cranks, and they exist in considerable numbers in every part of the globe; wherever there are malcontents; wherever there are those, and they are legion, whose abilities cannot keep pace with their ambitions; wherever there are those, and they are everywhere, who believe their comparative failure in the world to have been due to the evil machinations of their private enemies; wherever there are those who are small but think they should be big, who are ignored and think they should be dominant, who are poor and think they should be rich, who hate and who yearn for the opportunity to injure, wherever there are those who envy or who suffer, either justly or unjustly, then these damnable heresies of "communism" make their appeal.[22]

Berendsen had genuine oratorical skills and he learned all the tricks of effective delivery. At his best he was compared with Churchill; at his worst, after an anti-communist diatribe, he was likened to something out of Radio City Music Hall.[23] In 1945 at the San Francisco conference Sir Alexander Cadogan, Under-Secretary for State at the Foreign Office, noted in his diary of the Committee on Enforcement Arrangements on which he was sitting: 'the discussion dragged on, and eventually Berendsen, the New Zealander, chose to get up and make the regular sort of demagogic speech which he delights in. I lost my temper and went for him, which I enjoyed. He doesn't mind: I like him and we

22 Robin Kay, ed., *Documents on New Zealand External Relations Volume III: The ANZUS Pact and the Treaty of Peace with Japan*, Wellington, 1985 (hereafter cited as Documents NZEA III), No. 198, p. 525.

23 *New Zealand Herald*, 8 September 1951; Interview with Mr. Charles Craw, Wellington, 8 October 1985.

are very good friends!'[24] On this occasion New Zealand was trying so to alter Chapter I of the Charter as to include among the purposes of the United Nations: 'to preserve as against external aggression the territorial integrity and political independence of every member of the organisation'; a view of collective security in which every member would be bound to come to the aid of every other member.[25] Berendsen seems to have spoken for forty minutes on this amendment which of course represented one of New Zealand's efforts to get teeth into the new system of collective security and was therefore central in Berendsen's vision for the post-war world. His final peroration included reference to the graves of 'thousands upon thousands of New Zealanders throughout the world . . . undying evidence that New Zealand did not restrict her advocacy of the principles of peace, order and justice to mere words'.[26] One can feel a certain sympathy for Sir Alexander Cadogan.

Berendsen's speeches and despatches at their most elegant and forceful are all the more remarkable in that he was apparently not a deeply read man. He was never observed reading more than an occasional detective novel and a book on his obsession, baseball. This he read ostentatiously at the U.N. when he wished to bait the Russians. The book had a very bright cover and the title in large letters proclaimed *Balls Hits and Errors*. There were no books on the shelves of the library at the residence.[27] It seems, therefore, that Berendsen drew on the probably sound but certainly unremarkable education he had received in rural New Zealand and at Victoria University College in Wellington. He had a real, and apparently instinctive, feel for language. Berendsen never read background papers and never read U.N. documents, maintaining that these could tell him nothing he had not learned from *The New York Times*, which he did read thoroughly including the sports pages from which he may have obtained some of his racier images. He liked, in fact, to make sure he had one striking phrase in a speech so that it would be reported in *The New York Times*.[28]

24 David Dilks, ed., *Diaries of Sir Alexander Cadogan 1938–1945*, London, 1971, p. 744.
25 Bruce Brown, *New Zealand Foreign Policy in Retrospect*, Wellington, 1970, p. 6.
26 *The United Nations Conference on International Organisation: Report on the Conference held at San Francisco 25 April–26 June 1945 by the Right Honourable Peter Fraser, Chairman of the Delegation*, Department of External Affairs, Wellington, 1945, pamphlet No. 11, p. 25.
27 Information provided by Mr. Tom Larkin and Mr. Frank Corner, Wellington,.
28 Information provided by Mr. Jim Weir, Wellington, 8 October 1985.

Berendsen had written the papers and formulated policy for years before he came to Washington, was very familiar with the ideas and attitudes of Peter Fraser, Prime Minister from 1940 to 1949, and had a close relationship with Alister McIntosh who became head of the newly formed Department of External Affairs when Berendsen left for Canberra in 1943.[29] Berendsen was not interested in theories of foreign affairs: his ideas about international relations were simple, clear-cut, and firmly established by the time he reached the United States.

In his early years in Washington he reflected New Zealand policy very well and his telegrams tended to assume Wellington would agree with his observations.[30] As the time since he had been in Wellington increased, and as a new breed of better-educated idealistic young professionals began to be recruited into the Department of External Affairs, Berendsen's instinctive reactions were less and less those of Wellington, to which he became increasingly hostile.

In 1948 when back in Wellington for consultations Berendsen spoke to members of the Department of External Affairs, warning them, in one of his favourite phrases, that the world was faced with a choice between the secret ballot and the secret police. The tone of the questions which followed led Berendsen to accuse McIntosh of recruiting a bunch of communists. Latterly he had a list of 66 complaints about Wellington over which he would brood and he carried in his top pocket an envelope which he was wont to produce with a flourish, claiming that it contained his key card, his resignation.[31]

In Washington and New York Berendsen concentrated on what he saw as essentials: questions of political importance designed to make the United Nations do its job and keep the peace. He was not interested in questions of technical and capital assistance to the underdeveloped world and, as he disliked Bill Sutch, New Zealand's representative on the Economic and Social Council, who was stationed in New York, he seldom, if ever, went into the New Zealand office in New York.[32]

It was to be expected, given the pre-war experience, that Berendsen should, with Fraser, be determined to avoid for the U.N. the weaknesses

29 McIntosh, p. 18.

30 Interviews with Mr. Frank Corner and Mr. Jim Weir, Wellington, October 1985. Mr Weir said, 'Sir Carl *told* Wellington'.

31 Interview with Mr. Tom Larkin, Wellington, 7 October 1985.

32 Interview with Mr. Charles Craw, 8 October 1985.

they had detected in the League. They saw the failure of the League as a moral failure on the part of individual members who had chosen the rule of expediency over that of moral principles.[33] Berendsen and Fraser were consequently critical of the 1944 Dumbarton Oaks proposals for a United Nations Organisation on the grounds that no definite pledges were required of members to protect one another against external aggression, and on the grounds that the small powers were to have an inadequate voice.[34]

In April 1945 Berendsen accompanied Fraser to London to a Commonwealth Conference to discuss the Dumbarton Oaks proposals before the San Francisco Conference which was to be held in May. There New Zealand found itself, with Australia, in a fruitless fight against the Great Power veto. Berendsen wrote: 'We found ourselves being treated with that kind of friendly and patronising tolerance which adults extend to the fractious child. We were told, not of course in so many words, for that might be interpreted as impolite, that we were unrealistic, that we were not facing the facts of international life . . . we were urged, in the nicest possible and most indirect ways, to be good children and not to rock the boat.'[35] Apart from other considerations there is, implicit here, a certain attitude to British civil servants.

In spite of the warning, Fraser, 'that tiresome old New Zealand P.M.', as Cadogan described him,[36] did, in collaboration with Evatt, try to rock the boat and remove the veto – and failed.

The speech which Fraser made reads beautifully and bears all the hallmarks of the Berendsen style. For example: 'I am speaking for a country which, though small in area and population, has made great sacrifices in two world wars. I speak for the New Zealanders who have died and are buried thousands of miles from their own land in the cause they believed to be just. I speak for the millions of New Zealanders yet to be born.'[37] It is a pity to have to report that Fraser dropped and scattered the pages of this speech and Berendsen had the 'exquisitely painful' experience of witnessing Fraser, who was almost blind, peering short-sightedly at the pages which he scrambled together and proceeded

33 Statements 1943–1957, p. 85.
34 ibid.
35 Berendsen, Memoirs, Book III, Chapter i.
36 Dilks, p. 743.
37 Statements 1943–1957, p. 86.

to read in random order.[38]

It is said that after the San Francisco Conference Berendsen took a vow never to make a speech in which he did not mention the veto. He certainly found plenty of opportunities. Everyone in the office became very familiar with what they called his 'veto speech' which was made up and down the United States.[39] On one memorable occasion he even managed to work the veto into a speech proposing the toast at the marriage of a New Zealand Legation staff member to an American.[40]

In 1946 he reminded the General Assembly:

> The marriage of the veto to the Charter was a shotgun wedding. If this matter had been left to the free and untrammelled vote of the delegates to that conference, it would unquestionably have been defeated, and I venture to add that, were this matter put to the vote of men and women in the street throughout the world, then indeed the veto would be blown away in a gale of indignant repudiation . . . . It is in essence an application of the false and pagan principle that might is right. It is a negation in the international field of those principles of equitable democracy which are so dear to such a large section of mankind . . . .[41]

The message changed little over the years. New Zealand's demand, said Berendsen, was a modest one: 'we ask no veto. We ask no predominant or decisive voice. We ask for our proportionate voice in those Councils which will influence the affairs of man as far ahead as we can see – our proportionate voice, no more and no less.'[42]

Berendsen never doubted New Zealand's right to have its proportionate voice heard and his confidence harks back as much to the New Zealanders' view of themselves as co-decision makers on the board of the British Empire and Commonwealth, as to the New Zealand experience of the League.

The essence of the 21-point programme with which New Zealand and Berendsen had sought to reform the League Covenant was that the League should stand by its doctrines and be prepared to back them with force. After 1945 it was Berendsen's constant theme that the United Nations should show more backbone. By 1947 disillusionment

38 Berendsen, Memoirs, Personalities: P. Fraser.

39 Interview with Sir Guy Powles.

40 This story was related by everyone interviewed.

41 *The United Nations: Report of the New Zealand delegation on the second part of the first regular session of the General Assembly at New York, 23 October–15 December 1946*, Department of External Affairs, Wellington, 1947, pamphlet No. 33, p. 94.

42 ibid., p. 93.

was beginning to set in as it did not.[43] He blamed the use of the veto in the Security Council for the ineffectiveness of the system.[44] Berendsen was of course delighted when the United Nations intervened in Korea. He rang a colleague at the Embassy shouting in reference to Truman, 'The little man's done it!'[45] and, as Dean Rusk recalled, went straight to the State Department saying 'What can we do to help?'[46] Predictably he regarded the armistice, made when in his opinion the Chinese forces were on the point of being defeated, as wrong, and he also thought it was wrong to refrain from bombing Chinese bases beyond the Yalu. It seemed to him that appeasers among the Allies were 'hanging on to American "coat-tails" and holding the United States back'.[47]

The straightforward propositions that governed Berendsen's view of the world – that might is not right, that one must accept the consequences of one's actions – infused his speeches with powerful moral fervour. This is best illustrated in what some regard as his best speech, made in 1948 on the question of the partition of Palestine. In 1947 Berendsen had argued for New Zealand that the United Nations must be prepared to back up its plan for partition of Palestine with some enforcing organization. The proposals put to the Assembly did not contain such provisions and New Zealand first abstained on the vote in committee but finally was persuaded to support the partition.[48] In 1948 when the U.N. Assembly attempted to grapple with the situation following partition the United States, formerly a leading supporter of partition, put forward a plan for the administration of Palestine as a trust territory. This brought forth a passionate speech from Berendsen, who had not only disliked the partition proposal but had no time for 'weathervanes'. In a speech which effectively killed the American trusteeship idea he said:

> The New Zealand Government believed then that partition was the best solution and it believes the same thing today. It is our view that the Assembly decided to do the right thing the wrong way, and I am not expressing that view

---

43 *The United Nations: Report of the New Zealand delegation on the second regular session of the General Assembly held at New York, 16 September–29 November 1947*, Department of External Affairs, Wellington, 1948, pamphlet No. 60, p. 147.

44 ibid., p. 149.

45 Interview with Mr. Frank Corner, Wellington, 3 October 1985.

46 Information provided by Mr. Jim Weir, Wellington, 8 October 1985.

47 Berendsen, Memoirs, Book III, Chapter xiii.

48 Brown, p. 7.

> now with all the advantages of hindsight . . . . Up to the very last moment I asked whether the Assembly was prepared to gamble with the lives of innocent people in Palestine. The appeal fell on deaf ears. You were prepared to so gamble; we did gamble, and we lost. But we do not pay. You know today who is paying. The gambler's loss is being paid by the people of Palestine; it is being paid in part by the British boys dying at their post of duty, but for a much greater part it is being paid, and will continue to be paid, by the people of Palestine, be they innocent or guilty, be they Arab or Jew . . .[49]

In the United Nations Berendsen concentrated his efforts in the First Committee which considered political and security questions although he was sometimes active in the Fourth Committee, the Trusteeship Committee, where New Zealand had a particular interest through its trust territory, Samoa. Berendsen was chairman of this committee in 1947. He was by all accounts an excellent, if idiosyncratic, chairman and meetings directed by him finished in record time. There was general appreciation of his habit of deflecting matters back to the practical when discussions entered or seemed about to enter ideological clouds. He believed common sense was very uncommon indeed in such meetings.[50] Another area where his talents as a chairman were displayed was in the Far Eastern Commission to which he was appointed New Zealand's chief delegate in 1946. He was chairman of the Steering Committee.[51] He was very active in the first year of the Commission but quickly became frustrated with the United States attitude to the Commission[52] and with the tactics of the Chairman of the FEC, General McCoy, with whom he had some spectacular brushes.[53]

Berendsen's ideas about Japan, the Japanese and the Japanese peace treaty were typical of those of New Zealanders of his day. New Zealanders did not have much direct experience of Japanese people but broadly speaking they did not like Asians in general and, like Berendsen, saw in the populous lands to the north a threat to their

49 *The United Nations: Report of the New Zealand delegation on the second special session of the General Assembly held at New York 16 April–14 May 1948 to consider the future of Palestine*, Department of External Affairs, Wellington, 1948, pamphlet No. 61, p. 39.

50 Sir Cecil Day to A. McIntosh, 24 April 1947, MFA Archives 102/9/1, Wellington. Information provided by Mr. Charles Craw and Mr. Jim Weir.

51 Robin Kay, ed., *Documents on New Zealand External Relations Volume II: The Surrender and Occupation of Japan*, Wellington, 1982 (hereafter cited as Documents NZEA II) No. 181, p. 332.

52 Documents NZEA II, Document 200, p. 391.

53 Documents NZEA II, Document 269, p. 617.

relatively empty country.[54] Berendsen thought it was impossible for a westerner to fathom the oriental mind. He believed that the Japanese were warlike people, trained to a tradition of war and conquest, who had sought and would seek again to impose their will on the world.[55] Initially, therefore, he was in favour of a long occupation, harsh peace terms and, predictably, a commitment to the enforcement of such terms. In 1946 he felt twenty years was the minimum time before Japan could be expected to resume her place among peace-loving nations.[56]

The policy papers on the Japanese peace settlement came from Wellington and, while Berendsen's attitude about the threat from Japan was shared in the capital, there was general recognition by 1947 that New Zealand was ultimately dependent on American willingness to enforce any treaty with Japan. It was also recognized that it was not worthwhile to insist on including in the treaty provisions the United States was unwilling to implement.[57] The officials in Wellington saw that difficult choices would have to be made and by 1950 they knew that there was a good chance that the Japanese peace treaty would not advance New Zealand's security requirements.[58] For them, as for the Australians, it was a question of tactics vis-à-vis the United States. The Washington mission was involved in this discussion only insofar as it responded to instructions.

By 1950, however, Berendsen had reached his most sulphurous anti-communist phase. His disillusionment with the United Nations had grown steadily and he equated what he saw and heard with the 'dark forces' which had operated in Europe in the 1930s. As early as 1947 Berendsen was making virulent anti-communist speeches. At that time Soviet delegates were making speeches in which they denounced and named 'war-mongers'. Berendsen longed to be included in the list, for the company was, as he said, distinguished and included Churchill, Truman and Dulles. 'Who is there indeed,' he said, 'who would not be proud to have his name associated with that group of peace-loving

54 Berendsen, Memoirs, Book III, Chapter v, Chapter xv.

55 Berendsen, Memoirs, Chapter v.

56 *Dominion*, 1 March 1946; Memo by New Zealand Representative at the Far Eastern Advisory Commission, 6 November 1945, MFA Archives 268/9/9 Pt. 1.

57 The Enforcement of the peace treaty, memorandum, 27 May 1947; MFA Archives 102/9/38.

58 Colombo Conference (UK Delegation) to F.O., 13 January 1950, FO371/83828, FJ1021/4, Public Record Office, London.

men?'[59] In spite of his best vituperative efforts, however, the weeks passed and he was ignored. Finally he was denounced as a war-monger. Alas, the accuser was the delegate from Byelorussia. 'Not good enough,' said Berendsen, 'not good enough. War-monger third class!'[60]

By 1950, however, he might well have been declared a first class war-monger. He had become obsessed with the threat of Russian imperialism assisted by international communism, convinced that the world was moving towards a third world war, and conscious that the United Nations, which he felt had become nothing but a 'talking shop' because of the veto, would not solve the world's problems. In an enormously long despatch in his most purple prose he blamed the Soviet Union for this state of affairs: 'a group of international thugs and gangsters' who by a course of 'bluster, bribery, blackmail, chicanery and outright physical violence, torture and murder' were planning to seize Europe.[61]

This state of mind altered Berendsen's attitude to Japan and the Japanese peace treaty. He feared that 'if Japan should decide to join this communist conspiracy' the 'prospects in the Pacific would be gloomy indeed'.[62] He became convinced that, on the grounds of equity, fairness and expediency, a generous and friendly peace must be offered Japan. In addition in 1950 he advocated approaching the United States with the suggestion of a limited Pacific Pact, extending over the area for which the United States accepted responsibility for defence, and including Australia and New Zealand, which in return would join the United States in defending the Northern Pacific. Berendsen envisaged a treaty which might include the United Kingdom, Canada and the Philippines as well as Australia, New Zealand and the United States.[63] Such a treaty would be designed to stem the communist tide.

A treaty did eventuate in 1951 when Berendsen signed the ANZUS treaty on New Zealand's behalf. He did not claim to have had any real part in the formulation of this treaty[64] and it seems from the

59 *The United Nations*, pamphlet No. 60, p. 21.
60 Interview with Mr. Tom Larkin.
61 Documents NZEA III, Document 198, p. 523.
62 Berendsen, Memoirs, Book III, Chapter xv.
63 Documents NZEA III, Document 198, p. 533.
64 Interview with Sir Carl Berendsen, 10 September 1964, John Foster Dulles oral history project, Mudd Library, Princeton University.

evidence of the Wellington archives that his despatch on this matter was less influential there than in retrospect one might expect.[65] Perhaps this was in part because the despatch was so extraordinarily long. Berendsen's views had by this time become so extreme as frequently to be embarrassing.

Berendsen's last assignment of importance as Ambassador in Washington was the signing, on New Zealand's behalf, of the ANZUS treaty and the Japanese peace treaty at San Francisco in September 1951. It is often the fate of small countries and their representatives to be used by their more powerful allies. Berendsen had been an ally of the United States in the past and was again at the last. Dean Rusk, then Assistant Secretary of State, asked Berendsen to propose the adoption of the rules of procedure in order to forestall any attempt by the Russians to sabotage the proceedings in the absence of any accepted rules. The plan was put into action and Berendsen found himself brushing shoulders with Gromyko as he moved towards the platform. He wrote afterwards: 'I brushed better than he did, and I got there first without actually running or hurrying.'[66] To Berendsen's considerable pleasure, Russian obstruction had been thwarted.

Berendsen's speech at San Francisco was one of the most highly publicized and approved of all the hundreds he had made. Conscious as he was by now of the power of radio and television, he chose his time to speak at San Francisco with regard to Eastern Time, so that he obtained maximum coverage, and he records with satisfaction that over twenty million people saw him on television and another thirty million heard him on radio.[67] Berendsen himself did not feel his speech was particularly notable in part, one suspects, because this was one of the rare occasions when he had had some assistance in writing it.[68] The style is magisterial Berendsen. His tone to Japan is forgiving. 'We have no desire,' he said, 'to hold Japan in bondage nor to reduce a proud,

65 The Minister of External Affairs, Frederick Doidge, did not reply until 9 May 1950, two months later. See *Documents NZEA III*, Document 200, pp. 545–6. The department's comment on the despatch is dated 9 February 1952, almost a year later. See Summary of Sir Carl Berendsen's proposal for an alliance with the United States (9 February 1952), MFA Archives 102/9/46.

66 Berendsen, Memoirs, Book III, Chapter xv.

67 ibid.

68 ibid., and interview with Mr. Frank Corner.

energetic and capable people to a status of inferiority.'[69]

Acknowledging the risk in a treaty which left Japan the power to rearm he accepted responsibility for New Zealand in typical fashion: '. . . if it is a risk it is a risk that we in New Zealand have taken with our eyes open as an earnest of the intention of our small country to play its part as a good neighbour in the Pacific. The onus is on Japan to fulfill this trust as we hope and believe Japan will fulfill it.'[70]

His best shots were, as always, saved for the Russians who, he claimed, had come to San Francisco 'to do mischief' – a phrase picked up, not doubt to Berendsen's satisfaction, by the *San Francisco Examiner* in a flattering account of the performance of New Zealand's 'skilled and personable ambassador'.[71]

Berendsen's term in Washington ended on 30 January 1952. He had arrived nine years earlier when New Zealand's policy was in a state of flux. He left, having set the seal on a new era in New Zealand's foreign relationships. In his speech at San Francisco Berendsen made frequent reference to New Zealand as a Pacific nation[72] and, in retrospect at least, the Japanese peace treaty and ANZUS seem to mark the dawn of Pacific consciousness in New Zealand. Certainly they acknowledge publicly that the United States rather than the United Kingdom must be the focus for New Zealand's security. With ANZUS, in fact, New Zealand had joined a new team.

Berendsen's task had been to stamp New Zealand's presence and views on the consciousness of American politicians and officials. In this he had succeeded admirably. If, in the end, his flamboyance and obsessions came to embarrass his younger, better informed, and more cautious colleagues, he had, in fact, served his country well. There is no doubt that the New Zealand Foreign Service will not see his like again.

First published in *The New Zealand Journal of History*,
November 1986, Vol. 20, No. 2, pp. 167–180[73]

69 Documents NZEA III, Document 434, p. 1164.

70 ibid., p. 1165.

71 *San Francisco Examiner*, 15 September 1951, quoted in Documents NZEA III, p. 1168.

72 Documents NZEA III, Document 434, pp. 1164, 1166.

73 Professor Trotter published a second essay on Sir Carl Berendsen, entitled 'New Zealand in World Affairs: Sir Carl Berendsen in Washington, 1944–1952', in *The International History Review*, Vol. XII, No. 3, August 1990, pp. 466–489.

INDEX